# THE HEALTH CARE SUPERVISOR

# CAREER DEVELOPMENT



Edited by
*Charles R. McConnell*
Vice President for Employee Affairs
The Genesee Hospital
Rochester, New York

AN ASPEN PUBLICATION®
Aspen Publishers, Inc.
Gaithersburg, Maryland
1993

Library of Congress Cataloging-in-Publication Data

The health care supervisor on career development /
[edited by] Charles R. McConnell.
p. cm.
Includes bibliographical references and index.
ISBN: 0-8342-0364-2
1. Health facilities—Personnel management—Vocational guidance.
2. Supervision of employees—Vocational guidance.
3. Career development I. McConnell, Charles R.
[DNLM: 1. Career Mobility. 2. Health Facilities—organization & administration.
3. Administrative Personnel. 4. Personnel Management.
WX 155 H4343 1993]
RA971.35.H4 1993
362.1'1'0683—dc20
DNLM/DLC
for Library of Congress
93-195
CIP



Editorial Resources: Barbara Priest

Library of Congress Catalog Card Number: 93-195
ISBN: 0-8342-0364-2

*Printed in Canada*

1 2 3 4 5

# Contents

# Preface

## INTRODUCTION

*The Health Care Supervisor* is a cross-disciplinary journal that publishes articles of relevance to persons who manage the work of others in health care settings. This journal's readers, as well as its authors, come from a wide variety of functional, clinical, technical, and professional backgrounds. Between the covers of a single issue of *HCS,* for example, you can find articles written by a nurse, a physician, a speech pathologist, a human resource specialist, an accountant, a nursing home administrator, and an attorney. These authors, and the numerous others who write for *HCS,* write with a single purpose: to provide guidance that all health care supervisors, regardless of the occupations or specialties they supervise, can use in learning to better understand or fulfill the supervisory role.

Whereas most of the articles appearing in *HCS* understandably tell the supervisor what he or she can do to better serve the organization and its patients and employees, every issue or two there is an article intended primarily for the betterment of the supervisor. In this book, *The Health Care Supervisor on Career Development,* we have collected 20 of those articles that apply most directly in the growth and development of the individual as a skilled, knowledgeable, effective health care supervisor.

For the active manager at any organizational level the most effective form of development is self-development; one learns while doing, systematically applying that which is gleaned from the advice, experiences, opinions, and conclusions of those who have been there before. Individually, each of the articles that follow provides advice or perspective in some area of supervisory need. Taken together, they provide the supervisor with the framework for a well-rounded program of self development.

## CARVING OUT A CAREER PATH

"Health Care Supervision: A Special Kind of Management?" provides an overview of health care supervision as a line of work and begins to address the uniqueness of the health care environment. In "Career Planning for the Newly Appointed Health Care Supervisor", Jerad Browdy points out that one's first supervisory position could be but one of several career steps and that career progression is most likely to occur when it is planned and diligently pursued. Potential career hazards and the need for the supervisor to be flexible and adaptable as the times change are explored by William Umiker in "The Health Care Supervisor: Dinosaur or Superstar?"

Joy Calkin addresses the problems of making the transition from pure working specialist to supervisor in "Does an Effective Clinician Make an Effective Manager?" From "Finding the New Supervisor: Inside or Outside?" one learns how the forward-thinking organization strives to balance the advantages and disadvantages of recruiting from outside and promotion from within, and further comes to appreciate that sometimes one's best upcoming career step might lie in another organization.

In "Today's Supervisors Can Become Tomorrow's Health Administrators", Robert Boissoneau describes the range and variety of opportunities available through advancement in the ever-changing health care arena. Finally, in "Fitting Yourself to the Supervisory Role", the individual is guided through some revealing self-assessment steps that can help in identifying one's relative strengths, weaknesses, and preferences as they relate to a potential career in management.

## THE ART AND SCIENCE OF HEALTH CARE SUPERVISION

You will get no arguments as to whether supervision is exclusively art or science. We will recognize the science of management, however, as set forth by Leon McKenzie in "Supervision as Art: Imagination and Intuition", we will acknowledge the artistry of effective supervision. We will likewise acknowledge, through Howard Smith and T. Alan Jensen's "A Search for Excellence in Supervision", that excellence is not only a legitimate pursuit but a necessary striving. With "The Innovative Supervisor", Addison Bennett emphasizes the importance of open, creative thinking in day-to-day supervision.

In "The Supervisor as a Professional Manager" we are reminded that management is a profession in its own right, that one's approach to supervision should be fully as professional as the supervisor's former dedication to the occupation or specialty now supervised. That the supervisor is rarely if ever a solitary worker is emphasized by Howard Smith, Richard

Reid, and Neill Piland in "Building Productive Relationships With Movers and Shakers", suggesting that far more gets done through solid relationships with peers and colleagues than the supervisor could ever accomplish alone, no matter how diligent. These and other relationships are further explored by William Umiker in "Networking: A Vital Activity for Health Care Professionals".

## SELF-HELP IS WHERE YOU FIND IT

"Supervisor, Manage Yourself" suggests that one's own immediate surroundings and activities are where to begin conscientious practice as a manager. In "Time Management: From Victim to Victor", Victor Morano advises how to gain control of the supervisor's most important resource, and in "A New Look at Delegation: The Supervisor's Personal Approach", one learns how to manage the process that frequently represents the individual supervisor's greatest use of time.

"Improving Performance Appraisal From the Bottom Up" asks the supervisor to stand in the shoes of each employee and appraise employee performance with the same honesty, thoroughness, and timeliness that he or she would like to experience when appraised.

In helping look out for one's future career enhancement, William Umiker's "Does Your Resume Do You Justice?" reveals how to make this all-important door-opening document do the most effective job possible in a limited amount of space.

Our brief look at career development closes with consideration of two communication activities that those supervisors determined to rise in management will have to meet head on: speaking and writing. "The Supervisor's Guide to Oral Presentations" shows the individual how to come to grips with reservations about public speaking through preparation and practice, and "From Idea to Print: Writing and Publishing a Journal Article" suggests how to approach this process of sharing ideas and experiences with others and contributing to the literature of one's own line of work.

## CONCLUSION

In the years immediately ahead of us the opportunities in health care supervision will continue to multiply. As the population increases and forms of health care delivery continue to evolve and proliferate, an increasing number of responsible and demanding management positions will emerge. Individuals stepping into these future leadership positions will be those persons whose professional growth has paralleled the growth of modern health care and who have firmly and decisively taken charge of their own career development.

# Acknowledgments

It would not have been possible to assemble this book without the active involvement of the members of the guiding boards, past and present, of *The Health Care Supervisor*. As of this writing some of these valued advisors and authors are well into their second decade of service to *HCS*.

Our sincere thanks to the past members of the *HCS* Editorial Board, the members of the present *HCS* Advisory Board, and the present Board of Contributing Editors.

## Past Members of Editorial Board

Steven H. Appelbaum, Zeila W. Bailey, Claire D. Benjamin, Marjorie Beyers, Philip Bornstein, Leonard C. Brideau, Robert W. Broyles, Joy D. Calkin, Kenneth P. Cohen, Joseph A. Cornell, Darlene A. Dougherty, Kenneth R. Emery, Valerie Glesnes-Anderson, Lee Hand, Allen G. Herkimer, Jr., Max G. Holland, Bowen Hosford, Charles E. Housley, Loucine M. D. Huckabay, Laura L. Kalick, Janice M. Kurth, Marlene Lamnin, Joan Gratto Liebler, Ellyn Luros, Margeurite R. Mancini, Robert D. Miller, Joan F. Moore, Victor J. Morano, Harry E. Munn, Jr., Michael W. Noel, Rita E. Numerof, Samuel E. Oberman, Cheryl S. O'Hara, Jesus J. Pena, Donald J. Petersen, Tim Porter-O'Grady, George D. Pozgar, Ann Marie Rhodes, Edward P. Richards III, James C. Rose, Rachel Rotkovich, Norton M. Rubenstein, Edward D. Sanderson, William L. Scheyer, Homer H. Schmitz, Joyce L. Schweiger, Donna Richards Sheridan, Margaret D. Sovie, Eugene I. Stearns, Judy Ford Stokes, Thomas J. Tenerovicz, Lewis H. Titterton, Jr., Dennis A. Tribble, Terry Trudeau, Alex J. Vallas, Katherine W. Vestal, Judith Weilerstein, William B. Werther, Jr., Shirley Ann Wertz, Sara J. White, Norman H. Witt, and Karen Zander

## Present Advisory Board

Addison C. Bennett, Bernard L. Brown, Jr., Karen H. Henry, Norman Metzger, I. Donald Snook, Jr., and Helen Yura-Petro

## Present Board of Contributing Editors

Donald F. Beck, Robert Boissoneau, Jerad D. Browdy, Vicki S. Crane, Carol A. Distasio, Charlotte Eliopoulos, Howard L. Lewis, R. Scott MacStravic, Leon McKenzie, Jerry L. Norville, Stephen L. Priest, Howard L. Smith, and John L. Templin, Jr.

Our sincere appreciation as well to those who, in addition several persons mentioned above, participated in creating the articles that make up this present volume: T. Alan Jensen, Richard A. Reid, Neill F. Piland, and William Umiker.

# Part I
# Carving Out a Career Path

# Health care supervision: a special kind of management?

*Charles R. McConnell*
*Vice President for Employee Affairs*
*The Genesee Hospital*
*Rochester, New York*

## A LONG-STANDING CONTROVERSY

VARIATIONS OF the following argument are heard repeatedly:

Good management is good management no matter where it is practiced. What applies in one kind of organization should apply equally well in all other organizations. Knowledge of the techniques of management is more important than knowledge of the function that is managed.

Health care is different from all other organized business activity. Therefore, management techniques that apply in other businesses are inappropriate in health care. In a health care organization knowledge of the specific functions performed is of primary importance and one cannot bring so-called generic management methods into health care and expect them to work.

The foregoing controversy is also frequently summarized in comments

*Health Care Superv,* 1982,1(1),1–13

such as, "You cannot bring industrial methods into a health organization. After all, *our* business is human life."

**Health care versus industry**

There has indeed been a tendency among people working in health care to consider *health care* and *industry* as opponents in a controversy that has both philosophical and practical dimensions, with the term *industry* taking on the character of a dirty word. The anti-industry posture of some health care personnel has even been found in the titles of certain health care employees. For instance, when industrial engineering began to be used widely in health care organizations, it was found necessary to identify its practitioners as *management* engineers rather than *industrial* engineers.

As an organized activity, health care is the third largest employer in the country (exceeded in total numbers of employees by only government and manufacturing). By most standards then, it would seem that health care is an industry in its own right—an industry of considerable proportions. Despite the traditional connotations of the word, *industry* can no longer be thought of as simply *the commercial production and sale of goods*. Appropriate definitions of *industry* now refer to goods *and services*.

**Applicability of management practices**

Regarding the application of industrial management techniques to health care, the truth lies somewhere between the extremes of the controversy. Many management practices, even those that may first appear to be "industrial," are fully applicable regardless of the kind of business being pursued. Certain activities that cut across departmental or functional lines must take place. For instance, a supervisor must prepare and work with a budget, develop and implement schedules, perform employee evaluations and deal with personnel problems, regardless of whether he or she is supervising a team of registered nurses, a crew of transport aides, a group of medical record transcriptionists, or, for that matter, a team of employees who work on an automobile assembly line.

However, a strictly horizontal view—a view holding that all so-called management functions are equally applicable everywhere—is not fully appropriate in the health care organization. Health care is indeed different in many ways from other lines of organized activity. But neither is the strictly vertical view—that the kind of work done completely determines the type of management called for—true at all times. At some times, in some places and in

***A view holding that all so-called management functions are equally applicable everywhere is not fully appropriate in the health care organization.***

some ways, one or the other of the extremes described above can be true. However, most of the time the truth lies between the extremes. The problem is that often the supervisor does not know in which direction to lean.

## THE SUPERVISOR AND THE SETTING

Supervision can be vastly different from setting to setting, but the differences are not determined by the nature of the product or service provided and are certainly not due to the presence of some broadly defined activity such as *manufacturing* or *health care*. Regardless of how different any particular line of work may seem to be in outward appearance, all business activity actually takes place for the same reason: to provide something that people want or need. In this respect—their very reason for existing—all organized activities have something fundamental in common. Since organizations are in business to provide something for people, to stay in business all organizations must continue to satisfy human needs.

If one's business is the creation of a manufactured product, the customer—the user of the product—may well be remote and unseen, completely removed in time and space from one's work. Numerous steps exist between the start of manufacture and the use of the product. An assembler of waffle irons in California has no way of knowing that a complete stranger may first make use of the product to prepare breakfast two years later and 3,000 miles away. The connection between provider and user is remote indeed. However, even this remote connection can be important: If the customer is dissatisfied with the waffle iron, the manufacturer may receive a complaint, or the customer may refuse to deal with that company again. To retain their business, customers, however remote, must be satisfied.

On the other hand, in most subdivisions of health care the customer (that is, the patient) is physically present. This condition of immediacy makes the matter of need satisfaction much more important. Immediacy of contact is not unique to health care; immediacy is also a strong factor in retail stores, restaurants and other businesses. Generally, however, immediacy of contact—closeness in space and time between the provider of the service and the user of the service—is one of the factors that affects the special nature of health care organizations.

Just as all business organizations exist to fulfill people's needs, likewise all first-line managers exist to manage the people who provide products and services to the people who need them. The end product is people—those people whose needs are satisfied by the product sold or the service provided. The differences in management do not reside in some special attachment to the kind of product manufactured or the kind of service rendered; *all* business activity is basically people doing things for people.

For valid differences in management, it is necessary to look at many of the specific things that actually happen within a given organization and even within the various departments of that organization. It is useful to look at different kinds of organizations—looking not at *what* they do but rather at *how* they do what they do—and attempt to determine whether management exhibits different characteristics under different circumstances related to *how* they do business.

**Production-centered management**

Through no special effort on the part of the manager, a particular style of management can develop. The style is affected by the degree to which the manager's attention is focused on the output of the processes he or she manages. Under assembly-line concepts of management, especially those found in manufacturing, the people who do the work are as integral to the process as gears in a machine. Indeed, these workers often feel they are treated as no more than cogs in the works.

Organizational systems exhibiting assembly-line characteristics are not without their dehumanizing dimensions, and such systems often depend strongly on economic motives to keep running. That is, people show up for work, do as they are told and permit themselves to be swept along by the system, primarily for pay. The system may depend little, if at all, on the employees' initiative, judgment, motivation, or willingness to do what they do. The system is mechanical in the sense that scheduled output governs the provision of all inputs and generally sets the pace for the people. As far as the people are concerned, the work comes to them and goes by them, and they must continue to respond appropriately (and thus retain their jobs) or fail to respond (and ultimately be replaced by people who *will* respond).

The above description of *production-centered management* was perhaps extreme, but the message should be clear: The management focus is on output at a certain level, and the entire "machine," including the people, is geared to the production of that output. It is from this concept of production-centered management that many working managers have taken their notions about management. For most people who have lived in the nineteenth and twentieth centuries, the term *management* has a strong association with manufacturing and other forms of physical labor. Indeed, for many centuries when people worked for other people, they usually did so either making things or performing other physical work. It is only relatively recently that *service* industries have come into being, industries in which efforts are directed not at placing some physical product in a person's hands but rather toward performing a service that may be far less tangible than a physical product.

Archaic notions of management die hard, and today's archaic notions stem from long exposure to traditional production-centered management. Examples are plentiful of authoritarian leadership and plain bossism, much of it well-intentioned ("I'm paid to make decisions, so the buck stops here. I'll tell you what to do and you do it."). To many people, a more open, people-centered style of management—although essential in many of today's work settings—is seen as weak. Since many management role models were inclined toward authoritarianism, managers may be inclined to see open and participative management styles, try as they may to practice them, as representing abrogation of management's traditional responsibilities.

Recent experience has suggested that perhaps management started off "on the wrong foot" years ago. There appears to have been a vast inequity always present in production-centered management, an inequity recognized only in the last 100 years or so.

A necessary focus on production in "old time" manufacturing management caused a general failure to recognize the full importance of people. Full attention to the work caused the worker to be all but ignored. It is now commonly accepted that management of all kinds and in all organizational environments should have always been people centered to a considerable extent, but first-line managers (the supervisors of the workers) were simply swept along with the system in the same way the workers were.

**People-centered management**

People-centered management ordinarily prevails, or at least *should* prevail, when it is not possible for people to be swept along with the system and when the people themselves must make things run because input and output do not control the system. In other words, if a mechanized system cannot be relied on to drag the people along, then the people must be relied on to move the system.

People-centered management will generally prevail in systems in which people must be reasonably self-starting. In such a system much of the work will not be accomplished unless the workers do it willingly. Of course the economic motive for working is present, as it is in all organized systems, but there is also a need to depend heavily on the self-motivation of employees.

People-centered management is largely a product of the middle part of the twentieth century. It has been a long time finding its way into work organizations because of concepts of management and because management role models all came from an era during which production-centered management was dominant. However, management style is also influenced by the manager's reaction to organizational conditions and to certain aspects of the kinds of work performed and the skills and capabilities of the people who do the work.

## DETERMINANTS OF MANAGEMENT STYLE

There are a number of factors present in the organizational environment that help determine the appropriate management style. A supervisor's ideal style will necessarily vary at times according to the absence or presence of these factors and the extent to which they may be present.

One determinant of management style is the *immediacy* of contact between worker and consumer. In some industries, such as health care or retail trade, consumer contact is immediate. In industries such as manufacturing or government, consumer contact may be remote. When contact is immediate, management must be able to depend on the worker to deal with the consumer (or the patient) completely, equitably and courteously. When there is immediacy of consumer contact, employees themselves must be depended on to behave in a people-centered manner.

***When there is immediacy of consumer contact, employees themselves must be depended on to behave in a people-centered manner.***

Another important determinant of management style is *predictability*, or the ability of management to plan output in terms of quantity and time and to schedule the inputs required to produce the desired output. For instance, if an automated assembly line is to produce 25 typewriters per hour, the line speed can be set at that rate and all the materials and labor scheduled accordingly. The more predictable the output, the more production-centered the management style is likely to become. Conversely, less predictability of output generally leads to a need to focus more on personnel aspects of supervision.

The degree of *professionalism* of the employee group can also be an important determinant of management style. People who are trained in various professions are generally expected to exercise more self-determination than are untrained or unskilled workers. With untrained and unskilled workers, the supervisor tends to focus more on output and how it is achieved; with professional employees, the supervisor's focus shifts to how the workers approach their jobs overall, and less attention is paid to how specific output is generated.

Related to the foregoing but still identifiable in its own right as a determinant of management style is the amount of *structure* inherent in the jobs that must be done. Some jobs, such as those of manual laborers and unskilled workers, may be rigidly structured. For instance, at tray-assembly time the food service aide will stand in one place and make the same moves to accomplish the same task over and over again, and this procedure may be detailed with great accuracy in a set of specific instructions. On the other hand, the job of a registered nurse may be significantly varied and may involve reacting to such a variety of unforeseen circumstances that it is not possible to create detailed instructions for all tasks that might be encountered. The less structure present in the job, the more management will necessarily focus on people as opposed to production.

*Mobility* of one's employees can also be an important determinant of management style. If employees are legitimately mobile, moving about the institution in the normal performance of their jobs, the supervisor must be sure that they will do their jobs properly while out of sight. Thus the supervisor will focus more on who they are and how they conduct themselves and less on how they perform specific tasks. Conversely, if all employees spend their entire work time in the same physical area within the visual and voice control of the supervisor, then the problems that come with mobility are absent and the supervisor is situationally encouraged to focus more on output.

The degree of *variability* in the employees' work also exerts an influence on the management style the supervisor brings to the job. The more variable the work (the more different tasks that can come up at any time), the more people-centered the management style will necessarily become. On the other hand, when the work is repetitive and the same few tasks are performed over and over again, the supervisor tends to focus more on output.

The *quality* required in the performance of a given function and the likely effects of substandard quality also influence management style. The more important the quality considerations—and certainly there is no industry in which quality is of greater importance than in health care—the more the supervisor will find it necessary to lean toward people-centered management. Quality assurance programs and quality audits are much like final inspection in the factory setting; they are performed after the fact to determine whether something has been done properly. In manufacturing, output that does not meet standards is either discarded or recycled.

In health care, however, quality is a more important consideration, because if something is not accomplished correctly the first time, there may be no second chance. After-the-fact quality checks are necessary, but they do not *produce* quality. Quality must be *built* into the service; it cannot be *inspected* into it. Since the performance of work that meets quality standards is largely in the hands of the people doing the work, management must depend on the workers for quality. Requirements for high-quality output generally suggest the need for a greater degree of people-centered management.

There is no way to instruct a supervisor as to precisely what style of management to bring to the job. A great many different functions must be performed in a health organization, and the several determinants of management style may be present in those various functions in widely varying degrees. The degree to which these determinants are present in any activity, however, should suggest some general approaches that may be appropriate, depending on the employees involved.

For instance, it may not be necessary to supervise a staff nurse as closely as a nursing assistant in the same department. The former generally knows what to do a large part of the time; the latter may have to be instructed frequently as to what to do next. The activities of a therapeutic dietitian would ordinarily not be controlled as closely as the activities of a kitchen helper. The management style of, for instance, the supervisor of the medical record department, may be entirely—and legitimately—different from the style applied by the supervisor of engineering and maintenance.

## MOTIVATING A HEALTH CARE SUPERVISOR

Most people, supervisors included, experience a mix of motives that bring them to work every day. Without restating any well-known theories of human motivation, it can be assumed that most people who work for a living want various things from their work organizations. Listed in no particular order, the following are the wants or needs that most employees are attempting to satisfy, to some varying degree, through their work organizations:

- reasonable economic compensation in the form of both wages and fringe benefits;
- an acceptable degree of job security;
- the opportunity for advancement in the organization;
- fair treatment relative to other employees;
- recognition of their performance and contributions;
- respect and regard as individuals;
- a sense of accomplishment in performing useful work;
- the ability to see the results of their efforts; and
- interesting work experiences.

These needs are not experienced to the same extent by all persons. Neither, for a given person, are all needs usually satisfied equally well in all occupational fields or in all kinds of organizations.

It is important to consider the extent to which health care supervision seems able to satisfy these needs. The economic rewards, for instance, are generally comparable to what may be obtained in a number of other work environments, but health care is nevertheless lower paying than many fields. Job security, certainly related to material reward, may at least appear comparable to what is available in other kinds of organizations.

Advancement opportunity often appears to be modest and occasionally seems quite limited for the supervisor in a health care organization. Much of health care is made up of vertically short and functionally narrow career ladders that allow for little long-run career advancement. For instance, a medical record specialist in a medium-size hospital may find that there are only two levels of management involved in that specialty. When one eventually becomes manager of medical records, one has "topped out" in that organization. This fact suggests that if continued advancement opportunity is extremely important in that person's particular mix of needs, then the health care organization will probably not provide sufficient opportunity to satisfy that need, and the person will eventually feel limited by the circumstances under which he or she works.

Other reasons why people come to work can be seen as functions of the specific organization rather than functions of any particular line of business. For instance, fair treatment relative to other employees, recognition for one's contributions and respect and regard as an individual are determined by the employee relations philosophy of the organization. The presence or absence of such motivating factors will be apparent in the human relations approach of the people in the management hierarchy. An individual might be happy in one hospital and dismally discontented in another hospital.

On the list of motivators there are several items that seem to be of considerable importance to people who work in health care organizations. To people for whom these particular needs are strong, the health care organization often provides the opportunity for a high level of need satisfaction. For instance, the health care

***The health care organization provides significant opportunity for the supervisor to experience a sense of accomplishment.***

organization provides significant opportunity for the supervisor to experience a sense of accomplishment. Many people feel it is extremely important to be doing something that will allow them to accomplish something useful, something that is important to other people. Since health is very important to all of us, those who are able to work in the business of restoring health and preserving life have the opportunity to regularly experience a sense of accomplishment.

Also extremely high in the health care organization is the opportunity to see the results of one's efforts. Most of health care involves direct service to people. When health care supervisors or their employees do something, it is often done to, for or with the patient. There is considerable opportunity for immediate feedback regarding the work they perform.

Also a potentially strong attraction of health care is interest in the work. Many people are drawn into health care and remain there because they find the work interesting; the way they are put together as individuals says that this is important to them. Thus people with a strong need for interesting work experiences may seek careers in health care.

Much of what can be said about the mix of needs that brings people to work and the potential of health care to satisfy these needs comes down to this: People will like or dislike the organization they work for and the work they do depending on their particular mix of motives (their basic needs) and how well these needs are satisfied. Nobody can tell a person in advance what his or her suitability for health care supervision may be. People must go through the highly personal process of assessing their needs, determining how they react to their work and deciding for themselves.

## EVALUATING ONE'S SUITABILITY FOR HEALTH CARE SUPERVISION

One of the problems that afflicts many supervisors in a variety of organizational settings is fairly basic: They do not like what they do. They may believe they like being supervisors, when in reality what they like is the title, status, salary and other benefits that go with the job. Even recognizing that it is unlikely that everyone could possibly like all aspects of his or her work at all times, many supervisors nevertheless dislike doing certain fundamental management tasks and are thus unhappy in those aspects of their jobs.

If one is not prepared to assume the supervisory role—and many supervisors enter the job with no preparation at all, let alone being fully prepared—this will influence both one's liking for the job and one's success on the job. A person ill-prepared for his or her job may be faced with a familiar question: Do I dislike the work because I have not learned enough about it, or have I failed to learn enough about it because I inherently dislike it?

Matters of preparedness aside, however, much of people's happiness with their jobs will depend on how well their particular needs are met by the work and how they personally react to conditions encountered in the health care environment. A person can perhaps acquire a sense of how he or she fits into health care supervision by answering several questions that call for assessing one's capability of responding to both the requirements of supervision and the requirements of the health care organization.

*Can I cope with a pace that is often hectic, and can I accept problem after problem as a daily way of life?* To a considerable extent the health care supervisor is a frustration fighter; much attention will be demanded by emergencies, unanticipated problems, and a sometimes steady stream of interruptions.

*Do I have the ability to see each*

*employee as a whole person and not just simply as a producer of output?* Supervisors' willingness and ability to adopt a people-centered focus will in part determine how well they fit into the health care organization.

*Am I willing to work in one of the most regulated industries in the country?* Much of what is done in the management of a health care organization is done because federal, state and local governments so dictate. Supervisors do not need to accept or condone what many people see as obvious overregulation; however, they should at least be able to recognize the reality of regulation and decide that they will perform the best possible job of managing within the restrictions imposed by countless regulations.

*Am I sufficiently adaptable to be able to cope with rapid technological change?* Our general base of knowledge is expanding at an alarming rate, and in few areas is this expansion of knowledge more evident than in health care. Supervisors have to accept the likelihood that they may never acquire long-term familiarity with the equipment and processes of their occupations; the equipment and processes may change dramatically several times during the course of their careers. Also, supervisors must be willing to recognize that since social change always lags behind technological change, they will probably always face the problems of human resistance to change.

*Do I have adequate knowledge of and a genuine interest in the kind of work I supervise?* If supervisors disliked their own work before they became supervisors, chances are that they will not like it more when they must supervise others in those activities. A supervisor's interest or lack of interest in the work is likely to show up in the quality of the supervision he or she can provide to others.

*Do I have a genuine interest in working with people, as opposed to working alone?* Health care is people intensive, with many people working closely together to do things for other people in an immediate sense. Health care is generally not for the loner, nor is supervision in any industry for the loner, since it always involves getting things done *through people.*

*Do I have a genuine desire to do something that I consider to be important to people?* Many persons pursue successful careers in health care supervision comfortable in the knowledge that they are indeed doing something important. To people who remain in health care by choice, there is little that is more important than helping to preserve life, restore health and prevent illness.

*Do I experience a strong desire to see the results of my labor?* The opportunity for immediate feedback regarding one's work is more prevalent in health care than in many other lines of work.

*Do I thrive on variety in my work?* If so, a supervisor may be suited for supervision in the health care setting.

A health care supervisor must accomplish his or her work through employees who directly provide service for other people. The people a supervisor serves and the people he or she works with are all different from each other, and the problems they bring to the work setting are different. First-line supervision is fraught with variety, as is health care itself.

As a summary question, consider: *What is my individual focus?* Is this focus internal to one's self, such that one takes everything personally and is affected by what goes on? Or is the focus external, allowing one to consider all things that happen as external events? If the focus is internal, supervisors may find themselves in for some stressful times as they actually experience much of the pain and frustration of those around them. If the focus is external, however, supervisors will be more able to retain their objectivity and perspective relative to what is happening in their surroundings. The person with an external focus is better equipped for coping with the kinds of problems encountered in the health care environment.

Supervisors might also go on to judge whether their personal focus is narrow or broad. This dimension is closely related to several of the items mentioned earlier in this list. A person possessing a narrow personal focus functions best when able to concentrate for a considerable time on a single problem or task. A person with a broad personal focus is more able to cope with a variety of problems coming from a number of directions simultaneously. The individual with breadth of focus is generally more able to cope successfully with the demands of first-line supervision.

## A SPECIAL KIND OF MANAGEMENT

First-line supervision has its unique problems, and health care as an industry has its unique requirements. Generally, in health care the supervisor's primary emphasis is on people problems and human considerations rather than on so-called production problems. Furthermore, usually those difficulties that appear to be production problems are surface indications of people problems. One can certainly find pockets of production-centered activity in a health organization—for instance, routine, patient-room cleaning and meal-tray assembly are production-centered activities—but on the whole the health organization tends toward people-centered activity, and thus supervision must focus more on people than on output.

***In health care the supervisor's primary emphasis is on people problems and human considerations rather than on so-called production problems.***

Some people who have worked in health care supervision have ultimately abandoned health care and would not return under any circumstance. Those people have undoubtedly learned a few things about their likes and dislikes and about their personal coping styles. However, many people have become health care supervisors who would never care to do anything else.

Recall the earlier claim that all business organizations, health care and otherwise, have but a single common purpose: to fulfill people's needs. For those who work as health care supervisors and wish to remain health care supervisors, no other industry deals with more important needs. For them, health care supervision is indeed a special kind of management.

# Career planning for the newly appointed health care supervisor

*Jerad D. Browdy*
*President*
*Jerad D. Browdy, Inc.*
*Evanston, Illinois*

CONGRATULATIONS — you have just been appointed to your first supervisory position. You may be a working supervisor doing essentially what you were doing before but now having responsibility for several subordinates, or you may be a section head or department manager with responsibilities almost entirely supervisory in nature. Regardless of the scope of your responsibilities, however, a major change has occurred in your professional life and possibly in your personal life. It will become evident Monday morning when you report to the new job or begin your expanded duties that life will no longer be the same. You will no longer be one of the gang among your former associates.

Becoming a boss is a goal of most persons entering the work force. This is just as true in health care as it is in the industrial and business sectors. The staff nurse hopes to become a

*Health Care Superv*, 1985,3(4),31–41

head nurse, the laboratory technician aspires to the job of section chief and eventually laboratory manager and the physical therapist hopes to become a chief physical therapist. Certainly this is not true in all cases; some people have limited aspirations and goals and want to bear as little responsibility as possible. Sometimes, however, people find themselves forced to accept supervisory responsibilities, a situation which may be to the detriment and frustration of themselves and their subordinates.

Ambitious, highly motivated people in business and industry generally set their sights high. They view themselves as progressing through a hierarchy of increasingly responsible managerial positions until they arrive at or near the top. Few view themselves as remaining in their particular areas of specialization for a lifetime. This is true whether the individual is in sales, engineering, finance, production, marketing, human resources or any other specialty, but it is not necessarily true in health care. Few nurses may want to be anything but a nurse, few laboratory technicians see themselves in a role outside of the laboratory, and so on. While they may see themselves progressing within their particular disciplines and specialties, they do not necessarily see themselves as progressing beyond those disciplines into more general areas of management. While this is by no means intended as a negative observation, the pattern does hold important implications for the career-planning process.

## ROUTE TO TOP IS CHANGING

It is not our intent to dwell on the global issues affecting health care today. These issues are common knowledge. Suffice it to say that life for all levels of health care supervisors and managers is and will continue to become increasingly more complex. Those institutions that survive and prosper will be fiscally viable, competitive and managed in the same manner as successful major multimillion dollar business corporations without compromising patient care. The key to their success will ultimately depend upon the effectiveness and skills of the executive and managerial group, including first-line supervisors. This has profound implications for supervisors at all levels.

Traditionally, the road to upper-level executive or general management positions in hospitals and health care institutions has involved the pursuit of the Master's of Business Administration (MBA) or Master's of Hospital Administration (MHA) degree. Individuals aspiring to become chief executive officers usually begin their health care careers as assistant administrators then become associate administrators and eventually administrators of small hospitals before moving to progressively larger hospitals. This has been the traditional path to the health care executive suite, but it may not be so in the future. It is true that some present executives began their hospital careers at the department head or supervisory level, but most of the current senior-level health care executives entered graduate programs directly out of undergraduate school with little if any prior health care experience other than part-time positions held while in school.

An increasing number of executives are entering health care from business and industry. This is particularly true in the areas of marketing, finance, human resources and management information systems. Even more important, both trustees and chief executive officers alike are recognizing that while the graduate degree is an enhancement, it is not absolutely necessary for the successful manager or executive. Top executives are becoming more aware of the need to recruit and promote individuals having people skills and managerial talent rather than those having extensive technical experience and expertise, as has been the case.

Many chief executive officers and chief operating officers recognize that there may be supervisors well qualified for promotion to higher-level generalist positions in their organizations. However, many of these candidates for promotion do not aspire to be more than supervisors within limited functions. Thus when a vacancy occurs for a middle-level management generalist, a candidate from outside the organization is usually selected in spite of the fact that progressive and forward-thinking chief executive officers would prefer to promote department heads and even send them for further schooling if these people were to be so inclined.

Formal management development programs have been lacking in not-for-profit health care, but this is changing gradually. As the external management pool becomes smaller and reluctance to seek managers from outside the health care field continues, unquestionably, more institutions will turn to the supervisory ranks for potential middle-level executives. Career planning and assessment of career goals will become critical for the newly appointed supervisor who demonstrates excellent managerial skills, regardless of professional or technical specialty. These employees will be closely scrutinized for possible promotion to higher management positions.

Career planning should be an ongoing process for the health care supervisor. For the new or inexperienced supervisor, career planning should focus on goals based on the growing awareness of what the management process involves. Career planning at this stage is actually a matter of getting to know oneself; in other words, at the earliest stages of supervision, career planning should focus on critical elements of self-awareness and self-understanding, which fall into three major categories:

***Career planning and assessment of career goals will become critical for the newly appointed supervisor who demonstrates excellent managerial skills, regardless of professional or technical specialty.***

1. Why am I here and what am I doing?
2. Do I really know myself?
3. Where am I going and how do I get there?

One of the most exciting professional experiences can come at that moment when an individual is asked to accept a supervisory position. Sometimes this moment arrives as a complete surprise. Sometimes there are hints that something big is in the wind. Other times there is no secret that a vacancy resulting from retirement, separation or resignation is about to be filled, and in such instances people who want to be promoted may actively politic for consideration. Of course in many instances, especially at the lower supervisory levels, vacancies must be posted prior to external recruiting, and positions are filled through that means. Regardless of how he or she is appointed, however, the questions, "Why am I here and what am I doing?" can have a profound effect on the future professional growth of the newly appointed supervisor and can make the difference between a positive and negative mental attitude toward the responsibilities of the position.

## WHY AM I HERE AND WHAT AM I DOING?

It is absolutely essential that the supervisor understand why he or she was appointed to the position. Sometimes during the final selection process this will be explained in great detail by the appointing executive. More often than not, however, explanations are limited to vague and nebulous comments such as: "You deserve the job." "You're well qualified." "You've been here a long time and have earned it" (you got the job because of seniority). Although one is seldom told, "You are the only one willing to accept the additional responsibilities," this may indeed have been a primary consideration in the selection process. Sometimes this latter response may be offered facetiously though in all earnestness—but it is not a laughing matter. What the new supervisor is being told is that he or she was the candidate of last resort. In such instances, the newly selected supervisor may be under considerably closer scrutiny than someone entering the position under the halo effect of past achievements. The supervisor will have to prove himself or herself very quickly.

On the other hand, individuals are frequently told they have been promoted or selected for supervision because they are the best nurse, best laboratory technician, best buyer, best dietician. In other words, selection has been made on the basis of technical skills and expertise although these may have no bearing on supervisory talent or ability. The person selected for supervision for this reason may feel that he or she has to continue to prove to be the best in the particular specialty, often to the detriment of the fulfillment of supervisory responsibilities. Remember, supervision in its simplest terms is *achieving results through people.* The best technician who lacks the necessary people skills will fail as a manager.

The supervisor, especially in a health care situation, must wear two hats—that of the technical or professional specialist and that of the manager—but it is all too easy for the technical expert to forget to put on the managerial hat. In terms of self-analysis, the supervisor selected because of technical expertise must look inward to determine whether he or she has the temperament for dealing with people and motivating them. Some individuals do not find out that they have such ability until they have become supervisors. Others may inwardly know they do not have the patience or even the interest to direct others, yet they accept promotion because of pride or out of a feeling that the organization will be let down if they do not accept.

At the very beginning of one's supervisory career, technical expertise is of obvious importance. However, with the passage of time and with movement up the supervisory ladder, technical expertise becomes less important as the people, human relations and organizational skills become more important. The transition can be difficult for the professional or technical specialist who has not considered the need to grow into the broader role.

Assuming that you understand why you have been selected for supervision, the next question to be addressed is: Do you understand what you are doing and what is expected of you? Answering this question is critical to the career-planning process, especially for individuals with no prior supervisory experience. The way an individual approaches the first supervisory experience can be a major factor in developing a management style and in the future influence on subordinates. For example, a new supervisor thrown "into the breach" with little explanation of responsibilities, essentially placed in a sink or swim situation, may well treat subordinates in the same manner. On the other hand, the new supervisor who is coached, trained and mentored and enters the position fully understanding the scope of responsibilities may (but not necessarily will) be a more democratic and understanding supervisor.

The "What am I doing?" stage of career planning encompasses the following elements:

- What is the full scope of my responsibilities?
- What is my authority for hiring and firing?
- What is my authority for recommending salary increases?

In other words, what is the extent of my responsibility, accountability, and authority, and why is this an important aspect of the career-planning process? Simply stated, self-analysis is a critical element and includes understanding whether you really like the supervisory role and can adapt to greater responsibilities. As the full impact of supervision becomes felt in the months after promotion, one's attitude toward future expanded responsibilities may be established. Some individuals will be enthusiastic and excited and will begin preparing for future roles. Others will just wonder what they have gotten themselves into.

In the early stages of supervision (and even in later stages of development) individuals may make false assumptions about the extent and nature of their responsibilities. Some persons may not understand the full extent of their responsibilities and as a result will be reluctant to make decisions, or they may constantly ask their supervisor for help and guidance. Others may overestimate the extent of their responsibility, authority and accountability or may act hastily without apparent concern for consequences. Either of these conditions can occur when job responsibilities have been discussed only superficially or not at all. In either situation, the individual will make mistakes and may be criticized. To some supervisors, particularly those who were selected because they were the best in their specialties, this may be a new, traumatic experience. Others will obviously view such criticism as a learning experience and benefit from it. With respect to the career-planning process, these experiences can set the tone of and affect the supervisor's attitude toward decision making and risk taking.

Regarding the "What am I doing?" phase of self-analysis, one of the most dramatic revelations in today's health care environment is the supervisor's recognition of his or her impact on the financial condition of the organization, a situation that becomes increasingly evident when the supervisor is given budgetary responsibility. It can be a particularly traumatic experience for the newly appointed supervisor who (especially in direct patient care) has not had to think in terms of financial responsibilities. Again, some supervisors, particularly those with an entrepreneurial bent, thrive on running a business organization, but others find this distasteful and incompatible with their own personal philosophy or career goals. The responsibility for exercising some fiscal control and the impact and implications of this responsibility will be felt in the early stages of supervision. Consciously or otherwise, financial responsibilities will affect the future career plans of the newly appointed or inexperienced health care manager. This effect will become increasingly evident as health care supervisors at all levels and in all disciplines are held accountable for cost containment and fiscal performance.

Going through the considerations of "Why am I here?" and "What am I doing?" next leads to the most critical phase of career planning: self-understanding. "Do I really know myself?" In other words, a crucial element of career planning is an objective analysis and evaluation of one's own strengths, limitations, likes and dislikes.

## DO I REALLY KNOW MYSELF?

Experienced executives and managers may tell you there is probably no better way to really get to know yourself than to accept a supervisory position. You suddenly find yourself responsible for others, and regardless of whether the subordinates are unskilled workers or medical-scientific professionals, they are dependent upon you for their livelihoods and for the achievement of their own career aspirations. Some supervisors obviously thrive on such responsibility and dependency, but others find this such a heavy burden that they eventually prefer to return to nonsupervisory roles.

For the new supervisor, the "getting-to-know-oneself" stage focuses on several critical areas including organizational ability, management style, awareness of people and interpersonal skills. Successful executives, regardless of level or technical expertise, have developed the ability to organize and manage their time well. Knowing how to make the most effective use of one's time is a necessary skill for the new supervisor and requires critical self-appraisal, a step which has future implications. Much has been written and said about time management, and it is not our intent to dwell on this subject. It is likely that you as a new supervisor will be sent to a course or seminar on this subject. Just attending such a course, however, will not necessarily make you a particularly well-organized individual or an effective time manager. Effective time and organization management must be worked at with diligence and considerable effort. The need to do this may not become apparent until you are thrust into that first supervisory position; then it may suddenly seem as though there are not enough hours in the day. This will become especially evident at that time of year when budgets are prepared.

Effective time management becomes increasingly important with added responsibility. For some individuals this skill is easily learned or may already be a talent and may not be a problem. For other persons it is a skill never learned and a talent never developed. If you are overwhelmed by the need to organize and manage time in the early stages of supervision, the problem will be exacerbated with the passage of time. It is imperative, therefore, that the self-analysis phase of career planning recognize that time management and organization skills are needed and that these skills require effort, talent and patience to develop.

New supervisors who recognize the importance of time management and organization skills also recognize that they may not have the skill or self-direction to adapt by themselves. They often will—and should—take self-improvement courses either on their own or through the organization. Individuals who do not understand the importance of time management and organization skills or who do not recognize their deficiencies in this area may be unprepared for future and for more responsible administrative assignments. Even more important, persons who are aware that their skills are deficient may conclude that they do not want increased supervisory responsibilities.

When thinking about self-analysis

***For the new supervisor, the self-analysis process must include, in addition to time management and organization skills, an assessment of how one relates to people.***

and the assessment of one's strengths and weaknesses, it is not unusual to think in terms of academic criteria. You may ask, "Do I have the proper academic background or formal training necessary for a particular supervisory position?" This question deserves major consideration in the career-planning process, but for the new supervisor the self-analysis process must also include, in addition to time management and organization skills, an assessment of how one relates to people.

The ability to manage people is at least partly a talent. Some supervisors are "naturals"; others have to work at it and force themselves into molds that are unnatural for them. Others may at some point find the people-relationship aspect of supervision distasteful, if not impossible. Unquestionably, certain techniques of management and supervision can be learned or acquired through formal and on-the-job training, but the ability to transform what has been learned in training sessions into real-life situations is something else. For example, learning how to discipline someone or how to conduct a performance evaluation interview is completely different from actually having to do these things.

Learning how to conduct employment interviews for potential subordinates is completely different from actually having to fill vacancies, particularly when time constraints, Equal Employment Opportunity (EEO) or union regulations affect the employment process. Again, some individuals thrive in these areas and find them the most exciting and exhilarating aspect of the supervisory process. Others find this aspect of their job distasteful and procrastinate or otherwise avoid making decisions.

Probably one of the most difficult aspects of self-analysis is learning that delegation is a major element of the supervisory process. The realization that "I cannot do it all" can be one of the most difficult personal adjustments for a new supervisor. After all, no one can do the job as well as *you* . . . that is why you were selected for the position in the first place. This is the natural inclination of new supervisors. The mature and effective supervisor will grow into the role of delegator. The immature or distrustful supervisor, the person who does not want to let go for whatever the reasons, will eventually fail as a supervisor and will either be forced to delegate or forced to consider other career options. In career planning the question of knowing whether you are willing to give up what may be the most comfortable part of your job is all important. Some individuals may never discover this about themselves until they actually become supervisors. Others, however, know enough about themselves from their present and previous work experiences and from their life experiences to recognize how they will react to the need to delegate.

All the points discussed thus far relate to *management style,* which may ultimately prove to be the most critical aspect of the self-analysis process as it relates to career planning. For career-planning purposes you must early in your career understand which style is the most natural for you and works best for you. Frequently the style, whether positive or negative, autocratic or democratic, is an extension of the supervisor's personality. For some, however, the style is studied or forced, or the person playacts a supervisor role and is in his or her nonprofessional life a completely different person. Sometimes new supervisors try to emulate a role model or mentor. It should be recognized, however, that subordinates, regardless of their skill or intellectual level, can generally tell when a supervisor is only acting the part.

As an element of the career-planning process, understanding the role you are most comfortable with will likely affect your success or your future career as a supervisor and eventually as a middle-level manager or upper-level executive. Style is developed early, and some individuals may even try to play different roles until they find one that works best (autocratic managers are not necessarily bad managers, and democratic managers are not necessarily good managers). Developing a style is an evolutionary process, but the pattern is usually set in the supervisor's early stages. A certain degree of playacting may be necessary to be an effective supervisor, but for career-planning purposes such acting has to lie within the scope of one's own personality and psyche. In all probability, an individual cannot successfully pretend to be someone he or she is not and should recognize this fact.

In the self-analysis phase of career planning you will discover much about yourself only after you are actually on the job as a supervisor and are faced with situations you never before considered. However, you should know enough about yourself so that when faced with the prospect of becoming a supervisor you can ask yourself some basic questions like:

- Do I really like people and enjoy working with them?
- Am I more comfortable with "things" than with people?
- Am I tolerant and patient, particularly with individuals who are less skilled and perhaps less educated than I?
- Am I willing and able to delegate or give up some of what I have?
- How will I react the first time I have to discipline or perhaps discharge an employee?

Your responses could very well determine whether you are making the right move when considering a supervisory position.

## WHERE AM I GOING AND HOW DO I GET THERE?

"Where am I going and how do I get there?" concerns evaluating career-planning factors that are quantitative but also involves evaluating factors over which you may have no direct control. Thus, it is imperative that the career-planning process involve an understanding of the issues facing health care today. As hospitals change in structure, as more alternative approaches to health care delivery are developed, as increasing cost constraint requirements and competition become evident, the hospital in its present form may not exist five or ten years from now. It may be smaller, it may be highly specialized and in all probability it may be part of a health care conglomerate or system. Awareness of these factors must be a major consideration in career planning.

Individuals entering their first supervisory positions should understand that they must be prepared to make career changes. New supervisors who felt they would spend their entire working careers in a hospital may, at some point, have to consider careers in home health, outpatient care, or health maintenance organizations (HMOs). As more hospitals make the transition from single, freestanding entities to multifaceted health care corporations, supervisors may suddenly find themselves being transferred, not just between patient floors or from one department to another, but to health care delivery activities completely different from those to which they have been accustomed. This will occur more frequently as chief executives seek management talent to staff newly created organizations, facilities and programs.

In the large industrial organization, the corporate transfer is a way of life and this may begin occurring in health care, particularly for well-qualified, talented supervisors who aspire to general management positions. In fact, individuals unwilling to accept transfer may find opportunities for further growth limited.

As previously suggested, promotional opportunity in the not-for-profit health care setting appears to have long been limited. Generally speaking, middle-level management positions—for example, assistant administrators—have traditionally been filled through external recruiting rather than internal promotion. Except in the cases of certain positions that require a technical expertise such as finance, marketing or nursing, this pattern may change, particularly as hospitals make the transition to multi-entry health care corporations. Formal management development and management succession programs, common in industry but lacking in health care, will become more prominent. Various programs will be developed to help chief executive officers identify supervisors having the potential for advancement into higher management positions. Such management development programs will encompass various types of informal and formal training, including sending managers to school at the employer's expense for advanced degrees such as the MBA or MHA. Persons chosen for such programs may not have a choice as to whether they will accept. A supervisor who does not wish to accept additional responsibility or to transfer from specialist to generalist may no longer be acceptable to the employer. Having demonstrated appropriate managerial skills, the supervisor may be expected to subordinate his or her own professional career goals to the goals of the organization. Some difficult personal decisions will have to be made.

The most successful organizations will be those that remain financially viable without compromising or sacrificing the care quality. The institution must be profitable to survive. Unquestionably, many patient care executives are uncomfortable with the increasing emphasis on the bottom line. It is even predicted that within the next several years many not-for-profit hospitals may move toward for-profit status. Whether this occurs or not, financial control will be an essential element of management at all levels. Even the most altruistic and humanistic supervisor will need to understand the budgeting process and the basic economics of health care. Many supervisors will require additional schooling in basic accounting and hospital finance, and individuals may attend courses on the premises or be sent to courses at night. Supervisors are already beginning to voluntarily return to school in the evening to acquire financial knowledge.

Regardless of how the appropriate knowledge is obtained, advancement to higher management positions may be limited for those supervisors who do not understand the necessity for fiscal controls (and who indeed may resent such controls) or who do not avail themselves of the opportunities provided by their employers to gain the necessary knowledge. Recognizing one's interest or disinterest in further education is critical, and the need for additional formal schooling must be considered in the career-planning process.

The implications for career planning are plain. The newly appointed or inexperienced supervisor must understand the dynamic forces at work in health care today. A night or more of school each week, instead of the bowling league or one's favorite television shows, may become an important part of one's life style. The new supervisor must attempt to predict where he or she may be in five years and must begin to prepare accordingly.

Health care is a rapidly changing, dynamic field. Regardless of discipline or technical specialty, new and inexperienced supervisors seeking expanded responsibilities will find ample opportunities and awards available to them if they are willing to take the time to analyze their abilities and personal philosophies, assess their aspirations and prepare for the future accordingly.

# The health care supervisor: Dinosaur or superstar?

*William Umiker*
*Professor*
*Pennsylvania State University*
*Hershey, Pennsylvania*

THE 1980s HAVE featured a multi-tiered elimination of managers. Many chief executive officers (CEOs) and other executives are hurriedly updating their resumes and conferring with headhunters. When reductions in force (RIFs) are described as removal of layers of management, the reference is usually to middle managers. Middle managers are losing their jobs in droves.[1,2] Willis reports that an estimated 500,000 managers at more than 300 corporations have lost their jobs.[3]

Relatively little has been heard about the elimination of first-line managers, that is, foremen and supervisors. It may be appropriate at this point to define middle manager and supervisor. The latter, often described as the man in the middle, is the manager who is closest to where a product or a service originates. The middle manager, on the other hand, has supervisors, foremen, or other managers reporting to him or her. For the purpose of this article, a key difference is

*Health Care Superv*, 1988, 6(4), 39–44

that supervisors are usually capable of doing the work that their subordinates do; middle managers often are not.

Many health care supervisors are involved in more "doing" than directing. While Marvin found that industrial supervisors spend over 50% of their time administering, Templin claims that in a typical health care situation, supervisors spend only 4% to 10% of their time on staff duties.[4,5]

Are supervisors' jobs in jeopardy? Tom Peters seems to think so. He states categorically that there is no longer a role for the traditional first-line supervisor.[6] The Rohm and Haas Company has eliminated supervisors in its small plant.[7] All its employees play an active role in managing the plant. The Dana corporation improved productivity by keeping its plants small and shifting supervisory functions to the workers.[8]

## HOW WORKERS ARE AFFECTED BY THE ELIMINATION OF SUPERVISORS

Employees usually work in self-managed teams of four to seven people.[9,10] These teams perform holistic tasks rather than isolated components of these tasks. This provides a sense of ownership of the product of service, encourages quality work, and makes work more interesting.

Sometimes a lead worker or senior team member assumes more of the administrative responsibilities; at other times group leadership is by rotation. The supervisory or administrative functions that are not assumed by the workers are assigned either to a reduced corps of super-supervisors or to middle managers.

Sophisticated data processing systems facilitate production and quality control.[11] For example, user friendly terminals can be placed next to patients' beds, with function keys and numeric keypads replacing the keyboards of cathode-ray tubes (CRTs). Nurses record patients' vital signs, diet, input-output, hygiene, intravenous care, and progress assessments. These data are automatically recorded in electronic medical records at nurse stations. In one hospital this system saves over an hour per nurse per shift.[12]

Employment interviews, inventory control, and many other functions can be expedited by management information systems (MIS) using readily available software.

The training of these employees is extensive and has two major components. First, the workers learn a broad spectrum of technical or professional skills, often representing the content of as many as 30 different jobs.[13] These activities usually include equipment maintenance and repair, troubleshooting, and quality control. One of the goals for each member of a work group is to be able to perform all of the tasks assigned to the group. To achieve this, there is extensive cross-training and rotation of assignments. This training is provided largely by other members of the group, with little coaching by managers.[14]

Human resource executives like the fact that one of the outcomes of this approach is fewer job classifications. For example, in a General Motors plant in California, classifications decreased from 80 to 2.[15] The Rohm and Haas Corporation reduced job classifications from 100 to 20.[16]

The second training objective addresses the workers' need for managerial skills in order to perform duties previously handled by supervisors. Because the workers will select new employees, make their own decisions, solve group problems, evaluate each other, maintain inventory control, and prepare budgets, they must learn how to do these things competently.

## THE EFFECT OF MANAGERIAL CHANGES ON THE HIERARCHY

Certain variations of traditional managerial themes have surfaced in organizations in which supervisors either have been eliminated or have had significant role changes. Some of the more apparent effects of change are the following:

- Reduced hierarchical levels (flat organization), less bureaucracy, and fewer job classifications.[17–19] There are fewer layers of managers to filter, distort, or eliminate vertical information.[20,21]
- A major downward shift in responsibilities. Decision making is delegated to the action levels.[22,23]
- Increased span of control. Traditionally, managers have fewer than ten subordinates reporting to them. In supervisor-depleted organizations, 30 or more employees may report to a single manager.[24]
- An egalitarian shift towards Theory Z cultures. By adapting to colleagues and by working cooperatively, employees develop a flexibility like that of a basketball team; that is, they can move quickly from one formation to another.[25]
- Unbundling of large departmental functions into segments small enough to be identified as task clusters, which are then assigned to small teams.[26] For example, in a large health record office the function of patient follow-up can be sequestered into a group workstation. The team assigned to this workstation rotates through other sections of the department.
- Decreased specialization of workers. The employee, by developing a broad range of technical, professional, and administrative skills, becomes jack-of-all-trades.
- Increased specialization of the managers who serve as consultants, advisors, trainers, and facilitators.[27]
- Expanded training programs. In leading Japanese organizations and in better American corporations, employees spend 40 hours or more per year in classrooms. This is essential if workers are to assume supervisory responsibilities. The constricted management team must be made up of highly qualified professionals and leaders.[28]
- Increased leadership strategies of managing by wandering around, managing by objectives, or managing by exception.
- Delegation to the fullest, but while carefully avoiding abandonment of the delegates or confusing delegation with assigning busywork. If the managers serve as consultants and specialists, they must be visible and accessible.

## HOW WORKERS HAVE RESPONDED TO MANAGERIAL CHANGES

Reports are sketchy and largely anecdotal, but overall worker reaction to these changes seems highly favorable. The degree of positive response depends largely on what the situation was before the changes were introduced. When supervision had been perceived by employees as bureaucratic, autocratic, or incompetent, or when the work was monotonous and inflexible, the new systems were more likely to be greeted with enthusiasm.

***In leading Japanese organizations and in better American corporations, employees spend 40 hours or more per year in classrooms.***

The changes noted have been both motivational and operational. Motivational factors included closer identification with employers and management, stronger collegial relationships with coworkers, and greater appreciation for leadership problems. Operational factors were those dealing with communication, work organization and scheduling, and administrative responsibilities. Greater team identification, coordination, and cooperation were apparent. Some typical responses that were observed include the following:

- Improved morale, motivation, and self-esteem in the work force. These are manifested by increased productivity, fewer errors, less turnover, better attendance, and a marked decrease in employees' complaints and grievances.[29]
- Communication is facilitated. Employees feel they can better represent themselves in negotiating for increased pay and improved working conditions. It is easier to get complaints and criticism to higher authorities.[30]
- Employees have more input into what they do and how they do it. They report less red tape and nitpicking. This supports the currently popular cliche: workers want to be led, not managed.
- Employees like having more accountability and authority, making decisions, solving their own problems, selecting new hires, and doing things their way. They prefer being responsible for holistic tasks and a large menu of assignments.
- Employees applaud the augmentation of their vocational qualifications through education, cross-training, and job rotation.

## HOW MANAGERS ARE AFFECTED

The reduced managerial staffs, whether composed of middle managers or selected supervisors, find radical changes in their roles. These include the following:

- role as adviser, specialist, or troubleshooter rather than order giver;
- role as facilitator with the challenge of removing obstacles to help the work teams get their job done;
- role as trainer, planner, and strategist;
- greater use of computerized MIS to monitor productivity and quality, to help make managerial and administrative decisions, and to maintain records;[31] and
- utilization of delegation and MIS to free up time for other activities such as providing psychological support to the workers, engaging in research and development, or formulating comprehensive planning strategies.

## HOW SUPERVISORS CAN PREPARE FOR A POSSIBLE ROLE CHANGE

Some supervisors welcome the opportunity to surrender their managerial prerogatives, to return to being star performers. Many never wanted to be supervisors in the first place and dislike their managerial responsibilities. This situation is highlighted in colleges and universities when professors frequently resign their administrative posts as department heads or deans to resume teaching.

For the supervisors who opt to keep managerial duties, the opportunities for promotion may be better than ever. The following are some suggestions for individuals who are in this group:

- Sharpen all your general supervisory skills. Go to workshops, develop a management library, join professional societies that include management seminars at their meetings. Spend more time with fellow supervisors in other departments. Share problems and organizational information. Serve on committees and task forces.
- Serve as a good supervisory role model. Show personal interest in each employee, in what he or she does, and in what he or she is capable of doing.
- Support employees in their efforts to broaden their capabilities and responsibilities—their next performance review is a good time and place to start. Concentrate on their new goals and objectives and their plans and ideas for becoming more valued employees. Talk about cross-training, job rotation, training, and assigning of holistic tasks. Encourage intrapreneurship.[32]
- Discuss your problems with subordinates. Consider using quality circles and brainstorming techniques. At these meetings ensure that everyone is treated as an equal.[33]
- Keep lines of communication open and active. Tell associates what is expected of them. Provide positive and frequent reinforcement when they meet these expectations. Develop a high praise–criticism ratio.

• • •

A few industries have reported outstanding success in shifting operational responsibilities from managers to workers. In some of these organizations, supervisors have been eliminated or their roles have been radically altered.

Since this organizational revolution may spread to health care facilities, it behooves supervisors to be prepared to respond to the challenge.

## REFERENCES

1. Kutter, B. "The Declining Middle." *Atlantic* 252 (July 1983): 60.
2. *Fortune Magazine* 109 (February 6, 1984): 116.
3. Willis, R. "What's Happening to America's Middle Managers?" *Management Review* 76 (January 1987): 24–33.
4. Marvin, P. *Executive Time Management*. New York: AMACOM, 1980.
5. Templin, J.L., Jr. "The Impact of Nonwidget-Producing Activities." *Health Care Supervisor* 5, no. 4 (1987): 13–26.
6. Peters, T. "Seeking Improvement? Start with People."

*Lancaster New Era Newspaper*, 8 July 1987, p.1.
7. Nichols, D. "Taking Participative Management to the Limit." *Management Review* 76 (August 1987): 28–32.
8. Orchard, J. *Dana Corporation Plant Manager*, Lancaster, Penn., Personal correspondence.
9. Nichols, "Taking Participative Management to the Limit."
10. Geber, B. "Teaming up with Unions." *Training* 24 (August 1987): 24–32.
11. Willis, "What's Happening to America's Middle Managers."
12. Anderson, A. "Bytes & Pieces." *Physicians & Computers* 5 (August 1987): 6
13. Geber, "Teaming Up with Unions."
14. Ibid.
15. Ibid.
16. Ibid.
17. Willis, "What's Happening to America's Middle Managers."
18. Peters, "Seeking Improvement? Start with People."
19. Geber, "Teaming Up with Unions."
20. Peters, "Seeking Improvement? Start with People."
21. Whitney, J.O. "Organizing for a Turnaround." *Management Review* 75 (December 1986): 50–53.
22. Peters, "Seeking Improvement? Start with People."
23. Nichols, "Taking Participative Management to the Limit."
24. Whitney, "Organizing for a Turnaround."
25. Ibid.
26. Ibid.
27. Kutter, "The Declining Middle."
28. Nichols, "Taking Participative Management to the Limit."
29. Ibid.
30. Ibid.
31. Polakoff, J.C. "Will Middle Managers Work in the Factory of the Future?" *Management Review* 76 (January 1987): 50–51.
32. Umiker, W. "Do You Have an Intrapreneur in Your Lab?" *MLO* 18 (September 1986): 48–52
33. Ouchi, W. "Going from A to Z...Thirteen Steps to a Theory Z Organization." *Management Review* 70 (May 1981): 8–12.

# Does an effective clinician make an effective manager?

*Joy D. Calkin*
*Associate Professor*
*Nursing & Health Services Administration*
*School of Nursing*
*University of Wisconsin-Madison*
*Madison, Wisconsin*

A FREQUENTLY CITED criterion for the selection of head nurses and supervisors is that they be good bedside nurses and good staff nurses. When staff nurses and other health care providers criticize their first-line managers, these clinicians often claim that the managers do not really understand patient care needs or that they are too far away from real practice. Is it a myth that excellence in practice produces a better head nurse? Or, phrased differently, what kinds of staff nurse skills make a positive contribution to competence in nurse managers?

Similar functions and processes are performed by staff nurses and nurse managers. Hospital-based staff nurses are described as having a number of functions: assessment, planning, implementation and evaluation of direct patient care; communication with nursing and other health care providers regarding patient care; coordi-

*Health Care Superv*, 1982,1(1),26–37

nation of many services for their patients; and in some settings, organization and evaluation of the nursing care provided by aides and practical nurses. Managers are described as performing planning, organizing, communicating, controlling (e.g., evaluating), coordinating, leading, staffing and decision-making functions. With so many similar functions, why is the transition from staff nurse to head nurse often described as difficult and problematic?

There are similarities between able staff nurses and head nurses in relation to the overall organization, the nursing service department, the nursing unit and direct patient care levels. However, some issues are unique to first-line managers as they make the move from staff nurse to their new positions.

## THE OVERALL HOSPITAL ORGANIZATION

The two major reasons for the hospitalization of patients are the provision of highly skilled nursing care and the availability of sophisticated diagnostic and treatment modalities not available in a physician's office. The trend is toward more patients being hospitalized for shorter periods, requiring more intensive attention and needing more follow-up care after discharge. Almost one-third of patient care hours provided by nursing services are now in constant and intensive care units. Virtually all hospital departments have become more specialized; that is, each member of the hospital staff, especially in diagnostic and treatment departments, deals more and more with fewer and fewer aspects of patient services. In general, the larger the hospital, the greater the degree of specialization to be encountered.

All departments providing services to patients come to the patient to provide their services, or the patient is taken to the departments. Only the nursing unit is coextensive with the patient care unit. One might wonder why the nurse does not come and provide the nursing services required by patients and families, such as general hygiene, comfort measures and education for managing self-care, and then leave? (This notion is not far-fetched when one considers the care provided by a visiting nurse service, in which the nursing unit and patient care space are not coextensive in time and space.)

As a result of the historical development of hospital care, competent staff nurses have become skillful in fitting together the specialized functions of many hospital departments, for example, delaying breakfast while waiting for laboratory personnel to draw blood specimens. Staff nurses also take over specialized functions for other groups when they are absent, such as observing patient responses to medical therapy on behalf of the physician and doing respiratory therapy on the evening and night shifts.

As a result of these fitting-together and filling-in activities, better staff nurses become aware of the multiplicity and complexity of services provided throughout the hospital. The staff nurse has frequent communication with many hospital departments in coordinating patient services. Skillful and competent staff nurses have learned to coordinate services in ways that lessen the negative consequences on patients and families of the specialized, intensive diagnostic and treatment activities of the patient care environment. Conscious awareness of the functions of the overall institution is a strength of able staff nurses that is a necessary requisite for first-line managers of nursing units.

***Conscious awareness of the functions of the overall institution is a strength of able staff nurses that is a necessary requisite for first-line managers of nursing units.***

The professional staff nurse has a strongly developed commitment to patient care goals that go beyond nursing care goals. Recently, this author spoke with a group of 17 head nurses and 5 clinical specialists responsible for the administrative and clinical care aspects of patient care units. The nurse managers came from hospitals varying with respect to size, type of structure, degree of nursing care specialization, ratio of registered nurses to other nursing personnel and goals for nursing service. The length of time they had held their positions ranged from two months to 12 years. Three head nurses were from small, rural hospitals. The group with whom this author spoke identified this commitment to working with other providers and support staff as a characteristic of excellence in a nursing staff member. They indicated that this valuing of others' contributions to patient care and family care, when combined with sound conflict resolution[1] and other interpersonal skills, was often the single quality that set apart particularly effective nurses from their colleagues.

As one clinical specialist described it, "They seem to clearly believe that nursing goals are an important part of patient care. Yet, they consciously or intuitively check out others' goals, speak others' 'languages' and hang in and deal with perceived disagreements so that patients end up as the winners." The group noted that this kind of behavior, while important for staff nurses, was *essential* for head nurses, clinical specialists and other first-line managers because of nursing's coordinating function with respect to other departments or groups.

The transition from staff nurse to head nurse is facilitated by knowledge of the goals and values of hospital staff in other departments and how these are similar to and different from those of nursing. This knowledge, when combined with skill in conflict resolution and other interpersonal skills, seems to enable the head nurse to deal with the complex coordination needed by patients in most hospital settings. The larger the hospital, the greater the demands on this knowledge and skill.

## WITHIN NURSING SERVICE ADMINISTRATION

The fundamental purpose of the nursing department is the provision of planned, sound nursing care within the cost constraints imposed by the institution's budget. Some nursing departments establish safe care as a goal while others seek to achieve excellence in nursing care. Nursing departments may also have responsibility for maintaining an environment that facilitates educational experiences for students and encourages research in nursing. In many hospitals it is implicitly expected that the personnel of the nursing department will detect errors made by other departments and see that they are corrected so that patients, physicians and the hospital suffer no negative effects.

### Organizational structure

The structure of organizations and departments exists for the purpose of facilitating decision making appropriate to the size of the hospital. The structure of nursing departments varies widely from hospital to hospital and affects the way they plan, organize, control (e.g., monitor budgets), staff and specify who usually makes what kinds of decisions (e.g., hiring a staff nurse). The organizational chart provides a picture of the degree of nursing care specialization, the depth of the vertical hierarchy and the kinds of support units available (e.g., inservice education). The chart communicates something about specialization of nursing units and the nursing hierarchy, but it does not truly indicate which decisions are made by each position. The hierarchy of decision making and the responsibilities of different positions are found in formal policies and procedures. For example, policies indicate whether staffing of units is done in the nursing office, by the head nurse alone, or in some combined fashion.

There are currently two dominant tendencies in the structuring of nursing departments. Each type of structure is useful under different conditions.

#### *Centralized structure*

Traditionally, philosophy, goals, budgets, inservice programs, hiring and other decisions tend to be made centrally for the whole nursing department with varying amounts of input from the unit level. The head nurse is responsible for implementing the centrally made decisions and for the day-to-day running of the unit. The assumption is made that each succeeding level of the hierarchy supervises the next lower level. This traditional model is useful under conditions where well-prepared nurse managers and independent, self-directed staff nurses are believed to be lacking. It is also useful when there are few available registered nurses in settings such as many nursing home facilities. The centralized structure is, however, frequently used because the hospital and nursing service administrators are more comfortable with this level of control, because the structure is the same as that used for smaller and more routinely run departments or because an alternative structure has not been considered.

More recently, in many nursing departments overall departmental direction is provided, decisions are made, or major decision input is provided by nursing councils representing all levels of the hierarchy. Terms such as *participative decision making* and *professional practice models* describe these structures. Although major policy decisions are still centralized, in the council many more actors are involved.

Hospital size is not a major factor in the choice of this model. However, it functions better under conditions in which the nurse representatives are willing to study issues, discuss and make decisions or recommendations that reflect an understanding of both overall departmental needs and unit needs. The participative decision-making structure is useful when a hospital is committed to developing and maintaining responsible involvement of nurses in practice-related decisions. It also functions as a mechanism for gaining information from nurses about the effects of management decisions being considered. These structures are quite effective in increasing satisfaction with work and a shared commitment to the hospital and nursing unit goals.

### *Decentralized structure*

The second type of structure is generally called *decentralized.* There is variation in the level at which decisions are decentralized. The chief officer of the nursing department maintains final management authority; however, major authority and accountability for management is delegated to either the unit level (e.g., head nurse or clinical specialist) or clinical directors (titles vary greatly) of clusters of nursing units. Delegation to the unit level requires much greater management skill, both on the part of the first-line manager and the head of the nursing department, than does the traditional structure. Large and small hospitals may use this structure.

Decentralization to clinical directors is more common in large, complex hospitals. At the head nurse and staff nurse levels, this form of decentralization may not feel different from the traditional structure. This type of structure provides opportunities for developing more informed nurse managers and job enrichment for those to whom decisions are delegated. Transferring major accountability for decisions such as hiring staff and budget planning is a useful structure under conditions when there is a high level of unit specialization because of the differing needs of units. It should be considered when decisions are not being made in a timely fashion because of decision-making overload at top management levels. This structure does require well-developed managerial skills from the accountable decision makers.

**Effect of structure on preparation for management**

Why discuss these differences in structure when the focus of this article is the transition from staff nurse to head nurse? The way that information is gathered and decisions are made in the nursing service department has a direct impact on the opportunities for staff nurses to become involved in traditional management functions, such as making plans for nursing services, interviewing potential staff and becoming involved with committees within nursing and with other departments. High levels of staff participation in management decision making and problem solving better equip staff to understand organizational relationships and the numbers and kinds of factors that enter into decisions or influence the head nurses' decisions. As one staff nurse representative on a council commented,

> I had no idea how Medicare reimbursement cuts affected the budget nursing had planned for the year. The council had a very hard time recommending against starting the new quality of care review system we'd been planning for almost a year. The head nurse and I worked with the staff to develop suggestions for reducing unit costs, too. On top of all that our director reminded us that we should exercise caution in our recommendations so the kind of care we give wouldn't suffer. I think I learned more than I ever wanted to know about all the units and their money needs.

Staff nurses who have had practical experience with top-level decisions and problems bring an important perspective to the head nurse position. They have had to deal with the conflicting needs of different groups, collecting and using information in problem solving and negotiating with colleagues outside their own units. The greater the use of participative management structures and of decentralized management decision making in the nursing department, the more important it is to choose a staff nurse who has a broader view of departmental level issues for a head nurse position.

Staff nurses who demonstrate judgment, initiative and leadership skills with respect to patient care and the unit are a valuable nursing resource. Selecting or electing them for committees, advisory groups, limited assignments or projects is often viewed as a way of challenging them and maintaining their interest in their professional growth. These activities provide, in addition, a useful management "school" for potential head nurses. Staff nurses who are active in their professional association's committee work may develop skills in organizing, planning, communicating and leading—another excellent "school." They will gain more from these experiences if astute first-line supervisors, directors of nursing or others discuss what they are learning, not only about the work of the committee (e.g., how to perform a quality assurance audit) but also how the group functions, how leadership styles vary and how this work may affect patient care and nursing services.

The nursing department can provide formal opportunities for staff nurses to learn about broader management issues. Gerschefske describes an assessment program in which groups of selected staff nurses are given rigorous, relevant head nurse management exercises and feedback.[2] This program helps identify potential head nurses. This author is aware of one vice-president of nursing who selects a staff nurse to serve as an assistant to her for a defined time period. The assistant may assume responsibility for doing a project, gathering data for decision making and similar tasks. The assistant sits in on a range of meetings with the vice-president and in other ways develops a knowledge of nursing administration. The assistants then return to their staff nurse responsibilities with new awarenesses and skills. It is anticipated that a staff nurse with this experience would bring unique perspectives and strengths to a first-line management position.

Regardless of the particular goals and structures of a nursing department, it is possible to find opportunities for staff nurses to develop and test leadership and management skills. These "hands on" opportunities are an important way of learning about issues and problems about which many staff nurses are quite underinformed. Finally, effective staff nurses may be identified or may identify themselves as having potential for a first-line management position when they have the chance to exercise relevant skills.

## THE UNIT AND PATIENT CARE

The patient care unit is where goals and plans become actions or fail to become actions, where organizational goals (e.g., cost containment) and professional nursing goals (e.g., get patient needs met even if it means making exceptions to the usual system) sometimes mesh and sometimes clash, and where neophyte staff nurses enhance their direct patient care and patient care management skills or fail to do so.

Effective staff nurses and effective nurse managers have many tasks and skills in common. The amount of time they spend on those tasks and the demands on their skills may vary. Most often, of course, the head nurse maintains a unit view, while the staff nurse focuses predominantly on a group of patients and often the staff (practical nurse, nurse's aide) who assist with the patient care.

Both staff nurse and nurse manager require the knowledge base to make decisions and solve problems arising from patient care. Where they lack knowledge, each must possess skill in consultation with nursing colleagues, physicians and others. Each is more effective if able to adapt to rapidly changing unit conditions by altering priorities. The staff nurse who can effectively challenge assumptions has a skill important for nursing leadership. For example, is the traditional change-of-shift report really the most appropriate way to exchange information?

The way that staff nurses use their knowledge is one of the more important indicators of the likelihood of their success as nurse managers.

***The way that staff nurses use their knowledge is one of the more important indicators of the likelihood of their success as nurse managers.***

In general, one of the better predictors of future behavior is past behavior. Those staff nurses who see people's behavior as all good or all bad are unlikely to change that perception as head nurses. Nurses who carefully listen to patients' complaints about their roommates' annoying behavior and help the patients learn to deal successfully with the problem themselves are much more likely to manage staff complaints about their colleagues in a similar, growth-producing way. Nurses who carefully assess patient problems and evaluate a number of possible approaches to care before acting are likely to be more effective nurse managers than those who act on the usual approach or the first one that occurs to them. Staff nurses who plan in advance for possible patient care emergencies have been described by other staff as more effective in handling emergencies.[3] Similarly, nurse managers who anticipate and plan for unusual unit circumstances are more likely to deal well with problems if they occur. In sum, the ways clinicians consistently go about problem solving and working with others to resolve issues are likely to persist after they become head nurses.

## GOOD STAFF NURSE EQUALS GOOD HEAD NURSE: MYTH?

Myths contain a core of truth. Excellence in direct patient care is useful to the new head nurse for several reasons.

- Part of the position may include providing direct care.[4]
- Expertise is a source of power to influence others' behavior.
- Knowledge provides one source of judgment regarding quality of care on the unit for which the nurse manager is responsible.
- The nurse manager is the next step in the hierarchy for any patient care decision a staff nurse is unable to make.
- Problem solving, priority setting and interpersonal skills required for excellence often are brought to the new position.
- Excellence may give the new nurse manager a sense of self-esteem that facilitates adaptation to new functions.

However, if the new head nurse has received valued positive feedback for patient care behavior, there may be a tendency to cling to patient care activities to the detriment of other management functions. One can argue that excellence in general patient care may be more important than specialized skills for the new head nurse, provided the staff is competent and consultation is available to the new manager. For example, does the nurse manager on an endocrine service need to have had prior experience there? There has been no systematic study of this viewpoint with nurses.

Competence in patient care management activities transfers readily to requirements of the head nurse position. These activities include charting; referrals; consultation regarding care; admission, transfer and placement of patients; conferences with patients, families and other providers of care; evaluation of the quality of nursing care; and other activities that support and facilitate patient care.

Effective involvement for a staff nurse in hospital and nursing service activities is useful as the nurse becomes a first-line manager. The head nurse or clinical specialist is at the crucial level between administrative plans and patient care activities. Earlier experiences in productively representing the unit view of an issue to administration, or vice versa, will smooth the transition from nurse to nurse manager.

There is therefore an element of truth in the assumption that staff nurses' knowledge and skills make a distinguishable contribution to role transition. But good staff nurses may not become especially good nurse managers.

## TRANSITION FROM NURSE TO NURSE MANAGER

Unit level nurse managers almost uniformly state that a key problem in their transition is the change from being "one of us" (i.e., staff) to "one of them" (i.e., administration). This problem is described even by those who have not previously worked on the units where they are now nurse managers. The majority report that this role change is much more difficult than the change from student to staff nurse. Essentially, the nurses have moved from an "ingroup" to an "outgroup" position. The outgroup feeling is reinforced by the observation that staff reduce their "grapevine" communications, avoid spending more time with the manager than the rest of the staff, are more critical of the manager's patient care skills than of other staff, become annoyed when the manager "takes administration's side" and so on.

Managers respond by trying to remain or get into the ingroup (e.g., socially), avoiding negative feedback to staff about their performance, "feeling defensive," pretending they do not like their management duties (e.g., "I *have* to go to that boring meeting!") and doing the same work as the staff while fulfilling management responsibilities as well. Others react by identifying strongly with upper management and underattending the different needs of staff and patients.

### Goal orientation

There are resolutions to this conflict. Many nurse managers indicated they took their positions because they wanted to positively influence the unit environment and make things better. Those who kept this goal in mind seemed better able to cope with the negative responses they received. Several identified administratively solvable problems bothering the staff, dealt with them and told the staff how they thought they could continue to fulfill staff goals in their new position if they worked together. Managers who establish or join a small group of other managers for venting feelings and problem solving find they resolve their negative feelings more quickly and deal with staff's responses more objectively. One head nurse said she did not care what staff thought about her. She expected good care, she got that from staff, and although initial staff turnover was very high, "things have settled down now that I've hired my own staff."

### Problems of inexperience

None of the head nurses and few clinical specialists had experience in continuously dealing with the technical demands of their positions. Limited experience was the second barrier commonly confronting them: the more decentralized the management decisions, the greater discomfort with this lack. Competence in staffing and scheduling, developing and using budget information, handling personnel issues (e.g., hiring, evaluating, firing, monitoring collective bargaining agreements), knowing what issues should be reported upward and downward and facilitating group meetings were the areas of greatest difficulty noted. The direct result of such inexperience is that the manager cannot perform well. The indirect results are excessive hours spent in preparation, a loss of self-esteem and feelings of self-doubt.

Strategies to respond to this lack of technical skills are quite straightforward and often rewarding. A common initial strategy is to capitalize on the strengths of unit staff by asking them to assist with scheduling, interviewing potential staff and chairing meetings. Seeking consultation from experienced head nurses and others is very useful. "They were really supportive of me," one nurse noted. The advice of another nurse is, "Tell them to read, read, read—and practice, practice, practice—ask for feedback about how you're doing and go to every appropriate course or workshop until you can teach the stuff yourself."

### Time management

Time management is a challenge to all nurse managers. The greater the decentralization of administrative decisions and the greater the level of participative decision making, the greater the difficulty in resolving the problem. Feelings of being overwhelmed and unable to set priorities, of never finishing anything, and of doing a poor job and missing important deadlines are common symptoms.

An adaptive question is whether it is necessary for managers to perform all their tasks themselves and whether the tasks they are doing are actually necessary. Nurses who do simple time studies by jotting down their activities for several days find they can often better manage their work. Books about time management are a valuable source of new approaches.

Good basic mental and physical health care is an important element in dealing with time pressure. A clinical specialist advised that combining related and "even seemingly unrelated" tasks allowed her to survive time pressures. For example, she had clinical teaching responsibilities in addition to her direct care and management tasks. The staff nurses assumed some clinical teaching and supervision with her guidance, and that change contributed to staff development, student learning and, as it turned out, also raised everyone's satisfaction.

The students had projects to complete and selected them from a number the specialist had not had time to do. Several of the staff worked with particular students on the projects, took projects over when the students left and implemented the results. Everyone seemed to benefit from this more complex form of time management.

**Successful nurse managers**

Among the nurse managers interviewed were several who seemed exceptional. Like many others, they performed their technical and interpersonal management functions well. Yet, they seemed to have developed a different level of conceptualizing and carrying out their work. One characteristic was the ability to knit together multiple functions such as the clinical specialist described above. Second, their problem solving and decision making were remarkably complex and involved frequent consideration of short- and long-range goals. They perceived their jobs as complex and thought about them that way.

***The problem solving and decision making of the more successful nurse managers was remarkably complex and involved frequent consideration of short- and long-range goals.***

One woman was described by a nurse administrator as an excellent manager but she was "dragging her heels a bit on moving her unit into primary nursing." After an interview, it became apparent that she had set a late target date quite purposefully. She was working closely with staff members and several physicians to develop a shared, acceptable view of primary nursing because she had read that conflicting interpretation was a common problem in implementation. The staff wanted to evaluate two types of ten-hour shifts, and she believed the evaluation should be considered parallel to primary nursing. Nursing service was reevaluating job descriptions and had decentralized this work. She had raised the question with staff about whether they should have generalist and specialist staff nurse selection criteria and descriptions since the unit had several distinct patient populations. The solution to this question also had to "fit" with primary nursing.

The foregoing is but a sample of factors she was considering simultaneously in providing leadership for the unit. The staff on the unit, she thought, might be overwhelmed by all these "pieces." Interestingly, they saw these activities as part of the whole change to primary nursing.

The myth that skilled staff nurses make better nurse managers is partially true. However, nurse managers must gain technical, interpersonal and conceptual skills to deal consistently with the whole unit in the context of nursing service and the hospital. The manager is significantly different from the staff nurse. Management education, support from colleagues and the integration of many activities under one broad goal appear to be important strategies in successfully making this transition.

The many problems reported by new nurse managers from a variety of settings are remarkably similar. Yet, in spite of the pressures they experience, a large number of them like their work and want to remain in their job positions.

## REFERENCES


1. Filley, A.C. *Interpersonal Conflict Resolution* (Glenview, Ill.: Scott Foresman and Co. 1975).
2. Gerschefske, L. "Assessment and Development for Head Nurse Positions." *Supervisor Nurse* 11:2 (1980) p. 21–25.
3. Calkin, J.D. and Gulbrandsen, M.W. "Nursing Practice Decisions in Emergencies: A Course and How It Was Developed." *Journal of Nursing Education* 17:9 (1978) p. 30–37.
4. Barker, M., and Garti, A.R. "An In-Depth Study of the Head Nurse Role." *Supervisor Nurse* 11:11 (1980) p. 16–21.


## SUGGESTED READINGS


LeBreton, P.P. "A Council of Staff Nurses: A Proposal." *Nursing and Health Care* 11:5 (1981) p. 261–266, 285.

McCay, J.T. *The Management of Time* (Englewood Cliffs, N.J.: Prentice-Hall 1959).

Stevens, B.J. *The Nurse As An Executive* 2nd ed. (Wakefield, Mass.: Nursing Resources 1980).

# Finding the new supervisor: inside or outside?

***Charles R. McConnell***
*Vice President for Employee Affairs*
*The Genesee Hospital*
*Rochester, New York*

"SINCE RECEIVING my graduate degree more than a year ago, I have looked into every possible opportunity within this medical center for moving into a management position that would put me on a path toward administration. During that time there were several open positions that I believe I could have qualified for, but I saw all of these filled by people from the outside."

The foregoing paragraph appeared as the *reason for leaving* on an exit interview form. The person quoted, a registered nurse with a master's degree in public health administration, was leaving her employer of several years to take a management position in another organization. She had done reasonably well in graduate school, and, although she had never yet been tested in a position of significant managerial responsibility, she nevertheless had exhibited some of the signs of management potential.

For several years the medical center that lost the nurse had ex-

*Health Care Superv*, 1984,3(1),69–79

perienced a high rate of turnover among its upper level professional and technical employees—significantly higher than that of comparable institutions. This eventually caused the administration to seek the advice of a firm of personnel consultants. Through the use of a mechanism customarily described as an employee attitude survey, the personnel consultants developed conclusions suggesting, among other things, that qualified people were leaving the organization in unusual numbers because they saw the opportunity for advancement into higher management as extremely limited or nonexistent. Regarding turnover, it was pointed out that, although the medical center espoused a policy of promotion from within, in reality more than 90 percent of the center's management openings were filled through outside recruiting.

Based on the results of the attitude survey, the consultants were quick to suggest what was by then obvious: that the stated policy of promotion from within be made a reality by adopting the practice of filling a considerably larger proportion of management openings from within the institution. At about the same time, these same personnel consultants were telling another organization that too much emphasis had been placed on promotion from within. This latter organization, it was claimed, had fallen behind in the industry due to "management inbreeding and stagnation" that existed because of years of filling nearly all management positions internally.

Clearly, neither promotion from within nor recruiting from outside is always the right answer to a health care organization's management needs. There is indeed evidence to suggest that exclusive reliance on promotion from within eventually restricts the breadth and scope of management capabilities by limiting the introduction of new ideas and different ways of thinking. However, there is even more visible evidence to suggest that near-total reliance on recruiting from outside impairs the morale and thus the performance capabilities of the work group and saddles management with an image of instability.

Obviously, the question that arises is: What *is* the correct balance between the two practices? Unfortunately this question cannot be answered with specifically dictated proportions; that is, there is no sound basis for saying, "Make certain that *X* percent of new supervisors come from within the organization and the balance problem will be solved." Rather, it is necessary to examine the needs of each open supervisory position and follow a particular approach in attempting to fill that position. If the focus remains on each open position as it occurs, the long-run result will be neither all inside nor all outside recruiting.

## INSIDE VERSUS OUTSIDE: A CRITICAL COMPARISON

In this comparison of promotion from within versus outside recruiting, a number of pertinent characteristics of any given position are examined as they are affected by the advantages and the disadvantages of internal promotion and external recruiting.

**Recruiting considerations**

To first dispense with one of the more obvious areas of consideration: There is little or no recruiting cost associated with promoting from within. It is true that internal candidates must be screened, interviewed, and so on, but for the most part the costs involved are part of the overhead costs of the organization. That is, the internal posting system, the transfer application system, the personnel screening and interviewing process—the wherewithal to perform these and other related activities exists in the organization and involves costs that exist whether these activities are conducted or not. There is certainly a cost associated with handling an internal candidate, but it is not an out-of-pocket cost that can be avoided (unless of course internal transactions are reduced to such a level that a personnel interviewer can be eliminated).

Recruiting from outside involves direct costs in both time and money. Once again certain of these recruiting costs fall under the heading of fixed costs, but there are specific out-of-pocket costs as well, including advertising and perhaps interview travel and other related expenses. An informal survey of eight hospital personnel directors in a given region suggested that the filling of an open supervisory position from outside required an average of 8 to 12 weeks and cost approximately $2,000 out of pocket. "And we seem never to have enough time," said one personnel director. "With luck we get the requisition when the departing supervisor gives notice, usually 2 to 4 weeks before departure. More often than not the requisition is delayed and we have even less time in which to find candidates. But in either case it's rare that we can find an appropriate replacement in time to avoid a several-week period during which the position dangles open."

Often a department will drift with nominal supervision, acting supervision or no direct supervision at all while the outside recruiting process churns onward. And the potential for personnel problems and operating problems in a department lacking permanent leadership can be great.

In terms of both recruiting time and cost, promotion from within has the clear edge over outside recruiting.

***In terms of both recruiting time and cost, promotion from within has the clear edge over outside recruiting.***

**A significant change**

A change in the management of any work group is always a significant event in the life of that group and is virtually guaranteed to trigger certain forms of resistance to change.

Here again it is the insider who generally enjoys the edge. All other factors being equal, when the new supervisor comes from within the group, that individual is known by the people in the group and is thus less likely to be seen as threatening or potentially disruptive than the supervisor coming from outside the organization. To a considerable extent it is the *unknown* that people fear and thus tend to resist, and the supervisor coming from outside may be a totally unknown quantity. Even when the new supervisor is well known by the people in the work group, there may still be considerable resistance to this particular change. Some forms of resistance to the insider may perhaps be more troublesome than the resistance to the outsider if the particular insider had problems with the group before becoming supervisor, but for better or worse the insider has the edge over the outsider in becoming established with the work group simply because he or she is already known by that group.

### The supervisor's capability

If there are serious doubts or questions about the capabilities of available insiders, then outside recruiting may be the preferred way to go. Not every supervisory position can legitimately be filled from within the organization to best advantage; there simply are not always capable, qualified people available. By going outside, the organization can often obtain a new supervisor who has an established management track record generated through satisfactory performance in an equivalent or related management position.

The outside route is the way to go if special knowledge and experience is required that does not exist in the work group. This is often the case when new or expanded services or new technology has entered the operation of the department. For example, a materials management department that is preparing to institute a central transportation and distribution system would stand to benefit if its new supervisor had experience with such systems. As another example, a hospital pharmacy having a supervisory opening may deliberately look to filling that opening with someone experienced in unit dose systems if it is the hospital's intention to go toward unit dose in the foreseeable future. In short, judging the capability of a potential supervisor is up to higher management, but if it is clear to management that the capability does not exist in-house, then outside recruiting is clearly the only available way to obtain what is needed.

### The supervisor's credibility

Under some circumstances the person promoted from within may not be taken completely seriously in the department. The insider may have to overcome a long-standing image of being "just one of the gang" and may thus have to put forth extra effort to earn credibility as a supervisor. Some members of the work group may not be able to make the immediate transition from viewing the individual as a co-worker and organizational equal to viewing that same person as "the boss."

The supervisor from outside, on the other hand, may come into the work situation with a ready-made management image. The members of the work group will never have known the supervisor in any capacity other than supervisor, so the supervisor has no image problems to overcome.

There are, however, other dimensions to the credibility issue. While the outsider may be readily seen as a supervisor, that person may not be seen nearly as readily capable of rendering judgments regarding the organization's operations and activities. Thus the credibility issue may be addressed from either direction depending on the needs of a particular case. The outsider will generally be extended greater credibility as far as management is concerned; the insider will likely be regarded with greater credibility concerning knowledge and understanding of the organization's purposes and processes.

**Interpersonal relationships**

The supervisor who comes into the position from within the group will be supervising people who are friends or acquaintances as well as recent peers and co-workers. This invariably gives rise to the possibility of bias, usually unintentional but sometimes deliberate. Any person—and the supervisor of a work group is certainly no exception—will like some people more than others, will get to know certain people better than others and will tend to gravitate in relationships toward some people more than others. The work group is also a social group to a considerable extent, and it would be an extremely rare situation if the new supervisor's social relationships with all other employees of the department were equal. Even if actual bias does not exist, there will remain the real possibility of *perceptions* of bias or *charges* of bias based on peoples' knowledge of the supervisor's relationships. This can be fully as troublesome to the supervisor as reaction to actual bias.

Issues of bias aside, however, the fact remains that the supervisor promoted from within will be dealing with friends, acquaintances and recent peers and will be assigning work to these people, evaluating their performance, and occasionally criticizing and disciplining some of them. This dramatic realignment of interpersonal relationships presents considerable difficulty for many supervisors who come from within.

On the other hand, the supervisor who comes from outside of the organization enters with a clean slate as far as interpersonal relationships are concerned. This person is of course faced with the task of establishing relationships all the way around, but this is usually neither as difficult nor troublesome as the task the insider faces in altering existing interpersonal relationships. Thus the supervisor who comes from outside generally has the edge regarding interpersonal relationships by virtue of being unencumbered by preexisting relationships.

**Becoming fully effective**

In this particular dimension, the supervisor who comes from within has, in most instances, a clear advantage over the outsider. The insider is there and readily available. Promotion of the insider, if handled in a timely fashion, results in little or no lost time in the day-to-day management of the department. This can ensure continuity of department management.

In addition to being readily available, the insider already knows the people—their talents, their assets, their capabilities and their shortcomings. The insider also knows the work. The supervisor who rises from within the same department should be intimately familiar with the work methods, equipment and physical plan of the department. Even the semi-insider—the person who comes not from within the department but from another department in the same organization—is at least already knowledgeable of the policies, practices and objectives of the organization.

In short, the insider requires less orientation and can be expected to attain full speed much sooner than the outsider. The outsider has far more to learn, so the insider enjoys the edge in the ability to become fully effective much more quickly.

**The troubled department**

If a department has been experiencing managerial problems, performance problems or other difficulties that would suggest that a reorganization or general shake-up is called for, higher management might reasonably elect to recruit the new supervisor from outside the organization. If a department is troubled, it is highly likely that those persons who might otherwise emerge as internal candidates for the supervisor's position are themselves part of the problems or are at least affected by those problems to an extent that would impair their effectiveness at a supervisory level. In the troubled department, the insider is frequently hampered by differing interpersonal relationships and divided loyalties.

If it appears as though some degree of housecleaning will be required in the department—perhaps people will have to be released or reassigned, or reporting relationships and basic responsibilities will have to be altered—this is best undertaken by someone who has not been a part of the problem and who is unhampered by existing opinions, biases or loyalties. The supervisor from outside may enter the situation free from such encumbrances, so in most instances the supervisor from outside enjoys the edge in tackling the problem of the troubled department.

## MOTIVATIONAL CONCERNS

As alluded to in the opening example, problems will exist if employees see the practices of the organization running contrary to the organization's stated policies. Specifically, if there is a stated policy regarding promotion from within, there will be a problem of perhaps considerable dimensions if employees' perceptions run counter to that policy. A stated policy of promotion from within simply will not be believed if people see most desirable positions filled from outside, and having this policy in place under such conditions will be worse for employee morale than if there were no policy at all.

Employees will recognize growth opportunity within the organization if they actually see insiders rise not only into supervisory positions but also into higher-rated technical positions. The organization or department that appears to give serious consideration to internal promotion becomes, for many employees, a more desirable place to work. Consider, for example, the thirteen-member personnel department of a particular hospital. Within the course of one year, two key positions in the department—essentially the number two and number three positions in the personnel structure—turned over as two experienced supervisors left to assume personnel directors' positions elsewhere. Within this department attention had long been paid to the development of a knowledgeable backup for each supervisor, so promotable people were clearly identified. Each of the two instances of turnover triggered a chain of three internal promotions, and each resulted in the gap left by the departure being filled at the entry level (once by outside recruiting and once by transfer within the organization). Although the personnel staff stabilized following the second of these readjustments, in the months that followed, the unsolicited transfer inquiries—people in other departments inquiring into future opportunities to transfer into the personnel department—more than doubled. All persons inquiring about such transfer were asked why they were interested in the personnel department. Other than expressing an interest in personnel work, the most frequently cited reason was the observation that there appeared to be opportunity for growth and advancement in the personnel department. One individual summed it up well by saying: "People get promoted in your department. They know that as long as they perform they'll get a shot at the better jobs as they open up."

The opportunity for promotion and growth may be viewed as both a motivating force and as a potential dissatisfier; that is, as a reason for leaving one's employment. As a motivator the strength of this opportunity may be open to question; as a force that inspires people to work harder it is probably not as strong as many other forces. In a survey conducted a number of years ago by the United States Chamber of Commerce, the opportunity for promotion and growth fell into seventh place in importance on a list of the ten supposedly strongest motivating factors.[1] It fell behind some of the stronger psychological motivators (such as appreciation of work done) and behind material needs (good wages and job security). The presence of the opportunity for promotion and growth on the list of reasons why people hold onto their jobs is acknowledged, but it is far from being one of the strongest reasons.

Because the Chamber of Commerce survey was several years old and was conducted largely outside of health care, an effort was made to test the contentions of the survey by using the ten so-called motivating factors to sample the forces at work on health care personnel.[2] In minisurvey fashion, the ten motivating forces were tested against the preferences of several specific groups of employees in the hospital setting. For two pilot groups—a group of 24 medical laboratory technologists and a group of 27 registered nurses—the opportunity for promotion and growth again fell into seventh place on the list of the ten strongest motivating factors (with various people placing it as high as fifth on the list and as low as ninth on the list). The minisurvey was hardly scientific as surveys go, but it nevertheless suggested that there could be some validity to the relative position of this particular motivating force versus other more commonly accepted motivating forces.

***Among those currently employed, the opportunity for promotion invariably falls behind such things as good wages, appropriate benefits, appreciation of work done, job interest and job security as a motivator.***

One might conclude that the opportunity for promotion and growth may not be especially strong as a motivator; it invariably falls behind such things as good wages, appropriate benefits, appreciation of work done, job interest and job security. However, the aforementioned surveys dealt only with people who were actively employed and were probably expecting to continue in their positions. The results differ when one considers people who leave jobs and examines the reasons why they do so.

In another survey that concentrated only on persons who left their employment, the results were quite different concerning the opportunity for promotion and growth.[3] In this survey, of seven reasons why people leave jobs, "lack of advancement" fell into a strong second place (just after "lack of recognition" and immediately before "money"). These results suggest that although the opportunity for promotion and growth may not necessarily be a strong *motivator* it can nevertheless be a powerful *dissatisfier*. The opportunity for promotion and growth may not be availed of by many employees—and it will never be available to all, because supervisory positions are numerically few compared with nonsupervisory positions—but the opportunity must be present. If the opportunity is not present, it is possible that many employees will feel that there is a lid on their potential within the organization. They will see themselves as capped; they will know that they can go just so high (with "so high" usually meaning one's present position) and no higher. This feeling of being capped triggers discontent in many employees, a discontent that can grow more intense each time another desirable opening is filled by an outsider.

It is certainly true that not everyone will be capable of making it into management and that not everyone will ever have the opportunity to try. A number of people will not even particularly desire to advance. However, the average work group will include a number of people to whom advancement opportunity is important. These people, if they do not see advancement opportunity within the organization, will seek such opportunity elsewhere. Thus when an organization consistently fills supervisory positions and other desirable positions from outside, the organization is increasing the potential for the loss of good, ambitious, inside people. And usually it is the employees whom the organization should most wish to retain who are among the first to leave.

## OUTSIDE BY DEFAULT

Sometimes the choice of where the new supervisor comes from is forced to the outside by the failure of the previous supervisor to properly delegate to a subordinate and develop a potential successor. This failure can have an impact well beyond the immediate filling of the vacant supervisory position. Consider, for example, the situation presented when a specific hospital's business office manager left and that position became available. Neither of this manager's two assistants had ever been tested with any appreciable responsibility, and, because the manager's departure was abrupt, higher management had no knowledge of a potential successor in the department and no information about the supervisory potential of anyone in the department. Higher management felt compelled to go to the outside for a new business office manager rather than take a chance on a totally unknown quantity. Because this move was made, one of the two assistants lost out on the chance to become business office manager, and two lower-level jobs that could have been opened up by a promotional chain reaction remained closed. Thus three people missed out on possible promotions simply because one person had not practiced effective delegation.

When a supervisor fails to delegate to any appreciable extent and does not test subordinates with responsibility, often no one is able to emerge as a potential successor. There may be one or more potentially good supervisors lost in the confusion as higher management looks to the outside because they have no way of knowing what is available inside.

To assure that promotion from within works as intended, all parties concerned—each individual supervisor as well as each member of higher management—must be knowledgeable of the capabilities of persons in various positions in the customary promotional chain. In short, the organization should be reasonably prepared to promote long before the specific need to do so arises.

## NO PAT ANSWERS

Promotion from within assures valuable management continuity and stability that helps keep the organization functioning on a day-to-day, week-to-week basis. But new blood coming from outside brings with it new ideas and new approaches that are essential in helping an organization keep pace with the changing times. Clearly a balance between these two approaches to filling supervisory positions is desired.

When all new supervisors and managers come from within the organization, there is a tendency toward stagnation and a narrowing of management perspective. Managers tend to duplicate themselves in terms of style and approach as they promote subordinates, and subordinates tend often to pattern themselves after their role models.

On the other hand, an organization that fills all supervisory and management positions from the outside is inviting reduced employee morale, increased employee turnover and general organizational instability, as fresh ideas and new approaches continually clash with each other and the environment never fully settles down. The organization that relies wholly on the outside will also, as suggested earlier, lose many of its good people who will not remain where advancement opportunity does not exist.

A recommended approach for achieving a balance of inside versus outside in filling supervisory positions is

1. Under most circumstances, look first at the possibilities for internal promotion.
   —Look within the affected department, examining the true capabilities of available people (and not simply judging by longevity), and provide the initial opportunity to a qualified member of the work group.
   —If qualified persons either do not exist or exist but choose to decline the opportunity, broaden the search to include the rest of the organization (ordinarily done by way of a job-posting system).

2. If the foregoing steps produce no apparently qualified candidate, go to the outside.

If this process is pursued by higher management honestly and openmindedly, remembering that often a possibly qualified internal candidate constitutes something of a risk but that this is a risk worth taking for the sake of promotion from within, the majority of open supervisory positions will be filled from within, but a tolerable proportion (perhaps as high as 20 to 25 percent) will be filled from outside.

It is stressed that the organization should, in most instances, look first to the inside, going outside only after all reasonable internal possibilities have been exhausted. Furthermore, because the recruiting for an open supervisory position often includes consideration of both internal and external candidates, it is suggested that when there are both an internal candidate and an external candidate of equal qualifications, the nod should ordinarily go to the internal candidate.

Overall, the organization should initially go to the outside only if:

- the affected department is in a state of turmoil and it is clear that complete reorganization is required; or
- some special strength or expertise that does not exist inside is required.

This approach, conscientiously implemented, should provide a balance that strongly favors the filling of supervisory positions from within—thus assuring management continuity and stability—but that still brings enough outsiders into key positions of particular need to guarantee the regular infusion of new blood into the organization.

REFERENCES

1. Chamber of Commerce of the United States, Washington Report, 1966.
2. McConnell, C.R. "What Makes Them Perform?" Unpublished survey, Hospital Association of New York State, 1975.
3. Fournies, F. "The Real Reasons People Quit." *Administrative Management* (October 1969): 45–46.

# Today's supervisors can become tomorrow's health administrators

**_Robert Boissoneau_**
*Professor*
*Center for Health Services Administration*
*Arizona State University*
*Tempe, Arizona*

MANY OF yesterday's health care supervisors have become health administrators. At present, scores of people with experience in nursing supervision are seeking a master's degree in health administration in order to become cross-trained professionals. A large number of nurses and other health care professionals and personnel with supervisory experience could indeed become tomorrow's health administrators.

The purpose of this article is to analyze the career environment of the health administration field and its major components for the purpose of helping today's health care supervisors determine whether they should pursue upward mobility and become health administrators.

One point of view is that health care supervisors are already part of the broad field of health care management, as are health administrators,

*Health Care Superv*, 1986,4(4),44–54

because they do have management roles and responsibilities. A key difference is that health administrators are considered executives while health care supervisors are not.

## HEALTH ADMINISTRATORS

The executives among health care managers are known variously as health administrators, health care administrators, or health services administrators. Sometimes the word managers is used in place of administrators.

Executives are located in the upper echelons of management or administration. In health care organizations they are found above the department head level. Most often executives have line, rather than staff, responsibilities, although corporate-level human resources and marketing officials are also categorized as executives.

The most common way today for individuals to become health administrators is to obtain a master's degree from one of the graduate programs in the field. These programs are located in some of the nation's leading universities.

People graduating from these programs are occasionally referred to as professional health administrators. Many disciplines in the health care field are spoken of loosely as professions. The connotation of profession here is a field that is striving for a higher level of effectiveness rather than of a discipline that has reached its zenith.

While not widely accepted in the field of health care management where the practitioners have varying educational backgrounds, some observers consider individuals without a program degree, but belonging to one of the professional societies, such as the American College of Healthcare Executives (ACHE) or American College of Nursing Home Administrators (ACNHA), to be professionals. In addition, undergraduate programs in health administration have been developed during the last 15 years.

The field of health administration is gaining increased recognition on the national scene. In spite of administrators' characterization on several television programs as being little more than organizational hacks, business and industry, foundations, newspapers, government, and many citizens recognize that health care organizations are increasingly administered by professional health administrators.

## THE SUPPLY OF HEALTH SERVICES ADMINISTRATORS

Of considerable concern to many people in the health care field is the increasing number of professional health administrators, principally master's-degree graduates in health administration who work in the large hospital sector of the industry. The issue of supply is more emotional than rational.

The most comprehensive recent study, *The Report of the Commission on Education for Health Administra-*

*tion*, a project supported by the Kellogg Foundation, estimated that only 25 percent of the positions in the field were filled by program graduates in 1975.[1] Even if a large 10 percent increase was realized in the following ten years, some 65 percent of all practicing health administrators still do not have degrees in the field. Why then the concern about flooding the job market with new graduates?

In part, the reason is that most program graduates in health administration seek positions in large hospitals with 200 or more beds. Some 85 percent of the graduates seek employment in large hospitals.[2] Opportunities there are perceived to be the most challenging and such institutions pay the highest salaries for administrators in the health industry. Of course, the practicing hospital administrators who complain about the large number of graduates that the health administration programs are producing can readily observe these new people. The critics are not in a position to see the large numbers of positions in other parts of the health field that have difficulty in recruiting program graduates.

## RURAL HOSPITAL ADMINISTRATORS

One of the segments of the health industry that has experienced difficulty in attracting program graduates is rural hospitals. The great preponderance of rural hospitals are smaller than 100 beds. In the United States about half of all hospitals have fewer than 100 beds.[3]

Despite the large number of positions available in rural America, few are filled by professional health administrators. As a result many people have become concerned, especially some persons widely respected in the health care field.

The Kellogg-appointed Commission on Education for Health Administration finds that shortages exist in rural areas and in smaller organizations. In the Commission's view, the supply of new health care administrators from the nation's specialty programs is meeting conventional needs, but as the health care field changes with the development of new delivery organizations, medical care review establishments, regional health authorities, and health-related environmental management concerns, too few professional health administrators will be available.[4]

The Governing Council of the American Public Health Association[5] adopted a resolution declaring that rural health care systems may be poorly managed because they lack trained administrative personnel.

Finally, the Senate Health Subcommittee identifies health care problems as developing because of the geographic maldistribution of health professionals. The Subcommittee also states that cost and utilization controls require the best modern management systems and health professionals to implement them. This requires trained health administra-

> ***The Senate Health Subcommittee identifies health care problems as developing because of the geographic maldistribution of health professionals.***

tors with advanced management and planning skills because of new service programs, planning agencies, and regulatory commissions.[6]

**Rural quality of life perceived inferior**

While several reasons exist to explain the lack of educated health administrators in rural communities, the overriding answer is that the administrators themselves perceive the quality of life in rural areas to be inferior. Almost 90 percent of program graduates disclose that they would not seek a position in a small town.[7]

Most of these administrators have only a vague perception of rural living; they have never experienced it. Their experience has been in urban America. They spend their youth in a metropolitan community, marry a spouse from a city or suburb, receive a bachelor's degree from an urban-oriented university, and work between the undergraduate and graduate periods in a large community. Most know only about the country by driving through it.

Further disaffinity between prospective rural hospital administrators and rural communities is identified. Some disaffinity factors are community originated while others are concerns of administrators.

Perhaps the major practical disaffinity factor regards salary. Often the rural hospital is unable or unwilling to pay an administrator a salary that is considered competitive by professional administrators. Generally, salaries are lower in rural communities than in urban areas and so some discrepancies will be found as a result of the different market conditions. The problem is the degree of difference.

Even the minimum acceptable salary for the administrator may be considered excessive by rural hospital boards. Often rural board members have lived in the community for several years and have come to accept the salary structure. Having other experiences, administrators view the situation differently. Usually they are not as sympathetic to local limitations.

A deeper issue is whether relatively small and simple, rather than large and complex, rural hospitals require the management of a professional hospital administrator. Rural board members may think that their hospitals can be managed by just about any reasonably competent person.

Experts in the field seem to believe that rural hospitals do indeed need the knowledge and skills of professionally educated administrators. Even the small rural hospital is a more complex organization than most others and thus requires a more highly trained executive. Furthermore, the rural hospital will become increasingly complex as the health care field develops in new directions. Prospective payment with diagnosis related groups, joint ventures, and multihospital systems will certainly require a higher degree of administrative ability than was the case in years past.

Perhaps rural hospital board members have never been in a position to witness the advantages of working with a professional hospital administrator. Consequently, they may not know what they can expect. The administrative scope of too many practicing rural administrators is limited. Their restricted vision may be all that board members see.

### Rural populace may distrust outsiders

Another problem in rural communities may be a distrust of prospective administrators not personally known by citizens of the rural community. Ethnic groups and other minorities, along with administrators from an urban setting, may be the most distrusted of all prospective executives. Discomfort of board members with people from outside the community may lead to the selection of poorly prepared townspeople as the local hospital administrators. Unprepared ministers, bankers, and others have been tapped to lead community hospitals.

A further reason for the disaffinity between rural communities and prospective professional administrators is lack of respect for education. Often farmers and rural business people have become successful without having an education. Consequently, they may not understand the need for education among hospital administrators. They may not believe that both education and experience are important. Some successful rural people may say to themselves, "I have been able to do a good job with only my experience, and others can too, if they try!"

In addition, rural hospital administrators report professional shortcomings associated with working in such communities. Peer contact is limited simply by the fewer number of professionals in rural areas. Many professionals like the idea of having other individuals in the same or related disciplines available in close proximity so that professional communication can be facilitated.

## MULTIINSTITUTIONAL ADMINISTRATORS

Administrators who are employed in the health maintenance organization, nursing home, and acute and mental hospital systems spend their working lives in large corporations. Although technically meeting the "multi" definition, most urgent care center and home health care chains are much smaller organizations than the profit and nonprofit multihospital systems. All, however, must relate to bigness, a characteristic uncommon for most administrators of freestanding health organizations. Multiinstitutional administrators must relate to a corporate governance structure that, on one hand, offers staff support in finance, marketing, and other fields and, on the other hand, expects at least some degree of standardization from operating units. Operating-level administrators find that they must spend time placating corporate executives who make demands on them, such as completing written reports for which the operating officials do not always see the need. In short, a give and take relationship exists between the corporate and operating levels where the former occupy staff positions and the latter hold line positions. Another factor in the multi that is different in degree from what is often found in the freestanding unit is competition. Having larger numbers of employees unfamiliar with each other creates an environment of heightened competition. Overall, differences between multiinstitutional and freestanding facility administrators, as is the case between urban and rural administrators, are only degrees of difference rather than categorical differences or differences of kind. A thread runs through the heart of all health administration subspecialties as a thread runs through management specialties. In the case of the multiinstitutional executive, parallels can be drawn from the experiences of Ford and General Motors executives who must relate to bigness and to the special features of the corporate culture developed in such an environment.

## NURSING HOME ADMINISTRATORS

One factor indicating the increasing importance of the nursing home in the United States is the rapidity with which hospitals are buying such facilities. The primary reason is that under the diagnostic related groups prospective payment system, hospitals can make money under Medicare by transferring patients from the acute care hospital to the long-term care facility, a lower cost operation. The aging population in this country will further accelerate the importance of the nursing home industry.

In comparison to the acute care hospital, the nursing home is not as difficult to manage. Nursing homes are usually smaller and less complex organizations having fewer kinds and numbers of professionals and less technology. Physicians are not dependent on the nursing home to provide patient care the way they are dependent on the hospital. Also, nursing home administrators do not have to contend with the aberrations of a separate medical staff organization in the institution.

Since the typical nursing home organization is closer than the typical hospital organization to the simple organizational model, most practitioners do not need the more highly theoretical curriculum of the Master of Health Administration (M.H.A.) degree or the Master of Business Administration (M.B.A.) degree. A Bachelor of Health Administration degree or a Bachelor of Business Administration degree is sufficient formal education. Experience and continuing self-learning should be added to formal education in order to facilitate a successful career.

For much of recent U.S. health care history, the nursing home industry, and consequently nursing home administrators, has been relegated to second-class status. Partly because the industry is predominantly proprietary, many health care providers have been skeptical about whether nursing homes invest sufficient resources to provide optimum patient care.

However, two trends have emerged that, given time, will help elevate the nursing home industry to higher status in the health field, at least within management circles. First, the nursing home industry has made strides over the last 20 years in upgrading the educational component of administrators' backgrounds. Mainly through continuing education, rather than through degree-type education, the nursing home administration field has improved itself. However, not all has been smooth. The 1960s Medicaid legislation required that each state receiving federal matching funds develop a plan of continuing education for licensed nursing home administrators in the state. After the political infighting that normally follows such legislation in this country, many of the continuing education requirements were so diluted as to be meaningless. Too often the process has become little more than a number-counting game without the substantive educational content that nursing home administrators need. The sole unspoken purpose has seemed to be to gain enough hours to qualify for a license. Subsequently some states have changed their laws.

Despite problems with the licensure requirements and with resentment regarding mandatory continuing education, overall progress has been made.

Second, hospital proprietary chains have developed as a strong force in the health field. Their growth has given credence to the for-profit motive in health care, thus benefiting nursing homes. While still controversial in certain sectors after 20 years, the leading for-profit firms, Hospital Corporation of America, Humana, American Medical International, and National Medical Enterprises, have not only been accepted in health management circles but have even been acknowledged as leaders in several financial and productivity areas. The respect gained by the giant proprietary multis has improved the image of for-profit institutions in general within the health industry. Consequently, nursing homes have gained fallout respect by association.

## MENTAL HEALTH ADMINISTRATORS

While nursing homes are clearly part of the long-term care industry, so too are mental health institutions. The appropriate contrast is with short-term, acute-care general hospitals.

Across the spectrum of institutional treatment in the mental health field, length of patient stay seems to vary more widely than in the acute care hospital or in the nursing home. Length of stay depends on the patient's problem and the treatment of that problem. In fact, inpatient facilities within the mental health field use the terminology of both acute and chronic care. While not clear-cut, private psychiatric hospitals often provide acute care and state mental institutions usually offer chronic care.

In another view of the mental health field, private institutions care for the patients capable of paying for treatment while the state psychiatric institutions take care of people who cannot afford to pay for their care. In recent years, health insurance plans have included psychiatric coverage and so more patients are being treated in private hospitals.

The private psychiatric hospital field has so much economic potential that the major investor-owned chains are now buying into it. This development is occurring at a time in the United States when the stigma attached to mental health is dissipating, if only slowly. People are becoming more willing to undertake psychiatric treatment when needed.

Another trend in the mental health field is the deinstitutionalization of patient care. Whereas in earlier years patients were treated to a greater extent in state institutions, currently larger numbers of these patients are treated in community mental health centers and live in halfway houses—facilities halfway between institutions and completely independent living. Halfway houses offer some structure that is not found with fully independent living.

Implications for mental health administrators are that the patient census of large state mental hospitals has declined and that ambulatory care administrators are needed in the decentralized environment. (The work of ambulatory care administrators will be addressed in the next section.) Concerning the effect of decentralization on the administration of the state psychiatric hospital, it has generally been considered a positive development because of the reduced number of patients and the potential for better treating the remaining patients. Critics have long stated that some of the state facilities have been little more than warehouses for mentally ill people.

Mental health administrators, and to a lesser extent nursing home administrators, have been reluctant to identify themselves with the expanding field of health services administration and particularly with the process of educating men and women for the field.

At least part of the problem is that each subspecialty emphasizes its unique qualities. Mental health administrators point out that their patients have mental, not physical, difficulties. Patients sometimes require the care of professionals and modalities such as music therapy and drama therapy not found in acute care hospitals. Also, security is a much greater problem in certain psychiatric hospitals, particularly those treating the criminally insane.

Both mental health facilities and nursing homes are different from acute care hospitals because their patients remain in the hospital for a longer period of time and often are not as sick physically.

Sociologists refer to long-term care facilities, particularly mental hospitals, as *total* institutions. Total institutions have complete responsibility for the needs and wants of all patients for an extended period of time.

The relationship with patients in these facilities is much different than the relationship between the organization and patients in the acute care sector.

## AMBULATORY CARE ADMINISTRATORS

While long-term care and short-term care administrators deal with patients on a 24-hour basis for different lengths of time, ambulatory care administrators, by definition, do not address the hotel-type (sleeping and eating) concerns of patients that the others do. In this particular relationship with patients, patients come to the facility via an outside source, become involved in treatment, and then depart to return home or go to another location. Of course this arrangement is similar to the business service industry.

The outstanding position characteristic of ambulatory care administrators is the close proximity that these executives have with physicians. Most of the care given in this country in clinics, outpatient departments, and urgent care centers is provided by physicians. Although a greater amount of care in such ambulatory care facilities is given by nurses and allied health professionals, by far the most visible care is that given by physicians. In this environment, then, the linkage between the ambulatory care administrator and physician is decidedly different than between the typical institutional administrator and physician.

What makes it even more different, however, is that the ambulatory care administrator often works for a physician or several physicians as in the case of the group practice administrator. Reporting directly to a physician contains characteristics of the traditional employer–employee relationship.

This role is much different than the institutional administrator. Whereas the institutional health administrator usually reports to a part-time board with a part-time chairperson, the group practice manager reports to a full-time physician or physicians. Furthermore, the part-time board has no personal dependence on the administrator for the livelihood of members. Contrarily, physician members of the group practice or other ambulatory care facility of this type are dependent, at least in part, on the decisions made by the administrator for their own personal income. Consequently, it would seem that many ambulatory care administrators would work under conditions of far greater control from superiors than would institutional administrators.

***It is clear that in the practice of their disciplines physicians and administrators have different perspectives on some common issues.***

In a related matter, it is clear that in the practice of their disciplines physicians and administrators have different perspectives on some common issues. While the institutional administrator may use the size and complexity of the health care organization to buffer conflict, the group practice manager does not have this opportunity because of the organization's design and structure. Also, the ambulatory care facility is much closer in form to the simple organization than many other health institutions.

## OTHER HEALTH ADMINISTRATION SPECIALISTS

Health maintenance organization (HMO) administrators have many of the close working arrangements with physicians found in the job description of the group practice administrator and ambulatory care administrator. However, organizational buffering is found, too, as when the HMO is owned by an insurance company, for example. An even more complex role for the administrator occurs in the Kaiser Permanente Plan, which owns its own hospitals. Most HMOs do not own their own hospitals; instead, they contract with local hospitals for the inpatient care needs of subscribers. Of course, the HMO is developed on the ambulatory care base with inpatient care only as part of a comprehensive approach.

Home health administrators work with a myriad of services and providers to provide care to homebound people and to individuals who choose to remain at home rather than being institutionalized. Scheduling and developing relationships with a wide array of people are noteworthy characteristics of this specialty.

Finally, hospice administrators constitute the newest group of health administration specialists. While some hospices are physically located in hospitals and nursing homes, others provide services to terminally ill patients only in their own homes. As is true of management in general, the particular environment of the organization establishes the parameters for the health administrator's work.

## REFERENCES

1. Kellogg Foundation. *The Report of the Commission on Education for Health Administration.* Vol. 1. Ann Arbor: Health Administration Press, 1975.
2. Boissoneau, R., et al. "Factors Influencing Student Selection of Rural Health Service Administration." *Hospital and Health Services Administration* 26, special issue (1981): 56.

3. American Hospital Association. *Hospital Statistics*. Chicago: AHA, 1985, p. 196.

4. Kellogg Foundation. *The Report of the Commission on Education for Health Administration.*

5. "Resolutions and Position Papers Adopted by the Governing Council of the American Public Health Association." *American Journal of Public Health* 68 (February 1978): 188.

6. *Congressional Record.* 94th Cong., 2d sess., 1976. Vol. 122, pt. 5.

7. Boissoneau, et al. "Factors Influencing Student Selection of Rural Health Service Administration," 57.

# Fitting yourself to the supervisory role

***Charles R. McConnell***
*Vice President for Employee Affairs*
*The Genesee Hospital*
*Rochester, New York*

HAVE YOU EVER wondered whether you are *truly* qualified for the job you are performing? Or whether the job is causing problems for you because of its nature? Or that you are creating problems for yourself because of *your* nature? And then wonder, usually at a time when you are feeling overwhelmed by the problems of the job, what you could possibly do to the job—or to yourself—so you could better fit into the role you are expected to fill?

## BASIC QUALIFICATIONS

Not everyone is likely to fit well into every job. After all, dozens if not hundreds of jobs are not suitable because an individual does not possess the basic qualifications for employment.

However, even having the basic qualifications for a particular occupation or position still provides no guarantee that an individual is going to fit in and ultimately succeed. That

*Health Care Superv*, 1988, 6(3), 70–78

is, besides basic *technical* qualifications, there are "qualifications" of various sorts that are met not by credentials and work experience, but rather by aspects of personality and temperament.

Technical qualifications are for the most part simple to identify and understand. They are tangible. They might include so many years of schooling of a certain kind, a particular kind of degree or certificate, a specific license or registration, or a specified number of years experience doing a particular kind of work. Although these technical qualifications are sometimes subject to interpretation (e.g., deciding whether a particular educational path is applicable to a need, or assessing the relevance of some marginally appropriate experience), technical qualifications, by and large, are tangible and objectively measurable.

In addition to bringing technical qualifications to the job, every employee also brings a unique set of personality characteristics, inherent capabilities, and personal preferences. Everything that makes the individual unique merges with the person's particular technical qualifications to form the unique employee, the individual who is likely to be better suited for some kinds of work than others, and who is certain to enjoy certain kinds of tasks more than others.

***In addition to bringing technical qualifications to the job, every employee also brings a unique set of personality characteristics, inherent capabilities, and personal preferences.***

The supervisor can perhaps be described as requiring three kinds of qualifications. Two are the *technical qualifications* and *personal qualifications* already described. The third, wedged between the other two, might be described as *management qualifications*, or the technical qualifications of management (as opposed to the technical qualifications of the supervisor's basic field). For example, a head nurse would be expected to have a specified academic background, a nursing license, and a certain number of years of nursing experience (technical qualifications); some facility for management, whether through formal education or experience (management qualifications); and the apparent desire, personality, and temperament to function as a manager (personal qualifications).

In successfully filling entry-level management positions (i.e., first-line supervisory jobs), the technical qualifications of the job are the easiest conditions to satisfy. Unfortunately, most of the time the technical qualifications are the *only* qualifications that can be successfully judged in advance of placement in a supervisory position. The majority of a person's management qualifications—management courses aside, since head knowledge bears little relationship to ability to manage—do not begin to become assessable until the individual is actually working in a supervisory position. Personal qualifications (thoughtfulness, decisiveness, thoroughness, etc.), although sometimes responsible for getting a potential supervisor noticed, rarely exert their full potential impact until they are tested in practice.

Not all persons who work in supervision are equally good at all parts of the job. And certainly not all supervisors enjoy all parts of the supervisory job equally.

How well does any active supervisor fit into the supervisory role? It is possible to examine a few personal facts and conclusions and look at the way a person relates to the job so he or she can decide: How well do I fit the supervisory role? and How can I improve the way I fit the supervisory role? This assessment can be accomplished through a thoughtful examination of both personal and performance orientation.

## PERSONAL ORIENTATION

To a considerable extent, a supervisor will unconsciously approach everyday job activities in the same manner he or she approaches tasks and activities encountered in his or her personal life. The supervisor is the same person on or off the job, and unless conscious effort is put forth to behave differently in one or another area of life, the supervisor is likely to be governed by the same tendencies in all activities.

Personal orientation can be illustrated in simplified form as a graph with axes representing ranges of capabilities or tendencies (see Figure 1).

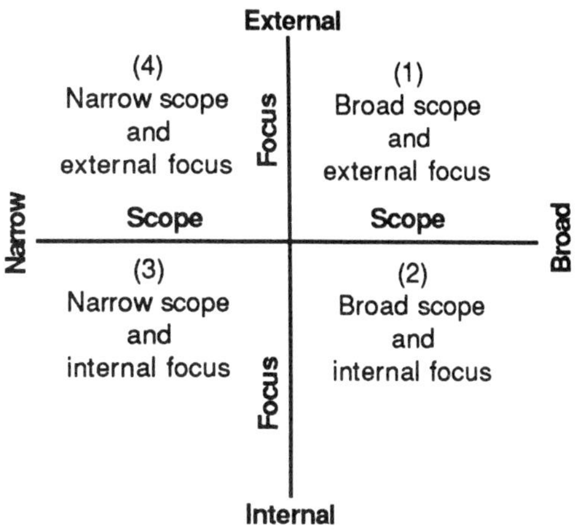


**Figure 1.** Personal orientation.

The vertical axis of personal orientation is *focus,* ranging from totally *internal* at the bottom of the graph to totally *external* at the top. Focus represents the extent to which a person is affected by or actively, emotionally involved in activities or events to which the person is exposed or is a party. External focus is typified by detachment; internal focus is represented by involvement.

As with any rendering of human tendencies or characteristics, this focus axis, as well as other supposed scales discussed in this article, represents a range with an infinite number of gradations possible between extremes. Rarely do the extremes apply in full. Rather, any person might show a tendency toward one end of the scale or the other.

### External versus internal focus

The individual with an external focus is not personally affected by matters in which he or she is involved, is witness to, or is otherwise party to. An external focus suggests the ability to keep from taking things personally. It also suggests the ability to better cope with stressful events and demands.

Internal focus is, of course, the opposite of external focus. The person who is internally focused is personally affected by most of what goes on. All events that the individual is party to are internalized, and the individual finds it difficult if not impossible to remain unaffected or unchanged by events.

This analysis is not an assessment of sensitivity or capacity for sympathy or empathy. It is possible to be extremely sensitive to another's problem, for example, and to engage in sympathetic involvement, without taking on the full measure of the other's pain. To the externally focused person, that which happens occurs in the world around the individual and is to be dealt with and coped with as necessary while being held at a safe emotional distance. To the internally focused person, the individual is inevitably affected by events and cannot deal or cope without experiencing others' distress.

### Supervisor's role

As far as the role of the supervisor is concerned, an individual who is totally externally focused might be able to cope rationally with a great many difficult matters, but the result might be a "supervision machine"—a decision maker operating on logic and fact, to the exclusion of intuition and all other human consideration. At the other extreme, a supervisor who is totally internally focused would probably not survive for any appreciable time. Considering the difficulties that arise in managing people, and recognizing the health care environment as one in which pain and suffering are commonplace, it is easy to accept the internally focused supervisor as a likely candidate for early burnout.

The most desirable focus orientation for the supervisor lies above the origin of the graph, a tendency toward an external focus and thus toward the ability to deal with the various events that come with the supervisory task and to cope with the many problems and other unpleasantries that are part of the job.

### Scope

The horizontal axis of personal orientation is *scope*. Scope simply refers to the kind or amount or variety of activity that an individual can best handle according to temperament or individual ability. The person with a broad scope can juggle, coping with a variety of tasks in bits and pieces, moving from task to task and back again, and solving unanticipated problems as they arise. The broad-scope individual can function in firefighting style without experiencing undue stress and without becoming overwhelmed by a seemingly unending stream of problems or by the inability to truly finish much of what is started.

At the opposite end of the horizontal axis are persons of narrow scope, those who cannot readily function in the scattergun fashion of the broad-scope person but who are most comfortable and whose talents are best applied to one specific task at a time.

Chances of long-run success in the supervisory role are enhanced if an individual possesses a broad scope and is generally able to constantly reorder priorities and cope with a continuous series of unanticipated demands. Supervision has more than once been described as a series of interruptions interrupted by interruptions, and although some days may see relative order and predictability, by and large the supervisory role includes sufficient variety and surprise to guarantee that the supervisor's attention will be drawn this way and that on a regular basis.

Persons of broad scope are best equipped to function as team members; persons of narrow scope are most likely to operate best as loners.

Combining the two axes used to describe personal orientation, a person is best suited to the supervisory role if his or her personal orientation lies somewhere in the upper right-hand quadrant of Figure 1, above the origin in terms of focus, and to the right of the origin in terms of scope. The person who is well suited to the supervisory role will tend to be externally focused, with the ability to deal with most matters at a reasonable emotional distance, and will be of broad scope, with the ability to take what comes as it comes. The supervisor whose personal orientation falls in any of the other three quadrants of Figure 1 may experience problems of orientation ranging from mild (e.g., having to remember to avoid giving in to a narrow-scope tendency and staying too long on a pet project) to severe (e.g., a stress reaction to the internalized pain of others).

## PERFORMANCE ORIENTATION

Performance orientation also can be described by a pair of perpendicular axes, with an infinite number of gradations along each axis (see Figure 2).

The vertical axis of Figure 2 presents *emphasis,* ranging from totally *personal* emphasis at the bottom to totally *functional* emphasis at the top. The higher the degree of functional emphasis evident in a supervisor's performance, the more visible will be that supervisor's degree of attention to activities of highest priority. The supervisor with a strong functional emphasis will ordinarily attend to the most important task at any given time.

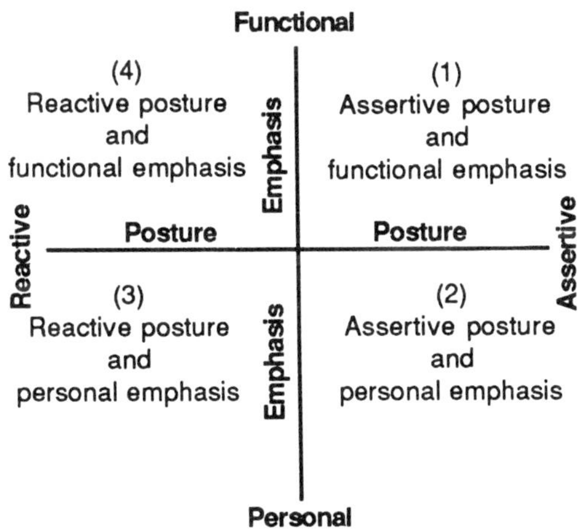


**Figure 2.** Performance orientation.

The more personal a supervisor's emphasis becomes, the more likely that supervisor is to give attention primarily to those tasks or concerns he or she prefers or enjoys. This orientation might be good when the supervisor likes to do what most needs to be done. However, most of the time the tasks the supervisor favors and the tasks that most need to be done are not the same. There is certainly no harm in occasionally falling back on a favored task for the sake of a change of pace or relief from stress, but working regularly with a predominantly personal emphasis guarantees that some high priority tasks will be slighted.

The horizontal axis of Figure 2 represents *posture* along a continuum ranging from completely *reactive* to fully *assertive.* The supervisor who tends to be assertive ordinarily initiates action, advances ideas or solutions, and moves to resolve difficulties in their early stages and head off problems before they occur. The supervisor who tends to be reactive ordinarily waits to be told what to do, procrastinates on important decisions until there is no more room for delay, and waits until a problem can no longer be denied before attempting a solution. The assertive supervisor deals in innovation and prevention; the reactive supervisor simply responds when pushed by circumstances.

The effective supervisor tends to be functional rather than personal in emphasis, and

***The assertive supervisor deals in innovation and prevention; the reactive supervisor simply responds when pushed by circumstances.***

more assertive than reactive in posture. However, emphasis and posture cannot be considered separate from each other; together they exert combined effects that can be described through association with each other in the four quadrants of Figure 2.

In the first quadrant (upper right), tendencies toward functional emphasis and assertive posture describe a supervisor who is generally in control of the job and who operates with a noticeable degree of autonomy. In this, described as the best of the four quadrants, the supervisor

- concentrates on high-priority tasks most of the time;
- tackles the important problems in timely fashion even though they may be difficult or unpleasant;
- experiences job satisfaction from accomplishment and achievement; and
- meets the needs of the organization in doing what he or she is expected to do as a member of management.

A supervisor functioning in the first quadrant is applying the right approach (assertive posture) to the right tasks (functional emphasis), moving in the right direction without being told to do so.

The second quadrant (lower right) suggests the combined effects of a tendency toward an assertive posture and a personal emphasis. A supervisor functioning in this quadrant may frequently be described as pursuing personal preferences or being out of step with reality. In this quadrant the supervisor may

- be unwilling to delegate, personally monopolizing preferred activities, or unable to delegate out of a sense of insecurity;
- take frequent refuge in preferred tasks of low priority to relax, achieve self-satisfaction, or escape;
- experience goal displacement, being unable to reconcile organizational goals with personal goals; and
- have little appreciation of job purpose, failing to see how this specific supervisory position is supposed to mesh with others as part of the organizational whole.

A supervisor functioning in the second quadrant is generally applying the right approach (assertive posture) to the wrong tasks (personal emphasis), moving without being told but going in the wrong direction.

The third quadrant (lower left) is the worst of the four general situations. The supervisor functioning in the third quadrant may

- appear to be running fast and working hard while going nowhere and accomplishing little;
- be unable to control interruptions;
- be unwilling or unable to say no to any request that comes along, no matter how unreasonable or intrusive it may be;
- avoid difficult, complicated, unpleasant, or potentially stressful matters whenever possible, taking the easiest route through most problems; and
- become disillusioned with the job and the organization.

A supervisor functioning in the third

quadrant is ordinarily taking the wrong approach (reactive emphasis) to the wrong tasks (personal emphasis), moving only when pushed and then going in the wrong direction.

Because a person falling into the fourth quadrant (upper left) will usually be doing most of the right things, the combination of emphasis and posture evident in this quadrant might present no problems at all if this article concerned people employed in any number of nonsupervisory capacities. However, the supervisor falling into the fourth quadrant may

- experience considerable frustration with a nearly complete lack of autonomy;
- feel out of control when reacting to the seemingly unending and unpredictable stream of demands made by others; and
- use time ineffectively, moving from task to task and crisis to crisis as directed, having no time left to plan and organize.

A supervisor functioning in the fourth quadrant has the proper functional emphasis (assertive posture) but is applying an improper reactive approach. This orientation may be acceptable in some nonsupervisory employees. Although assertiveness is desired in many employees, supervisory or otherwise, there are still many jobs in which an employee may best serve by performing as directed. But while a reactive posture may be appropriate—or at least tolerable—in many nonsupervisory employees, such a posture is contrary to what is expected of an effective supervisor. A supervisor functioning in the fourth quadrant is operating on what might be called the *wheelbarrow principle*—doing the job, but only when loaded, aimed, and pushed.

## HOW WELL DO YOU FIT?

Many people who do not fit well into a supervisory role have either voluntarily abandoned supervision or have failed as supervisors. Many others who also do not fit especially well into a supervisory role have nevertheless remained supervisors, with widely varying degrees of success. It is highly likely that so-called perfect fit supervisors are a minority of the supervisory population of any organization. Therefore, most supervisors probably have weaknesses that can potentially affect their performance and perhaps ultimately determine whether they succeed or fail.

Simply identifying individual weaknesses is a large part of the struggle for improved personal effectiveness. Once these weaknesses are identified, the next essential process is recognizing the difference between those things that a person can actively change and those things that a person cannot readily change but must compensate for or otherwise work around. The final step in the process is acting to remove or guard against personal weaknesses.

### Your personal orientation

How do you believe you must place yourself in regard to *personal orientation*? You may find, as most do, that you have more control over your scope than you do over your focus. Although both scope and focus are rooted in personality, focus is much more emotionally based and is therefore much more difficult to alter. If you are strongly internally focused and truly sensitive to the point of creating intolerable stress within yourself when having to apply firm disciplinary action, you are more prone to minimize this aspect of the supervisory role and thus impair your effectiveness in handling problem employees. Since your focus is emotionally based, unless you are sufficiently near the middle of the graph to allow you to accommodate the occasional emotional stresses of the job, you may be consigning yourself to a working life of strain and unhappiness by remaining in supervision.

Since scope is less emotionally tied than focus, more can be done to control this dimension of personal orientation. Broad-scope people are team members; narrow-scope people prefer to function as loners. The supervisor needs to be a team member. However, it is acceptable to give in to a tendency to enjoy working as a loner once in a while, as long as you are conscious of the need to be a team member and to willingly function as a team member whenever circumstances demand (which, for the typical supervisor, is most of the time).

### Your performance orientation

Aspects of personality ordinarily have a great deal of influence on both major dimensions of *performance orientation*. Of the two dimensions, posture is probably more deeply rooted in personality than is emphasis. Surely there are some people whose posture is essentially reactive because they are self-doubting and insecure. Just as surely, however, there are others who are reactive because they lack goal orientation or because they have never been given any clear idea of what is expected of them. Perhaps individual insecurities can be overcome with a great deal of effort and the right kind of assistance and support. Developing goal orientation—not nearly so difficult as overcoming an insecurity—can surely be done if an individual wants success strongly enough, and can pointedly ask for higher management's expectations.

***The person who would aspire to manage others must first become proficient at self-management.***

Although unavoidably influenced by aspects of personality, emphasis is more readily altered by the individual than posture. The key to emphasis is self-discipline, the ability to give the most attention to the highest priority tasks at hand. The supervisor who enters each workday asking, "What is the single most important task I need to accomplish today?" and plans to get that task done and proceeds to do it, is on the path of effectiveness. Even the supervisor whose workload may seem overwhelming is making progress if he or she is always at work on the highest priority task of the moment.

To develop a true functional emphasis, add to self-discipline a consideration of the need to plan, to organize, and to control interruptions while concentrating on priorities.

This self-discipline is crucial to the improvement of personal orientation and performance orientation. To develop an improved personal orientation and to adopt a more appropriate performance orientation is to put yourself in the position of becoming a more effective supervisor. Self-discipline as applied by the effective supervisor is self-management, and self-management precedes the management of others. The person who would aspire to manage others must first become proficient at self-management.

• • •

In determining how well you fit the supervisory role, it is necessary to assess both your personal orientation and performance orientation and decide

- Am I sufficiently externally focused to cope with the pressures of the job, and is my outlook broad enough in scope to allow me to meet the demands of the job?
- Am I capable of bringing a predominantly functional emphasis to the job, and can I consistently behave more assertively than reactively?

Once you are able to answer these two questions affirmatively, there remains only one additional question to consider: *Most of the time, do I truly enjoy what I do for a living?* If you can answer with an honest yes, you are properly fitted to the supervisory role.

# Part II
# The Art and Science of Health Care Supervision

# Supervision as art: Imagination and intuition

*Leon McKenzie*
*Director*
*Human Resource Development*
*Indiana University Hospitals*
*Indianapolis, Indiana*

NEARLY THREE decades ago, C.P. Snow published a landmark work in which he described the humanities and the sciences as two cultures separated by a gulf of incomprehension.[1] Snow was a scientist by training and a novelist by vocation; he lived in both cultures and experienced their dominant, and often conflicting, values.

The idea of the two cultures is relevant today. Both cultures find expression in the behaviors of individuals. Some persons are governed by a concern for objectivity, reason, systematic procedures, logical analyses, and rigorous techniques. Others prize subjectivity, spontaneity, feelings, imagination, insight, and free-wheeling creativity. What is essentially a distinction between scientific and artistic approaches to reality finds current support in brain-dominance theory.

*Health Care Superv*, 1988, 6(2), 1–12

Writing about brain hemispheres and behavior, Jeremy Campbell noted that the left brain prefers tightly organized, sequential patterns of relationships. The right brain specializes in meaning networks and is more conceptual than computational. Campbell explained, "In the integrated brain, these two polar styles coexist and collaborate to a greater or lesser extent."[2] While personal style may be influenced by the degree to which the left or right brain is dominant, care must be taken not to oversimplify a complex matter by pressing the distinction too vigorously. Nonetheless, there are probably grounds other than behavioral observations that support Snow's idea of the two cultures.

The contrast between the two cultures may be helpful for gaining a more complete understanding of supervision. Some people tend to view supervision as a science; others see supervision as more artful than scientific work. The regnant assumption is that supervision can be thoroughly rationalized. That is, it is assumed that the supervisory process is highly rule bound; the rules for effective supervision can be identified scientifically by research. To be effective the supervisor need only follow prescribed rules and guidelines. What is essential for the supervisor, it is often assumed, is a command of scientifically determined techniques. All problems will yield before the supervisor who uses the methods and procedures that arise out of management science.

The impetus for viewing supervision as a science came chiefly from Frederick W. Taylor earlier in this century. Taylor's major work, *The Principles of Scientific Management*,[3] is generally evaluated today as simplistic, something that reflects the superficial thinking of nineteenth century positivists who framed all human questions in terms of a narrowly conceived scientism. The impact of this one-dimensional world view, however, has left its mark. The notion of supervision as artful behavior is largely neglected in articles and training programs that purport to help supervisors become more effective.

This problem is somewhat exacerbated in respect to health care supervisors. Because of the biomedical academic backgrounds of many health care supervisors, there is a tendency to look at supervision through the prism of the so-called scientific method. The concepts of supervision and art are seldom linked. The forging of such a linkage is the burden of this article.

## ART: IMAGINATION AND INTUITION

Anyone who has been involved in any kind of artful work, on reflection, knows the place of imagination and intuition in this work. Artful work, in the present context, does not refer restrictively to the production of an oil painting, the composition of a piece of music, the writing of poetry, or other activities that are commonly recognized as artistic. The concept of art used here is inclusive and embraces a host of ordinary, everyday activities. Artistry comes into play whenever someone arranges furniture in a room, decorates a cake, presents a speech, or selects clothes to wear. A day does not pass but that most people engage in some kind of artful, creative work that implies the use of imagination and intuition.

The capacity for imagination allows images to be visualized in various juxtapositions. A person can visualize what happened in the past or what might occur in the future. A person can imagine scenarios that are factual or purely fictional. A person can create "stories" in his or her mind or display designs that are pleasing or repugnant. Imagination is virtually limitless in its creative potential.

Nor is intuition lacking in daily artful works. Intuition has been defined as a kind of "seeing."[4] Intuition presents quick and ready insights into problems and situations. Most behaviors each day are not founded on well-reasoned and complex arguments but derive out of a more or less immediate sense of what is appropriate.

Imagination and intuition join in any creative act. Intuition, a process not clearly understood, presents insights and images; imagination takes what intuition provides and "plays" with these elements in an attempt to elaborate a coherent inner vision. This is not to say that reason and logic have no place in a person's mental construction of reality. What is emphasized, however, is that the importance of imagination and intuition is seldom recognized in the orientation of thinking and performance.

It would be interesting to discuss the process of artful work in greater detail but such an excursion would travel beyond the purposes of this article. A more practical question is this: How can imagination be used by the health care supervisor to make supervisory work more effective? Imagination can be employed in at least two ways: (1) as a means of rehearsing for situations that can generally be anticipated, and (2) as a means of evaluating a situation that has already occurred.

## Imagination and preparation

"We normally anticipate what form the future might take," wrote Edward Casey, "so as to be in a better position to deal with the projected object or situation if and when it does arise. Hence the primary aim is not to increase knowledge but to induce more skillful or suitable action."[5] John Dewey expressed a similar idea when he discussed the deliberative process in terms of imagination. Deliberation, for Dewey, was a dramatic rehearsal in one's imagination, "an experiment in finding out what the various lines of possible action are really like."[6]

Suppose a supervisor is to conduct an appraisal of a subordinate's performance. In preparation, the supervisor can visualize the setting in which the interview will take place. An imaginary scenario will also include elements of the expected dialogue, a sense of the prevailing mood that surrounds the dialogue, and an anticipation of the feelings of the subordinate. When the interview is played out in advance, the supervisor will be better prepared to face contingencies that may arise. The imaginary scenario will also help the supervisor become attuned *affectively* to the situation.

But what if the imaginary scenario does not resemble the eventual actual interview? The predictive accuracy of the imaginary scenario depends in large measure on the supervisor's experience in constructing these scenarios and on his or her familiarity with the situation. A supervisor who knows subordinates well and is accustomed to a particular work setting will generally be more accurate in anticipating encounters through imaginary scenarios.

The imaginary scenario will never predict the actual event perfectly. The purpose of the imaginary scenario is to explore various lines of possible action, to experiment with different alternatives, to prepare in a general way for a supervisory situation, and to enhance the deliberative process. The imaginary scenario can be helpful even if its predictive quality is imperfect.

Just as it is important to anticipate situations involving subordinates, it is also important to prepare for meetings with superiors. Once again, the preparation should transcend pure discursive reasoning and logic. In the imaginary scenario, the supervisor should attempt to achieve a sense of the tone of the meeting, an insight into the feelings of the superior, and an appreciation of the interpersonal climate that will probably control the meeting.

The rationale for the use of imaginary scenarios as preparatory tactics can be simply put: The meetings that take place between supervisors and others are not conducted in vacuums merely at the level of abstract concepts and logic. To prepare adequately for any situation requires that the health care supervisor try to achieve a "feel" for the situation that takes into account the major factors involved in human relationships. This preparation is best accomplished using imagination.

### Imagination and evaluation

If imaginary scenarios can be used to prepare for supervisory situations, imagination also can be used as an approach to self-appraisal. One of the defining characteristics of a professional person is self-appraisal. The professional is a person who reviews his or her performance in such a manner as to learn maximally from experience. Imagination can be used for purposes of evaluation much in the same way it is employed for purposes of preparation. While imagination directs itself to a future situation for purposes of preparation, imagination joins with memory and directs itself to the past for purposes of evaluation.

Imagination enables the supervisor

to "play back" and review important situations. During the debriefing process that takes place in imagination, the supervisor can extract new meanings and render new interpretations of the remembered event. It is often difficult to interpret a situation adequately as the situation is enfolding; things happen too quickly. In retrospect, however, it is possible to use the theater of one's imagination for more deliberate interpretations of what actually happened. A supervisor can effectively weigh his or her performance after "seeing" the "tapes" of a particular situation that reside in memory and imagination.

In the preceding paragraph, imagination is treated as an analogue of the video cassette recorder (VCR). The capacity of the imagination for creativeness, however, is not available in the replay of a video cassette. The supervisor can play out in imagination various "what if?" scenarios. What if I had said this instead of that? What if I had approached the discussion of an issue from a different perspective? How would the consequences of the situation have changed given a different performance on my part? Creativity in the review process helps the supervisor apprehend the alternative possibilities that were present in the situation.

The distinction was made between using anticipatory imagination for preparation and using retrospective imagination for evaluation. In a broader sense, however, even the use of imagination for debriefing and evaluation can be acknowledged as preparation. Performance is evaluated not as an empty exercise in curiosity but as a remote preparation for contingencies that may arise in similar situations in the future. In some sense, professional self-appraisal always looks to improved performance in the future.

Two examples have been provided to illustrate the uses of imagination and visualization in supervisory work. Many more opportunities can be identified. Imagination can come into play profitably whenever the supervisor engages in deliberative activity. Supervisory judgment and decision making can be enriched through the use of creative imagination.

## THE CONCEPT OF INTUITION

Intuition is a broad concept that defies precise definition. Intuition has at least three connotations: (1) a belief or hunch not preceded by inferential reasoning, (2) an immediate apprehension of the truth of a proposition, and (3) knowledge of a concept that does not entail the ability to define the concept.[7] At root, intuition refers to a more or less spontaneous acquisition of knowledge that bypasses the ordinary manner of reaching conclusions. Intuition can be likened to a kind of immediate knowledge that arises out of accumulated experience.

The intuitive process is complex and obscure but it is not occult or magical. Intuition is a kind of recognition that arises in consciousness as a precipitate of accumulated experience, a kind of recognition that emerges from a person's storehouse of memory and knowledge given certain triggering events.

Intuition has been described frequently as insight. Gestalt theorists have noted that learning involves insight, that "the learner who has insight sees the whole situation in a new way, a way which includes understanding of logical relationships or perception of the connections between means and ends."[8] Insight occurs suddenly and immediately, and usually after a time of incubation while attention is not directed to the situation or problem at hand.

***Insight occurs suddenly and immediately, and usually after a time of incubation while attention is not directed to the situation or problem at hand.***

Over 2,000 years ago, Plato discussed the immediateness of intuition. After much study, reflection, and discussion about a particular topic, a flash of understanding "blazes up, and the mind, as it exerts all of its powers to the limit of human capacity, is flooded with light."[9] In this instance intuition is seen as the outgrowth of intense striving. A person expends much mental energy in pursuit of understanding. When conscious effort stops, and after a period of incubation, a flash of recognition occurs in a dramatic way.

Intuitional insight also presents itself to consciousness in a less dramatic, almost commonplace, manner. Plato also pointed out that individuals can arrive at knowledge of a particular subject through a long acquaintance or a "close companionship"[10] with the subject. What Plato meant is best exemplified by contrasting the behaviors of the novice and the expert in any line of work.

A novice usually pays close attention to the guidelines that have been identified by others. The behavior of the novice is rule bound; the novice carefully follows predetermined procedures. On the other hand, the expert works almost casually and with the confidence characteristic of a master performer. The difference between the novice and expert lies in the fact that the work, whatever it may be, has become second nature to the expert. The procedures necessary to complete the work, for the expert, are not extrinsic to the expert (e.g., written in a book) but have become an actual part of the expert's personal makeup. The expert's effortless performance is guided largely by the intuitional insights that flow from his or her accumulated experience and close companionship with the work at hand.

In the work of the expert there is a diminishing consciousness of the science (systematic knowledge) that supports correct performance and a correlative increasing attention to the intuitions associated with artful behavior.

In summary, insight is an enlightenment that comes unbidden to a person either after an intense struggle to master an issue, problem, or situation or after a person has developed a close affinity with the issues, problems, or situations associated with a particular kind of work.

## SUPERVISION AND INTUITION

Three related questions come to the fore in any discussion of the use of intuition in supervisory work: (1) How can a supervisor distinguish between an intuitional insight and a mere transient whim or impulse? (2) Under what conditions is it appropriate to base supervisory decisions on flashes of insight? (3) To what extent should supervisors rely on intuition rather than logic?

### Intuition or whim?

There is no easy way to discern the difference between an intuitional insight and a fanciful impulse except by means of *ex post facto* validation. Action based on authentic insight is usually productive and correct; action based on a whim is ordinarily unfruitful. This observation, of course, is of little practical utility to anyone trying to determine in advance the difference between intuition and whim, but it is an important observation and worthy of further discussion.

While it is not possible to distinguish intuition from whim with absolute prior certitude, it is possible to identify situational elements that are almost always associated with intuition. These elements have already been noted briefly. First, intuition arises in consciousness usually after a person has been immersed in the problem that is to be resolved; intuition visits only those who have concerned themselves with the issue at hand with some degree of intensity. Intuition is largely the byproduct of serious thought, vivid imagination, and hard work. What arises in the consciousness of the person who has not wrestled with a problem is ordinarily a thin caprice.

Second, intuitions are more likely to come to supervisors who have benefited from accumulated supervisory experiences. The supervisor who has had little experience, or the supervisor who has not reflected seriously on his or her experience, would be well advised to assume that what arises spontaneously in consciousness is probably a whim. This inference derives from viewing intuition not only as an afterproduct of hard work but also as the precipitate or fallout of experience.

It is altogether possible that a penetrating insight can come to an inexperienced supervisor who has not analyzed a situation thoroughly, but it would be imprudent to reach such a conclusion given the difficulty of distinguishing between insight and whim in such a case.

### Conditions

In his study of how top executives use intuition in decision making, Weston Agar reported that intuitive ability seems to function best when exercised under certain conditions. Intuition works best: (1) under conditions of uncertainty and when there is little precedent for decision making, (2) when facts are limited and do not point clearly to a particular solution, (3) when there are several alternative solutions to a problem all of which seem equally plausible, and (4) when there is pressure to make a decision within a limited time frame.[11]

The foregoing conditions can be reduced to a single principle: The supervisor may rely on intuitional insight in situations that are highly ambiguous, situations in which no particular alternative course of action is seen clearly as most appropriate. What this principle says, in effect, is that a supervisor may rely on intuition when all other avenues are blocked. As such, the principle, while it may be somewhat helpful, is too conservative.

There may be occasions when the situation does not seem ambiguous, when facts appear to point in a particular direction, when logic suggests a definite supervisory response, and when reliance on intuition for a different supervisory response is not inappropriate. A situation may appear unambiguous only because it has not been scanned for its true depth. Some facts may point in a particular direction, but there is no assurance that all of the facts of a situation have been uncovered. At times fallacies in logic are so subtle that poor reasoning may be mistaken for valid reasoning. The use of intuition in supervisory work can never be governed entirely by referring to ideal conditions under which intuition seems to work best. The supervisor who is practiced in the use of intuitive ability may sometimes transcend logic and resort to a higher norm: the intuition itself.

Earlier it was noted that the use of intuition is validated *ex post facto*, that is, action based on an insight is eventually evidenced as correct. The supervisor whose insights have been repeatedly validated over time, the person who has a consistent track record of supervisory effectiveness and a high degree of confidence in his or her intuitive ability, should not flinch from depending on this ability even when logic seems to dictate a different course.

### Supervisory work: Intuition and logic

A person's response to a set of circumstances is influenced by the cultural context in which the person lives. Contemporary culture has been shaped by historical forces that celebrate logic, objectivity, and science. Contemporary culture teaches that logic is more important than intuition. Any suggestion, therefore, that intuition may sometimes be more valuable than logic will be received with reluctance, if not outright suspicion.

In many subtle ways, contemporary culture teaches that intuition, imagination, and feelings are not totally trustworthy. Logic is the court of last resort in problematic situations.

And yet the insights that come via intuition are valuable sources of correct performance. Intuition and an artful approach to supervisory work are at least as crucial for effective supervision as logic and science.

***Intuition and an artful approach to supervisory work are at least as crucial for effective supervision as logic and science.***

It is not argued here that supervisory decision making should be solely a matter of following one's feelings or that intuition is demonstrably more worthwhile than logic. What is argued on behalf of intuition is modest: Supervisory work that excludes the use of intuition on principle neglects a valuable human potential and often compromises the quality of the work itself. There is room for creativity in supervisory work and creativity, more often than not, springs from reliance on intuition.

Creativity in supervisory work entails a degree of risk taking. Dependence on intuition opens the possibility of error, but reliance on logic alone assures neither infallible judgment nor correct performance. What is needed is a balance between science and art, a partnership between logic and intuition. Intuition preserves logic from sterility; logic provides intuition with discipline.

The supervisor who taps his or her intuitive ability is not advised to abandon self totally to a general feeling that a certain line of action is most appropriate. Intuitive insight, once entertained, requires critical thoughtfulness. The possible consequences of any supervisory decision, whether the decision is based on logic or intuition, must be anticipated and studied prior to the implementation of the decision. At all costs, however, feelings that represent the emergence of intuitive insight must not be dismissed as unscientific illusions.

To state that a balance must be achieved between the use of logic and intuition in supervisory work implies the avoidance of two extremes. To view supervisory work only in terms of logic assumes that human beings inhabit a purely cerebral and rational world. On the other hand, to base supervisory work simply on intuitive insights assumes human beings perform best in a world of impulse unguided by reasoning. Each of these extremes is to be avoided precisely because humans, in the real world, operate most effectively as beings who have achieved an integration of reason and insight.

## Gaining insight

What procedures can the supervisor follow to achieve insights into supervisory work? There are no definite rules for generating insights and no procedural models for eliciting intuitions. Artful work is not the same as scientific work. The artist does not follow step-by-step directions to produce the intuition on which a creative expression is based. A painter may follow technical rules in the execution of a painting, but the intuition that precedes the laying of brush to canvas is not so easily captured. Insights, it will be remembered, ordinarily arrive spontaneously in consciousness.

There are no explicit rules for the production of insights, but the supervisor can cultivate certain dispositions that seem to be associated with the emergence of creative insight. These dispositions include: (1) trust in one's previous experience, (2) confidence that one has learned from previous experience, (3) attentiveness to the issue at hand, and (4) receptiveness to intuitional prompts.

Intuitional insights are, in large part, the fruit of previous experiences. The supervisor who trusts that his or her previous experiences have been rich and varied is more likely to be visited by insights than the supervisor who lacks this trust.

Trust in the quality of one's previous experiences is yoked with confidence that one has learned from these experiences. It has been stated that the intuitive approach to decision making "can involve a telescoping of years of observation and experience. Many managers have a great capacity to learn from past failures and successes and to apply this knowledge to new, but similar, situations."[12] The possibility also exists that some supervisors, habitually uncritical, have learned dearly little from previous experience. Simply living through certain experiences is not a guarantee that a person has grown, developed, and become more competent.

The supervisor who wishes to develop intuitive abilities would do well, first of all, to evaluate his or her previous experience and reach a firm judgment as to the quality of these experiences. Next, the supervisor must respond honestly to the question, "To what extent have I learned about supervision from previous experience?" Insight comes to those who expect insight; this expectation, in turn, issues from a sense of one's competence, from a realization that one has profited from a broad range of experiences.

It was suggested above that intuition is not magical and that insight frequently comes to those who have immersed themselves in a particular problem. Attentiveness to the problem at hand and concentrated study of the problem are often precursors of insight. Intuitive ability is not the product of lazy inattention to details. The supervisor who hopes to gain insights into supervisory work must, as a matter of course, analyze situations critically and studiously. Attentiveness to the problem at hand, of course, is a disposition closely related to learning from experience.

Finally, insights can be gained through the disposition of receptiveness to intuitional prompts. Trust in the quality of previous experiences, confidence that learning has occurred through these experiences, and habitual studiousness are necessary but insufficient dispositions for the acquisitions of insight. The last dispositional requirement is that the supervisor becomes receptive to insights through relaxation.

A now-forgotten speaker once related an apposite illustration. It seems that a tribal people long ago trapped monkeys by placing nuts in specially prepared tree holes. A monkey would reach into the hole and grasp a nut. As long as the animal held the nut with clenched fist, it could not remove its hand from the small hole. When the hunters came, with much noisy celebration, to take the monkey, the animal grasped the nut even more tenaciously thereby ensuring its capture. The moral of the story is evident: Sometimes the only solution to a problem is to let go of it and relax.

Insight often arrives as a surprise in a moment of relaxation after strenuous mental activity. Sometimes the churning of the mind is like heavy static that prevents the supervisor from tuning in the promptings of intuition. Relaxation and the intentional disposition of passivity sometimes provides an opening for insight.

• • •

Apollo and Dionysus were two prominent figures in the pantheon of ancient Greek deities. Apollo was the patron of intellect, order, clarity, and control; he resided at Delphi and, through his priests, was the imparter of wise counsel. Dionysus, known to the Romans as Bacchus, was the patron of wine, celebrations, festivals, and spontaneity; he was the god who counseled surrender to instinctual feelings. According to mythology, Dionysus would appear and disappear suddenly. History relates that the cult of Dionysus was spread by societies of artists.

Returning again to Snow's description of the sciences and humanities as two disparate cultures, it is easy to imagine Apollo as presiding over the former culture and Dionysus as reigning over the latter. It is more important, however, to see the two mythological figures as metaphors for two kinds of human experience and performance. Both metaphors are valid given different human contexts. There is a season for supervisors to depend on science and discursive reasoning; there are also times for supervisors to rely on imagination and listen attentively to intuitional prompts. In short, there are times when situations call for supervisors to be artists. Over the long haul of a supervisory career, it seems appropriate that Apollonian and Dionysian tendencies come to coexist in a suitable balance.

## REFERENCES

1. Snow, C.P. *The Two Cultures and the Scientific Revolution.* London: Cambridge University Press, 1959.
2. Campbell, J. *Grammatical Man.* New York: Simon and Schuster, 1982, 252.
3. Taylor, F.W. *The Principles of Scientific Management.* New York: Harper & Row, 1911.
4. Noddings, N., and Shore, P. *Awakening the Inner Eye: Intuition in Education.* New York: Teachers College Press, 1984, 43.

5. Casey, E. *Imagining: A Phenomenological Study*. Bloomington, Indiana: Indiana University Press, 1976, 115.
6. Dewey, J. *Human Nature and Conduct*. New York: Henry Holt and Co., 1922, 190.
7. Rorty, R. "Intuition." In *The Encyclopedia of Philosophy*, vol. 4, edited by Paul Edwards. Reprint ed. New York: Macmillan, 1972.
8. Hill, W. *Learning*. 3d ed. New York: Crowell Co., 1977, 117.
9. Plato, "Letters." Translated by L.A. Post. In *The Collected Dialogue of Plato*, edited by E. Hamilton and H. Cairns. New York: Pantheon Books, 1961, 1591.
10. Ibid., 1589.
11. Agar, W. "The Logic of Intuition: How Top Executives Make Important Decisions." *Organizational Dynamics* 14, no. 3 (1986): 9.
12. Steiner, G., and Miner, J. *Management Policy and Strategy*. New York: Macmillan, 1982, 207.

# A search for excellence in supervision

*Howard L. Smith*
*Associate Professor*

*T. Alan Jensen*
*Assistant Professor*
*Department of Health Administration*
*Medical College of Virginia*
*Virginia Commonwealth University*
*Richmond, Virginia*

HEALTH CARE organizations, like organizations in other sectors of the economy, are vitally interested in improving performance in productivity and profitability. Management in nursing homes, hospitals and health maintenance organizations are concerned with getting the most output from all clinical and ancillary personnel. As the hospital field moves progressively toward prospective payment systems, fiscal control is becoming a major concern for all health care organizations, forcing these organizations to stress bottom-line results and perform in a more businesslike fashion.

In the presence of the financial slack inherent in cost pass-through reimbursement systems, health care organizations have been managed primarily with quality of care in mind. Now, however, they must balance quality of care with cost control, a difficult assignment because the ex-

*Health Care Superv*, 1985,3(4),58–66

pectations for high quality of care will not simply disappear. If anything, concerns about quality of care are likely to be intensified as health facilities devise and implement plans for holding down costs. Higher productivity is desirable only if quality of care can be maintained and economic costs controlled.

This situation puts health care supervisors under pressure to achieve rather extraordinary results with few additional resources. In some cases they are being asked to make do with less and produce at levels that are commensurate with past performance. These demands must be met by appropriate tactics at the work unit and departmental levels. Health care supervisors are wondering how they can make their employees more productive and control costs without sacrificing high quality of care.

## THE NEED FOR EXCELLENCE

If ever there was a time when health care organizations needed excellent performance from employees, that time is now. The transition from cost-based reimbursement to prospective payment will be traumatic to many health care organizations. Unless that transition is managed effectively, fiscal solvency will be jeopardized. Mental health institutions, medical clinics, long-term care facilities, medical suppliers and the other health care providers not experiencing prospective payment are also confronted with this message: Now is the time to begin managing with a greater focus on performance—and excellent performance at that.

With respect to this challenge, health care supervisors are asking a number of questions:

- What is excellence in supervision?
- What is excellence in employee performance?
- Is excellence in supervision just another fad, or is it a new idea?
- Is excellence attainable, or is it merely the promotion of productivity and work quality among employees?
- Is there anything unique about health services management that prevents it from pursuing concepts of excellence?
- How long will it take to develop a program of excellence in supervision?

The answers to these questions are especially relevant to health care supervisors who recognize that they are responsible for motivating employees toward higher productivity. Employees are the first line of defense in the battle to lower costs without impairing the quality of service.

## THE CONCEPT OF EXCELLENCE

In *In Search of Excellence,* Peters and Waterman[1] have presented some provocative concepts and lessons from American industry on managing performance. They have analyzed 43 of the most successful companies in America, seeking to define the common denominators that define excellence. They specify eight principles that differentiate excellent companies from corporations that are merely good. The principles state that companies should:

- have a bias for action;
- remain close to customers;
- encourage autonomy and leadership;
- respect employees;
- have hands-on, value-driven management;
- stick to the knitting;
- remain simple in form, have a lean staff; and
- tolerate simultaneous loose-tight properties.[2]

The applicability of these principles to health care organizations is worth exploring. Would a search for excellence in health care supervision reveal a similar set of principles? Can these ideas be transferred to the supervisory level? What recommendations can be made for attaining excellence in supervision?

It is likely that with minor modifications the eight principles Peters and Waterman have specified for organizational excellence can be applied to health care supervision. It is also likely that health care organizations are especially subject to this application given pressures for higher employee productivity, lower costs and stable quality of service.

Clearly, some major problems of definition arise when anyone begins to discuss excellence or recommends methods by which excellence can be achieved. For discussion purposes, excellence can be viewed as desired performance levels that are superior to previous levels of performance. Note the transitory nature. On the one hand, excellence is a state to be attained; on the other, it is a process. Once having reached perfection, a person, work unit, department or organization is at a new beginning in the process, and the cycle continues through progressively higher levels of excellence.

It is clear that there is no single finite definition of what constitutes excellence in supervision. Neither is there a single best—and maximum—definition of excellence in employee performance. There are only successive attempts to raise performance beyond previous levels. A termination point is never attained—only new beginnings are reached.

With these thoughts in mind, it is appropriate to review the specific elements in Peters and Waterman's model of excellence and to apply them to health care supervision.

## EXCELLENCE IN CORPORATIONS

### Bias for action

America's best-run companies use eight basic principles to guide their operations. The first is having a bias for action. Such a bias ensures that something will be done. An integral part of this bias for action is good communication. Formal channels of communication are required, but functional informal channels must also exist. The manifestation of these informal channels of communication are best observed in daily operations that cultivate communication (e.g., first-name basis for all employees, open-door policies and physical layout that promotes interaction). Informal communication networks within organizations lead to more interpersonal contact and finally to more action. It is this bias for action that separates the excellent companies from the others.

**Close to customer**

The survival of every successful corporation ultimately depends on the corporation's remaining close to its customers. The second principle that guides the activities of America's excellent companies is dedication to the customer. This emphasis is succinctly translated as service, which must be an obsession if an organization aims to remain close to the customer. The essential ingredient of good service is follow-up. Not only is the customer sold a service or product, but the customer must be sold a piece of the business as well. At no time should the customer feel that the buyer–seller relationship ends with the sales transaction.

Management must make a clearly defined commitment to the customer, and it must be clear to the customer that not only does the department with which he or she deals care about his or her satisfaction, but the entire corporation cares. Thus management style affects the company's ability to stay close to the customer as much as does good service and genuine caring.

**Autonomy and entrepreneurship**

Excellent companies consistently endorse an organization structure and environment that induces innovation. These companies identify and support champions. Champions are people who, though they might seem eccentric, irrational and unorthodox, provide products, services and ideas that set the company apart from all others. Excellent companies believe in experimentation and are constantly seeking the new or innovative.

**Productivity through people**

If a company is to be excellent, it must realize that employees are assets who must be treated as partners, with dignity and respect. Employees are the primary source of productivity. A commitment to this principle is shown by respecting the individual; this is a pervasive theme in excellent companies. A redefinition of the worth of employees improves employee self-perceptions and materializes as greater profits through increased productivity for the firm.

**Value-driven**

The excellent company is guided by clearly defined values. Management in excellent companies does not treat values lightly; they make it a point to sort and select their values meticulously. Values provide motivation and guidance for the firm, dictating the direction the firm takes in a changing, uncertain environment. To be excellent is to be value-driven. Excellent companies know themselves.

**Stick to the knitting**

There is a tendency in every company to diversify. Excellent companies diversify but still remain close to their mission (i.e., knitting). A key objective of the successful company is to diversify around a single skill. As might be expected, the least successful firms are those that diversify into a wide variety of fields. Some diversification is necessary if the organization is to remain stable as it adapts to a changing external environment, but the magnitude of change must be tempered by the realization that the corporation cannot be everything to everybody.

**Simple form, lean staff**

Many firms make the common mistake of developing complex systems and structures to accompany increasing size. The lesson to be learned from this mistake is: keep things simple; especially strive for simplicity in form. Simple form implies a small (or lean) staff.

Dedication to this principle increases organizational flexibility. Excellent companies use ad hoc committees and task forces and are also constantly reorganizing. Most of this flurry of reorganizing activity occurs on the fringes—the basic form rarely changes.

***Dedication to this principle of simple form and lean staff increases organizational flexibility.***

**Loose-tight properties**

Finally, excellent companies are tightly controlled when it comes to the customer or its image. Corporations exercise a high degree of central control in order to ensure that customers receive the best service or product. They are loose when it comes to allowing internal anomalies like the champion discussed earlier. In other words, there is a high degree of tolerance for autonomy within the corporation, but this autonomy is integrated with, never separated from, the core values of the corporation.

## EXCELLENCE IN HEALTH CARE SUPERVISION

How can the concepts presented by Peters and Waterman be translated into guidelines for health care supervisors? Table 1 relates Peters and Waterman's principles of organizational excellence to excellence in health care supervision.

**Action**

Excellence in supervision is predicated on action. Supervisors must emphasize to employees the importance of successfully completing tasks. Simultaneously supervisors should continually seek better ways

**Table 1.** Achieving excellence in health care supervision

| Characteristics of organizational excellence | Equivalent implication for health care supervisors |
|---|---|
| A bias for action | Underscore the importance of attaining work objectives while continually seeking better methods of serving organization and clients. |
| Stay close to the customer | Create an atmosphere of service to other departments and to patients. |
| Autonomy and entrepreneurship | Think independently within the framework of an organization. Build an entrepreneurial work unit but not at the expense of organizational performance. |
| Productivity through people | Reinforce the attitude that a higher standard of performance is always attainable through the best efforts of people. |
| Hands-on, value-driven | Communicate work unit goals to others, and seek information on how the work unit can work better with others. |
| Stick to the knitting | Focus on the work of the department or work unit without trying to be everything to everybody. |
| Simple form, lean staff | Use a simple form for organizing and coordinating tasks. |
| Simultaneous loose-tight properties | Develop dedication to central organization values. |

Source: The characteristics of organizational excellence are defined and explained in T.J. Peters and R.H. Waterman. *In Search of Excellence* (New York: Harper & Row Publishers, 1982).

to serve patients and clients. A supervisor must strive to help the work team or department achieve not only the highest level of operating efficiency and productivity but higher levels of service as well. There must be an openness in the department to innovation and change that might help better achieve these objectives. This implies a willingness to look for opportunities for improvement, accompanied by the courage to implement changes when they seem to be justified.

For health care supervisors, a bias for action can be particularly important at critical times when constraints are seemingly growing faster than resources. This is especially true for most ancillary service departments in hospitals confronting prospective payment. However, supervisory obsession with action is justified with or without the constraints of prospective payment. All health care supervisors should be alert to opportunities to help employees better service patients and clients.

## Orientation toward service

Health care supervisors pursuing excellence must create an orientation toward or attitude of service within their employees, an attitude that should extend not only to clients and customers but to other departments in the health care organization. It is too easy to interpret the application of Peters and Waterman's findings as suggesting that supervisors direct their employees to focus on serving only clients. Customers, patients, clients and other purchasers of health care services are the main reason for the existence of the department or work unit; however, it must be remembered that a health care organization is often comprised of many work units that must collaborate to produce a product or service.

These ideas are perhaps more easily understood by health care supervisors than by supervisors in manufacturing settings because of the extensive coordination already existing in most health care organizations. Few ancillary departments in nursing homes or hospitals have not been integrated with other departments in serving patients or clients, a coordination that is an outgrowth of the tolerance for only the highest quality of care and relatively centralized methods of administration, which promote integration rather than division.

This spirit of cooperation among health care personnel must be maintained but must not be allowed to prevent improvement in service orientation. Supervisors should not expect subordinates to magically become more concerned with service. To maintain such an orientation, the director of nursing services, for example, must carefully coach nursing staff in daily activities and patient interactions.

**Entrepreneurial independence**

Supervisors must help their subordinates think independently. This idea does not conflict with the need for integration—it supports integration and adds vitality. Supervisors must build an entrepreneurial work unit: a unit that, in order to maximize performance, is always alert to the probabilities of innovation and risk taking.

Standard operating procedures may be discarded as the work unit devises new ways to produce a good or service. For example, a billing office in a mental health facility might revise its bill preparation process in order to shorten the collection period, beginning by processing data upon initial patient visits rather than waiting until a case terminates. Whatever the improvement, the work unit is striving toward better performance.

Health care supervisors must encourage their employees to think like entrepreneurs but without jeopardizing organizational performance for work unit performance. Supervisors' responsibility is to overall organizational goals rather than specific supervisory goals, even if they and their employees are penalized by the compensation system for less-than-optimal performance. In that case the reward system needs revision, but department goals still take priority over work unit goals.

**Improvement is always possible**

Excellent health care supervisors reinforce the principle that a work unit's excellence is attained through the best efforts of employees. For example, in the laundry and linen department of a nursing home the department head must help aides remember that it is people, not machines, that produce clean linen. The department employees determine whether the laundry is clean, how much and how fast it is cleaned, and how much it costs to achieve those results.

Keeping this principle in mind may be difficult when medical technology overshadows the efforts of people. Technology is expensive, impressive and results oriented. But technology is worthless without people to run it. The lesson is simple: Supervisors must believe that employees contribute more than technology and manage accordingly.

### Communication

Organizations that are value-driven (i.e., that are guided by clearly defined values) perform better. Health care supervisors must be value-driven. They must inspire others to attain work unit goals, they need to be prime advocates of the department and its accomplishments, and they must let other departments and work units know of their successes. At the same time they should seek information on how their unit can work better with other departments. A measure of excellence in health care supervision is whether a department can achieve excellence while helping others do the same.

### Retain focus

Excellent corporations stick to what they do best. This is a critical lesson for health care supervisors to learn. They must help their departments focus on accomplishing realistic goals and realize that, particularly at the work unit or team level, a group cannot be everything to everybody. For example, when the food service department in a hospital expands from serving patient meals to serving staff and visitor meals, department focus has been broadened, and the performance level of the expanded service must reach excellence before the department branches out further.

### Simple form

Like excellent corporations, health care supervisors must use a simple work unit structure for organizing and coordinating tasks—a simple yet powerful idea that is easier said than done because simultaneous pressures for cost containment and productivity drive departments toward technological solutions that often confuse the process. For example, matrix organization structures can be used in most health services organizations to provide specialized services derived from main, ancillary and clinical services. This complex structure may corrupt the fairly routine and simple organization of laboratories, food service, pharmacies and other departments.

The drive to computerize most standard or routine processes is a well-intentioned trend that assumes more technology is better but that can require complex form when simple form may present a more satisfactory solution. For example, a hospital's secretarial pool may constantly upgrade its knowledge of word processing equipment and software but never reach optimum performance before new changes are introduced. Incorporating less technology and attaining greater stability might produce better results.

### Dedication

Finally, health care supervisors must promote dedication of the work unit to organizational values as excellent corporations do. What supervisor has not witnessed within a department an "us" versus "them" orientation toward the rest of the organization? Employees must be dedicated to central organization values, not just individual values or departmental values. Congruency between individual goals and organizational goals is critical if departments are to achieve excellence.

Supervisors must help employees to understand that they are an important part of the organization and to align their individual goals with organizational goals. This is particularly important for health care supervisors in light of the high rates of absenteeism, turnover and alienation among health care workers.

## FINDING EXCELLENCE

Even a manager or supervisor of a successful health care organization should continually want to improve performance. Excellence is always attainable because it is a fluctuating reward standard. Excellence is more than promoting productivity and quality work. Finding excellence depends on how well health care supervisors articulate and implement in their organizations the principles of excellence used by successful organizations.

Clearly there is nothing unique about health care services management that prevents the pursuit of excellence, and there are no solid reasons why health care supervisors cannot pursue and achieve excellence in supervision just as organizations pursue and attain excellence. Principles of excellence can be implemented by health care supervisors, even though health services often are under constraints other organizations may not face.

How long will it take a health care supervisor to find excellence? The answer should be readily apparent. Excellence is both a goal and a process. A search for excellence in health care supervision begins with this realization and continues through successive refinements and progressively higher levels of excellence, but never ends.

REFERENCES

1. Peters, T.J. and Waterman, R.H. *In Search of Excellence.* New York: Harper & Row, 1982.
2. Peters and Waterman, *In Search of Excellence,* 13–15.

# The innovative supervisor

*Addison C. Bennett*
*Consultant to Management*
*Los Angeles, California*

THERE IS NOT ONE aspect of human activity that is not touched and altered by the culture of the organization—how people express themselves, how they think, how they function, how they solve problems, and how they deal with change. Concern and consideration for establishing an environment for meaningful change should compel the leaders of an organization to focus their attention on creating an innovative culture. Surely leaders need to do this if they want the pursuit of ideas to be a continuing purposeful process rather than a fragmented chance occurrence and if they wish to focus the minds and energies of their people on innovation. The true source of innovation is people, and the act of innovation is not only a contributing force, but is also a cohesive force. Innovation is a force that abounds with endless possibilities, allowing the entire organization to

*Health Care Superv*, 1986,4(2),1–12

capture the excitement of discovery. Taking joy in the search for solutions is indeed the province of the total organizational membership, with the supervisor as a key innovative player within this membership.

The introduction of newness is a happening inspired by a corporate culture fashioned in a mode of innovation. It also can be stimulated and affected by innovative supervisors. In a new book entitled *Boss Kettering*, Charles Kettering, General Motors' legendary wizard of research and innovation and founder of New York's Sloan-Kettering Institute, states that he attributes his success to luck—adding with a wink: "The harder I work, however, the luckier I get."[1] Like Kettering, if hospitals can get supervisory management to work harder at innovation, hospitals are bound to get luckier as well—and more competitive at the same time.

Yet, being lucky and working harder at newness are still not quite enough to gain substantive contributions from supervisory personnel. The ingredient that remains wanting is the preparedness of those in supervisory positions to be truly effective at innovating.

For purposes of this discussion, the definition of the term *innovation*, as proposed by Rowe and Boise, will be: "Managerial innovation may be defined as those decisions and tasks which are new to an organization and which result in the successful solution of one or more problems related to management's responsibilities."[2]

To bring increased newness to an organization, which brings with it successful solutions to managerial and operational problems, educated supervision needs to embrace three interrelated dimensions: (1) a foundation of beliefs, values, and expectations, (2) a capacity for extension of experience and knowledge, and (3) a set of essential skills and abilities.

## A FOUNDATION OF BELIEFS, VALUES, AND EXPECTATIONS

An underlying proposition to this first area of need for the innovative supervisor is the indelible inscription, "Know thyself," a saying attributed to the seven sages of antiquity. It remains today as a cornerstone of superior performance at any hierarchical level of leadership.

Knowing oneself, an indispensable characteristic of an innovative supervisor, finds its source in the beliefs, values, and expectations that the individual holds, and which in turn fashion his or her attitudes and behavior.

The innovative supervisor knows the need for a positive attitude toward change and endeavors to create a climate appropriate for the implementation of new and better ways of doing things. The supervisor's own attitude toward change may be measured in terms of certain beliefs considered to be fundamental to the search for newness and novelty. Such beliefs are included in the following list.

- It is change—with improvement—that enables the organization to be of service to its patients in new and better ways.
- Improvement in hospital operations cannot be left to chance—improvement requires conscious and continuous attention.
- Development of new ideas and the embodiment of these ideas in practice are two of the primary functions of management at all levels.
- There is always a better way.
- An open-minded attitude—the willingness to challenge custom and to try new ideas—is essential to growth and progress.
- An improvement for the future is not to be viewed as a criticism of the past.
- The person doing the job is capable of making a contribution to the improvement of the job and therefore should be consulted.
- A point of view that considers the good of the entire operation rather than that of any one department or individual is essential in developing organizational improvements.

The extent to which those in supervisory positions hold and practice beliefs such as these is a test of their individual capacity for change and innovation.

The innovative supervisor understands the importance of the central belief that changing things for the better is an objective worthy of his or her best efforts. Undergirding this belief is the acceptance of certain fundamental values that need to be subscribed to and activated not only by the supervisor, but also by the organization in which the supervisor serves as an effective change agent. The behavioral and managerial activities of the innovative supervisor will surely mirror the five values described here.

1. The value of balance encompasses several meanings. First, there is the balance of tradition and newness. Tradition should not be the enemy of innovation. At the same time, if individuals confine themselves to organizational patterns and practices of the past, they remain prisoners of the familiar and lose the chance of a century to take the next step to development. The innovative supervisor, although endowed with "now sight," knows how to bring into balance a sensitivity to the importance of the insight that comes from a reverence for the past and a backdrop of experience. There, too, is a criticality in attaining an intellectual, acute balance between the exercise of ordained power and the sharing of power. The innovative supervisor comprehends and is willing to accept the basic thought that the most effective way for one to gain power is to share one's power—a rather simple lesson to be learned and applied by any manager who wishes to ex-

tend his or her innovative power.

2. The value of unity helps the innovative supervisor to create within the work place an environment of unity and reciprocation in which collaboration, integration, and coordination can flourish.
3. The innovative supervisor manifests the value of sharing in many ways: the sharing of knowledge with others so that ignorance is not institutionalized; the sharing of skills so that people will succeed in what they do; and the sharing of trust so that the essential human connection is sustained.
4. The innovative supervisor subscribes to the value of excellence in performance as an obligation. This supervisor is well equipped to put forth some hard, tough questions about his or her own practices in honoring the excellences that are most fruitful for continued renewal and vitality of the organization.
5. A primary value for the innovative supervisor is the value of giving the highest of priorities to the hospital's human capital. Such a supervisor fully understands that his or her own humanistic behavior is the very foundation of a quality of work life in which excellence in employee performance is reared and nurtured.

Innovation begins with people, so values such as these will always be found supporting the human actions and behavior of the innovative supervisor.

Closely linked to beliefs and values is the idea of expectations: administration's expectations; nonmanagement employee expectations; and the supervisor's self-expectations.

The administration's expectations of its managers are clearly articulated at the Inter-Community Medical Center in Covina, California. Not only has the Medical Center's administrative team communicated in writing the expected qualities of its management people (one quality of a set of nine is problem solving and idea development), but it also has given proper emphasis to innovation as it declares its first patient-care–related goal for 1985 through 1986 to be: "To explore and implement innovative ways of extending the concept of quality and cost-effective behavior in Patient Care Services."

Nonmanagement expectations voiced by the majority of members of today's work force are of major concern to the innovative supervisor. Expectations identified in these generalizations include using one's mind; continuing development; recognition as individuals; worthwhile accomplishment; the right to know; a voice in decision making; and work that challenges. It is the innovative supervisor who recognizes the need to match this philosophy of entitlement with a sense of enlightenment. The supervisor's self-expectations bring us full circle to the imperative of

"Know thyself," an idea that can embrace several levels of self-examination: the act of making clear and distinct one's response to the questions "Who am I?" and "What must I do to be myself?"; of focusing on maximizing one's potential and level of achievement; and of gaining a self-awareness of one's strengths and weaknesses.

Capacity for self-discovery is a characteristic of the innovative supervisor; effective change seekers and change makers use a number of questions in their continuing self-assessment such as:

- How much of an innovator am I?
- How well do I do in maintaining the attitude that I "just want to keep improving"?
- How aware am I of who I am? Of what I must do to be myself?
- How aware am I of where I am? Of where I want to go?
- How aware am I of my strengths and weaknesses?
- How good do I feel about myself in terms of my level of performance?
- How effective have I been in motivating my employees to seek out new ideas and approaches?
- How well do I react and respond to unexpected occurrences in innovative and creative ways?
- What are the beliefs I hold with respect to the search for newness?
- Do I truly believe that changing things for the better is an objective worthy of my best efforts?
- What are the central values to which I subscribe and the evidence of these values in my actions and behavior?
- Do I consider the pursuit of excellence in performance to be a continuing obligation and responsibility of mine?
- Am I clear as to what is expected of me as a member of supervisory management?
- How responsive am I to the expectations of my employees?
- Have I, in the past, shown a capacity for self-assessment and self-discovery?

***To be innovators, supervisory managers need to be visionaries who bring achievement out of dreams; who see what others do not see; who hold perceptions linked with the future; who make the most of a slight edge.***

## EXTENSION OF EXPERIENCE AND KNOWLEDGE

To be innovators, supervisory managers need to be visionaries who bring achievement out of dreams; who see what others do not see; who hold perceptions linked with the future; who make the most of a slight edge, not just by giving the organization a new look, but by giving it a new outlook.

The innovative supervisor knows that the human capacity to create newness rests with the domain of knowledge, awareness, and experience one possesses, and knows all too well the avenues for gaining extensions to these qualities that are accessible in today's cultural environment. It is imperative that such extensions be sought, because the type of thinking required in the future on the part of executive leadership at all levels of the health care institution demands the presence of more management visionaries—those who can lead people to future breakthroughs because they have an acute sense of dynamic possibilities coming together through concepts, networks, analogies, parallels, and linkages.

What are the opportunities for extension readily available to today's supervisor? Here are a few:

- traveling to new places; experiencing varied cultures; seeing new faces;
- attending outside conferences and seminars that focus on varied subjects;
- networking with business and industry;
- taking on new and challenging tasks, both inside and outside the work place;
- seeking opportunities to speak or write on a variety of topics outside one's particular specialty, but which are worthy of exploring;
- carrying on good conversation with people who have the ability to think abstractly or profoundly;
- engaging in constant development of the skill of asking special questions so as to get special answers; and
- reading or scanning the most informative newspapers (surely, *The New York Times* and *The Wall Street Journal*); the best of health care and business journals; the books of greatest value—the writings that offer the prospect of a new idea, a new discovery, a new connection, a new principle of thought. Perhaps some of these are the more traditional texts on management. More likely, they are to be found in a diversity of fields of human activity and interest that are indeed complementary to the task of managing.

Innovative supervisors tend to be attracted to several areas of reading and there are several kinds of books they ought to be perusing if they wish to join the "innovators' circle."

### Art

The vision and creativity of an artist can help supervisory managers in advancing their effectiveness of working through people in imaginative and humanistic ways.

In Robert Henri's book, *The Art Spirit*, there appear a host of interesting insights about art and the artist. Henri provides a moment of wisdom at the very beginning of the text. He states,

> Art when really understood is the province of every human being. . . . It is simply a question of doing things, anything, well. It is not an outside, extra thing. . . .

When the artist is alive in any person, whatever his kind of work may be, he becomes an inventive, searching, daring, self-expressing creature. He becomes interesting to other people. He disturbs, upsets, enlightens, and he opens ways for a better understanding. Where those who are not artists are trying to close the book, he opens it, shows that there are still more pages possible.[3]

### Philosophy

To gain a brilliant and concise account of the ideas of the great philosophies, Will Durant's writing, *The Story of Philosophy*,[4] is one of the great books of our time. Today's and tomorrow's manager, to be effective, to be successful, needs to be a philosopher. "To be a philosopher," said Thoreau, "is not merely to have subtle thoughts, nor even to found a school, but so to love wisdom as to live, according to its dictates, a life of simplicity, independence, magnanimity, and trust."[5]

The writings of Mortimer J. Adler, America's most popular educator and philosopher, which consider the more practical sides of philosophy, are also highly recommended.

### Science

Well-written books deserving the attention of health care managers are those authored by Jacob Bronowski (*A Sense of the Future*;[6] *The Ascent of Man*[7]) and W.I.B. Beveridge (*The Art of Scientific Investigation*[8]). The innovative supervisor needs to have some insight into the creative, human nature of the scientific enterprise and how the human mind can best be adapted to the process of discovery.

The recently published book, *From Knowledge to Wisdom*, by Nicholas Maxwell, is an excellent addition to anyone's bookshelf.[9]

### Sociology

A landmark work by Paul Starr, a Harvard sociologist, is his book, *The Social Transformation of American Medicine*.[10] It is the first authoritative account of how physicians, hospitals, health plans, and government programs in the American health care system have evolved over the last two centuries. It is important reading for those holding leadership positions in health care organizations.

### History

The innovative supervisor can receive inspiration and guidance from many good contemporary writings that offer new values in the examples presented through historical perspectives. Two such works are *The Lessons of History*[11] by Will and Ariel Durant and *Practicing History*,[12] a set of selected essays, by Barbara W. Tuchman. As articulated clearly by these historians, a sense of history can very well change the structure of new developments.

### Management

One must be highly selective in reaching out to the multitude of management texts being written.

In today's work world, it is imperative that the innovative supervisor not only understand the organization's role in the health care system, but also understand the social, economic, and educational forces that affect the operation of the health care system. In addition to this externally directed vision, the supervisor also needs to view the organization itself as a system in which all the components must interact and interrelate in order to effectively direct the organization's resources to the treatment of the patient.

To assist the supervisor in gaining this broader vision, C. West Churchman's *The Systems Approach*[13] is recommended. This soft-cover book, published by Dell (New York), attempts to examine what the "systems approach" means, and fosters the idea of decision making in a logical and coherent fashion that avoids the fallacies of narrow-minded thinking. The systems approach is a way of thinking that is imperative to discovery.

Another recommended book in the management arena is Peter Drucker's *Managing in Turbulent Times.* One certainty about the future in health care is that the times during which managers will have to work and perform will be turbulent. Drucker declares in his introduction that in turbulent times "the first task of management is to make sure of the institution's capacity for survival, to make sure of its structural strength and soundness, of its capacity to survive a blow, to adapt to sudden change, and to avail itself of new opportunities."[14]

## Innovation

Two excellent books are offered as suggested readings. The first is Alvin Toffler's *The Adaptive Corporation*,[15] which is filled with insights on how to think about rapid change. It explains the impact of "newness" on any organization—whether new employees, new values, or new products. It is a thought-provoker for the innovator.

The second book is written by Rosabeth Moss Kanter and is entitled *The Change Masters.*[16] Contained in this writing are detailed analyses of both the pathways and pitfalls in the search for innovation at some of the most important companies in America. The book looks behind the scenes in these firms and describes what they are doing to free the powers of innovation and the entrepreneurial spirit within their own people. There is a wealth of information for the innovative supervisor.

This discussion of writings is not meant to be narrowly prescriptive, but to enable the supervisor to stretch out beyond his or her area of specialization—to extend his or her depth and breadth of vision in order to gain a global perspective. That, in turn, can aid in solving local problems more effectively, efficiently, and innovatively.

Returning once again to the idea of self-assessment, following are a few questions that need to be asked.

- How would I characterize the extent of my world of knowledge and awareness?
- Do I truly view myself as a visionary? Do I tend to see what others do not see?
- Do I fully understand and accept the relationship that exists between the extent of knowledge, awareness, and experience one possesses, and the degree of one's capacity to innovate?
- How purposefully active have I been in seeking out extensions to my own knowledge base?
- When I analyze situations and happenings, do I tend to think in terms of networks, analogies, parallels, and linkages?
- Do I need to do more traveling? When I have traveled in the past, has it helped me see the world in new and different ways? If so, in what ways? If not, why not?
- Have I made a concerted effort to expose myself to new dimensions of learning beyond my specific area of expertise?
- Have I aggressively sought new and challenging tasks, both inside and outside my work environment?
- Do I seek the kinds of thinking people with whom I can have a dialogue, and from whose knowledge, intellect, and experience I can gain personal growth?
- What other sources of extensiveness have I put to use? Is there more I can and should do in this regard?
- What is the amount of time I devote to reading? Is it adequate? If not, how can I make more time?
- What am I reading or scanning? Is it the best for striking the right balance between what is required to help me develop as a total human being, and that which is needed for personal enjoyment and relaxation?
- To what extent have I delved into the arts, philosophy, science, sociology, history? Other areas of human activity or interest?
- How good am I at asking new, different, or special questions? At adding other queries to this list that may reveal some further insights about my innovative tendencies?

## A SET OF ESSENTIAL SKILLS AND ABILITIES

The discovery of vision through extensive knowledge and experience is indeed linked to increasing supervisory skills and capabilities, not only in terms of how best to use one's own skills and abilities, but more importantly, in terms of the value of a global perspective that allows the supervisor to clearly understand all purposes served by assigned tasks and where these tasks fit into the full scheme of things. These are payoffs essential to the cause of innovation. What are some of the areas of supervisory skills and ability central to innovation?

First, there is the idea of viewing the organization as a total system that operates as a part of a larger system.

Innovative supervisors are capable of doing new things because creativity and ingenuity are nurtured through a concern and commitment that go beyond the narrow limits of the functional boundaries of the work unit for which they are responsible. Second, innovative supervisors have the skill and ability to establish and achieve innovative goals that evolve from foresight with respect to advancing organizational performance. Third, these supervisors possess the ability to maximize performance of available human resources. The innovative supervisor knows that fulfilling the role of manager rather than "part-time worker" allows worthwhile extensions to helping employees not only to handle problems, but also to participate in all parts of the problem-solving and innovative process. Fourth, supervisors who are innovative handle and impart information that is not only essential when considering that employees change their attitudes and their expectations, but that is also essential when creating an environment in which newness and novelty can flourish. Fifth, this innovative leader effectively manages human affairs at work, counteracting such barriers to change as the absence of a unity of purpose, threats to harmonious relationships, resistance and resentment, incompetence, or workers' unwillingness to produce.

Underlying these basic requirements for innovation in supervision is the need for problem-solving ability—being able to take a problem and develop its issues and dimensions, generate alternative ideas for solution, and derive feasible initiatives from the alternatives. To make this change process work well, the effective, innovative supervisor does eight things. This innovator

***Underlying basic requirements for innovation in supervision is the need for problem-solving ability—being able to take a problem and develop its issues and dimensions and derive feasible initiatives from the alternatives.***

1. recognizes when the problem in question is *really* the problem;
2. opens the mind to ideas;
3. provides sight, insight, and excitement;
4. focuses on the unusual, seeing what others have ignored;
5. tempers innovativeness with practicality;
6. engenders cooperation and coordination;
7. thinks through the work needed to turn an idea into meaningful action; and
8. asks the right kinds of questions in different ways.

The list of questions is as follows:

- Do I believe in the old saying, "Problems have a way of working themselves out if you leave them alone"?
- Have I ever caught myself saying

"We tried that, but it did not work"?

- Do I prefer waiting for someone else to try a new idea first, rather than take a calculated risk on it myself?
- Do my people show any fear of being threatened by new ways of doing things?
- What is the degree of my discomfort about the anticipated complexity and uncertainty that lie ahead? What has been the degree of pleasure associated with my past problem-solving opportunities?
- Do I perceive problem solving as a discrete activity or as an integral element of the management process?
- Do I really hold to the belief that "the best is yet to be"?
- What level of value do I place on my current skills in identifying problems requiring solution? My skills in devising successful methods to solve these problems? My skills in gaining acceptance and support from people affected by, and involved in, change?
- In my past problem-solving efforts, how well have I applied the principle of systematization?
- Have I ever chosen a solution, yet realized I still had a problem?
- How active and successful have I been this past year in producing new ideas?
- How good am I at noticing details ignored by others?
- Am I functioning as a manager or as a "part-time worker"?
- When solving problems, do I approach the need for change with confidence, hope, and enthusiasm?
- Do I approach problems with an open mind, with an absence of any preconceived notions, and with an organized plan of questioning? Did I, in fact, ask any good questions today?

Interesting stories about the innovators abound in the motion picture industry. For example, there is the story about Sam Marx, a highly creative Hollywood producer who has spent a good many sleepless nights trying to figure out how much wisdom can be crammed into four words. In God we trust. Still waters run deep. Bad news travels fast. Nothing succeeds like success. Charity begins at home. Politics makes strange bedfellows. Nothing ventured, nothing gained. Man proposes, God disposes. Let sleeping dogs lie.

A great deal can be said in just four words. The following summation of thoughts expressed in only four words is meant especially for the health care supervisor:

- Innovation is a process.
- Innovativeness requires systemic perspectives.
- Supervisors are key contributors.
- Innovation is everyone's business.
- Innovation begins with ideas.
- Ideas begin with people.

## REFERENCES


1. Stuart, W. *Boss Kettering*. New York: Columbia University Press, 1983, p. 45.
2. Rowe, A., and Boise, W.B. *Organizational and Managerial Innovation*. Pacific Palisades, Calif.: Goodyear Publishing Company, 1973, p. 7.
3. Henri, R. *The Art Spirit*. Philadelphia, Pa.: Lippincott, 1960, p. 15.
4. Durant, W. *The Story of Philosophy*. New York: Simon & Schuster, 1961.
5. Ibid, 1.
6. Bronowski, J. *A Sense of the Future*. Cambridge, Mass.: MIT Press, 1977.
7. Bronowski, J. *The Ascent of Man*. Boston: Little, Brown, 1973.
8. Beveridge, W.I.B. *The Art of Scientific Investigation*. New York: Vintage Books, 1950.
9. Maxwell, N. *From Knowledge to Wisdom*. Oxford, England: Blackwell, 1984.
10. Starr, P. *The Social Transformation of American Medicine*. New York: Basic Books, 1982.
11. Durant, W., and Durant, A. *The Lessons of History*. New York: Simon & Schuster, 1968.
12. Tuchman, B.W. *Practicing History*. New York: Knopf, 1981.
13. Churchman, C.W. *The Systems Approach*. New York: Dell, 1968.
14. Drucker, P. *Management in Turbulent Times*. New York: Harper & Row, 1980.
15. Toffler, A. *The Adaptive Corporation*. New York: McGraw-Hill, 1985.
16. Kanter, R.M. *The Change Masters*. New York: Simon & Schuster, 1983.

# The supervisor as a professional manager

*Charles R. McConnell*
*Vice President for Employee Affairs*
*The Genesee Hospital*
*Rochester, New York*

IN A SURVEY conducted in a number of health care organizations and updated several times over a period of years, a number of working health care supervisors were called on to describe what they did for a living in as few words as possible. Undertaken as part of the opening sessions of a supervisory skills development program, the survey attempted to determine if there was any noticeable consistency in how supervisors viewed themselves, and to determine, if possible, what supervisors identified with or associated themselves with in describing themselves and their roles.[1]

In most organizations in which supervisors were requested to "describe what you do in as few words as possible," supervisors tended to identify most strongly with their basic occupations, secondarily with their departmental functions, and only thirdly with supervision. Identi-

*Health Care Superv*, 1986,4(3),59–71

fication with one's basic occupation or profession—for example, registered nurse, laboratory technologist, medical record practitioner, accountant, and so forth—tended to be strongest among educated technical specialists. That is, the people who had invested considerable time and effort in acquiring education, qualifications, and experience in a given specialty tended to identify more strongly with that specialty than with department, organization, or supervisory status.

Identification with a specific departmental function appeared to be strongest among supervisors who had risen to their positions through unskilled or semiskilled occupations. For example, the housekeeping supervisor who began work as a housekeeping worker, the business office supervisor who began work as a file clerk, and the maintenance supervisor who first began work as a mechanic's helper—these supervisors, having no "specialty" other than that which they learned on the job, tended to identify most strongly with the departmental function as a specialty.

In most of the survey responses, identification with occupation and identification with departmental function seemed to be far stronger than the supervisor's identification with supervision or management (a few notable exceptions to this will be discussed later). It was also clear from the supervisors' responses that most of these people considered themselves to be professionals in their basic occupational fields. Again this was especially strong among supervisors who had risen to their positions through one of the health care technical specialties. However, it also appeared that many of the supervisors surveyed did not view supervision as a professional activity, or saw supervision and management as two different activities, with supervision the decidedly less important of the two.

It should be stressed that the survey was far from scientific, consisting simply of a few questions asked of all new attendees at a supervisory skills development program that was conducted some 40 times for supervisors from 50 to 60 different institutions over a period of six years. Scientific or not, however, the same kinds of responses occurred often enough to lend credibility to the following general conclusions:

- The majority of supervisors do not identify with supervision nearly as strongly as they identify with their basic occupations.
- A great many supervisors do not see themselves as full-fledged members of "management."

The premise of this article is that the supervisor is a manager, management is a profession, and the supervisor can become a professional manager largely through his or her own efforts. However, becoming a professional manager requires overcoming some longstanding misconceptions about management, and becoming a professional manager may also mean overcoming some organizational barriers to the full development of the supervisor as a manager.

## MANAGEMENT'S "CASTE SYSTEM": FALSE DISTINCTIONS

Some of the more widespread misconceptions about management hold that the various levels in the organizational hierarchy are populated by different kinds of people who perform distinctly different functions. While the word management is almost always used as the generic term that it really is (although it is often qualified, as in top management, middle management, first-line management, etc.), the specific label of manager is frequently applied only in describing people in the middle ranges of the hierarchy. Because of this strong use of the term manager, associated with only the middle part of the managerial hierarchy, we are led toward the impression that "manager" is different from and greater than "supervisor." Similar reasoning leads us to regard "executive" (or whatever other term may be applied to the upper reaches of the hierarchy) as different from and thus greater than both supervisor and manager.

The tendency to think of management in terms of strict hierarchical distinctions is regularly reinforced by academicians, management theorists, and other writers. For example, one widely distributed publication spoke of ". . . the strength of (the organization's) executives, managers, and supervisors," and also of a "clear distinction between executives, managers, and supervisors."[2]

Within many works on management one can find a glaring inconsistency that occurs over and over again: Most such works use "management" as a much-needed generic term to describe the business of running the organization or any of its parts, but then proceed to use "manager" in a less-than-generic sense to describe a particular level of the activity broadly referred to as management. Thus have so many fallen into the labeling trap.

### The labeling trap

Certainly there are differences among the duties and responsibilities of people at different levels in the management hierarchy. However, all managers are there for the same basic purpose—to manage; that is, to get things done through people.

Thus, misconceptions arising from false distinctions between levels in the hierarchy come largely from the inconsistent use of management as a more generic term and manager as a strongly entrenched, level-specific label in organizations (with the problem compounded by the fact that the organizational label may apply to different levels from one organization to the next). Within any particular organization a variety of management titles will exist. For example, we may find, among those people responsible for getting work done through others, the supervisor, the manager, the director, the executive director, the department head, the vice president, the president, and a variety of others. However, one overall label applies to this entire collection of titles—all are managers, but the list includes *manager* as well. Therefore, manager is both a generic label for any practitioner of management, as well as a specific title found in most organizations.

In any specific health care organization, the supervisor usually cannot correctly be called manager in a position-title sense; but the supervisor is a manager in the generic sense of the term and is legitimately a member of the body of management. It is essential to recognize that supervisor has come to be regarded as something less than manager by many people purely because of the weight given manager as a position title in the hierarchy. It simply does not occur to most people to think of the same term as both a specific label and generic term, so other labels to which the generic might apply are shortchanged (at least the labels below manager in the hierarchy are shortchanged—it matters not that president or executive director likewise do not automatically equate to manager; because of their hierarchical position they are automatically perceived as "more than" manager just as supervisor is perceived as "less than" manager).

As an important first step toward professionalism, the supervisor must accept the contention that he or she is indeed a manager. The supervisor might be the lowest manager in the organization's hierarchy, but that person nevertheless is a manager.

**A constant balancing act**

Because of his or her basic technical specialty or function, the supervisor is usually part nonmanagerial worker as well as a member of management. To an extent that may vary from one supervisor's position to another's, supervisors are expected to follow instructions—as indeed all employees are—and to adhere to established procedures in seeing that employees do the same (follow instructions and adhere to procedures) in getting the work out. Because the supervisor's role ordinarily includes doing some of the work as well as getting work done by others, the supervisor is frequently caught between the conflicting roles of technical specialist and manager. The roles of technical specialist and manager are described as conflicting because their very nature and structure set each apart from the other.

***Because the supervisor's role ordinarily includes doing some of the work as well as getting work done by others, the supervisor is frequently caught between the conflicting roles of technical specialist and manager.***

The technical specialist's role is completely vertically integrated. One's technical knowledge is built on a specific base and is always applied within the same general context. That is, much of one's technical specialty will not be transportable across functional lines. Using one's specific technical background, for example, a radiology technologist can work nowhere but in the department of radiology, a laboratory technologist can work only at some aspect of laboratory work, and a registered nurse can work in that capacity only in some position that calls for a registered nurse. Vertical integration essentially defines a specialty; knowledge is built on knowledge, all deliberately channeled within a particular discipline.

On the other hand, the managerial role of the supervisor is horizontally integrated. The general tasks that managers do and the techniques they use apply across all functional lines. Managers are concerned with the likes of budgeting, planning, staffing and scheduling, performance evaluation, employee counseling, and handling disciplinary matters and other employee relations problems. All of these tasks are such that they apply horizontally across functional lines. Every department, regardless of its specialty, requires a budget; every department has employees, and these employees require periodic performance evaluation and occasional counseling or disciplinary action.

The technical specialist who enters supervision has to make a significant adjustment. Where one's role was previously all vertically integrated, one will now be expected to function half or more of the time in a role that is horizontally integrated. More often than not, one's preparation for the new, horizontally integrated role is severely lacking.

Role preparation, which is quite thorough for the technical specialty, is frequently minimal or nonexistent for management. It has happened since time immemorial and will continue to happen—the technically good performer, well trained in a basic field, is promoted to supervision and given a title and new and expanded responsibilities without appreciable preparation. The usual absence of preparation may also contribute to the reasons many people do not think of management as a profession. Because the organization is continually putting new managers in place with no particular preparation, the organization may appear to be saying through its actions that management does not amount to a great deal because no special preparation is needed.

A supervisor must contend with the conflicting roles of technical specialist and manager. Furthermore, the supervisor is usually highly trained in the technical specialty and trained little or not at all in management. Thus the supervisor wears two hats and is put in a position of attempting to balance two important roles, although he or she is far better prepared for one role than for the other.

In dealing with the problems that arise day to day, the supervisor frequently finds that the majority of the frustrations and seemingly insoluble problems encountered come from the management side of the job. Because the supervisor may not have been prepared to succeed—or even to survive—in the management role, he or she will frequently shy away from the responsibilities of management and take refuge in some aspects of the work of the technical specialty. Every supervisor is required to wear two hats, but when difficulties arise most will tend to favor the hat that fits best.

Balancing the technical and managerial roles usually means forcing some elements of one's technical specialty to secondary consideration. This is not to say that one's technical specialty should be discarded when entering management; rather, simply that when entering management, one's first concern should turn more toward "how to get it done" than "how to do it." In addition to pulling away to some extent from some elements of one's specialty, successfully balancing roles means pursuing management training and development, often at one's own initiative.

Often much of one's own supervisory development must be accomplished in the face of apparent organizational indifference to management development. Hardly a professional working in a technical specialty would deny the importance of continuing education within that specialty; however, it is perhaps another indication of the failure of many to see professionalism in management that continuing education for management is not taken especially seriously. It constantly seems as though a large part of the working world of management will always remain too busy working to learn how to manage more effectively.

Effectively balancing one's technical specialist role and the management role requires that one deliberately adopt management as a second career of fully equal importance as one's primary career field. Often the supervisor's overall professionalism will be a direct reflection of how well he or she balances the two roles.

## Authority: a critical element

A publication cited earlier also includes the following passage: "To the extent that a supervisor is provided with the environment and the responsibilities and accountability to achieve the organization's objectives, he or she is an integral part of the management team."[3]

The foregoing is true but only as far as it goes—it is completely true only if we may assume that "environment" is the total organizational environment and that this includes the supervisor's authority to act. Although authority was not specifically mentioned in the quoted passage, it must be made clear that every supervisor needs to be given a certain amount of authority.

Responsibility—or accountability, which is a state of being obligated to fulfill one's responsibilities—is the load that the individual must carry. Authority is the container or conveyance with which that load is carried.

It is fundamental to the appointment of duties and responsibilities that authority be apportioned consistent with responsibility. At all levels of the organization it is essential that anyone who is given a task to be accomplished must also be given the wherewithal to accomplish that task. Authority is essentially the hard currency with which something may be bought. Consider as a simple parallel the matter of going to the grocery store to bring home the bread. Securing the bread and bringing it home is the responsibility; the money with which to purchase the bread is the authority, the wherewithal for fulfilling the responsibility. Were one to go to the store without the money—that is, without the authority—the responsibility could be fulfilled only indirectly and with considerably more effort, perhaps by begging, borrowing, stealing, or bartering.

It may seem rather basic to suggest that no one would send someone to the store responsible for returning with bread without providing the money (the authority) to secure the bread. Yet in many work organizations people in supervisory positions are continually made responsible for accomplishing various results, but they are not given appropriate authority to enable them to do so. Consider the supervisor who may be charged with solving a problem of apparent excess absenteeism in a department. If this supervisor is free to counsel and to warn and to apply a standard disciplinary process, then the supervisor has sufficient authority to fulfill the responsibility. However, if the supervisor is under the gun to reduce excess absenteeism but finds that higher management controls the disciplinary process and limits supervisory action to counseling only, then the supervisor is left with less than the complete wherewithal required to do the job. Overall, any supervisor should be in possession of just enough authority to fulfill the responsibilities of the position—no more, and most certainly no less.

How does one obtain authority? First, one should not assume that he or she does not have authority. A detailed review of one's job description will reveal that this none-too-complicated document actually contains most of the individual supervisor's authority to act. If on review, however, a job description seems to contain gaps and shortcomings, the supervisor should take the initiative to review this with the immediate superior and recommend revisions as necessary. In short, if the supervisor does not have enough authority to get the job done properly, he or she should ask the boss for it. Because authority is delegated through succeeding levels down the management hierarchy, the boss is usually in possession of the additional authority required and can parcel out (delegate) this authority accordingly.

As an absolute last resort, and only in the absence of clear direction from one's superior, one may simply assume a reasonable amount of authority required to get the work done and to fulfill the responsibility. However, simply assuming authority can be hazardous and one should never assume more authority than is needed, should never knowingly stray into the territory (or more specifically, into the job description) of another supervisor, and should always advise one's own superior, preferably in writing, of what was done and why it was done.

This matter of authority often marks the most pronounced difference between the true professional manager and the manager-in-title-only who has neither sought nor achieved professionalism. The professional manager recognizes the long-run hopelessness of trying to fulfill a certain level of responsibility with an inadequate amount of authority, and will either strive through channels to obtain sufficient authority or will simply assume sufficient authority when the matter of the moment seems to warrant such action. Either of these courses of action failing, the professional manager may well seek new employment. Under the same circumstances the less than professional manager will do a great deal of complaining about having to work with both hands tied, but will do little or nothing to attempt to secure a proper measure of authority.

## WORKING THROUGH OTHERS

Management is frequently described as the process of getting things done through people. This is a simple description, until one considers the different ways that people of differing viewpoints qualify that statement. One view holds that "people" consists of only the employees in the work group beneath the supervisor, not including the supervisor. Under this view the employees do all of the hands-on work and the supervisor is an overseer only, a giver of orders and instructions as necessary. This is a literal interpretation of "through people" that excludes the supervisor from consideration. Those holding this view often attempt to distinguish between "pure" supervisors and those others who do some supervising as well as doing some of the hands-on work. Thus we encounter labels such as working supervisor that attempt to identify those individuals who are not pure managers. (Problems of a different kind arise with terms like working supervisor. This label suggests that if some kinds of supervisors are working supervisors, there must be others who are nonworking supervisors. Thus the indirect suggestion of the term working supervisor is that there are also some supervisors who do not work—at all.)

Other views of getting things done through people more realistically concede that the manager of a group may often, perhaps even routinely, do part of the hands-on work of the group. This is a more practical view, suggesting that the manager gets work done by and through others and self as necessary. This view also suggests, far more accurately than the opposing view, that pure managers are not particularly common. One need examine only a select few positions in an organization's management hierarchy to discover that few if any pure managerial positions exist below the level of top management.

The professional manager will as necessary consider himself or herself to be a member of the work group as well as the group's leader. The professional manager will also recognize that the work is considerably more important to the organization than is the group's manager. Through their normal knowledge of what to do and when to do it the members of a work group can accomplish a fair amount of useful work without the manager, so one can say that to a certain extent the work group can function without its manager. However, the opposite is not the case—a manager can function little or not at all without the work group.

The professional manager will be all manager when necessary, but will also be one more pair of hands in the work group when needed. The manager's intent in behaving either way will remain the same—to ensure the accomplishment of the work of the group in the most timely and efficient manner possible.

## BEHAVIOR VERSUS TREATMENT

Professional behavior and professional treatment are equal but apparently opposing sides of the same coin.

The work organization has a responsibility to treat as professionals those workers who it wants to perform as professionals. Often, however, the organizational attitude requires professional treatment to be earned by employees through professional behavior. That is, the attitude of the organization often says, "Behave as a professional should behave, and then we will treat you as a professional."

On the other side of the argument, the employee who wishes to be considered as a professional should perform and behave as would be expected of a professional. Often, however, the individual seems to be demanding that his or her appropriate professional behavior must be purchased by the organization through appropriate treatment. This attitude says in effect, "Treat me as a professional, and then I will behave like one."

***In truth there are, in health care organizations, more supervisors—that is, more first-line managers—than any other kind of manager in the organization.***

The matter of behavior versus treatment may not present a problem in some organizations, but it is indeed a problem in many organizations that do not treat their supervisors as though they were true members of management. In truth there are, in health care organizations, more supervisors—that is, more first-line managers—than any other kind of manager in the organization. Yet frequently the hierarchy of middle-to-upper-management, often supported in their attitudes by the upper ranks of professional workers, do not regard these supervisors as managers.

Although managers who have come up through the ranks are to be found at all levels in nearly all organizations, it is becoming more and more common for middle and upper-middle managers to enter the organization at managerial levels with formal education in management. However, most supervisors—again, first-line managers—have almost exclusively come up through the ranks, directly out of their own work groups in most cases, into management. Most of these supervisors are also still involved to some extent in the hands-on work of their work groups. These supervisors are thus seen by others as more associated with nonmanagerial work than with managerial work, and thus upper levels of the management hierarchy tend to treat them as something less than professional. A normal, understandable reaction to such treatment is, for many supervisors, to feel like something less than professional and thus to act as something less than professional.

In the opening discussion concerning the factors that supervisors identified with (occupation, department, and management), the notable exceptions hinted at were found in organizations in which supervisors were treated as full-fledged members of management. The more an organization treated its supervisors as true members of management, the more those supervisors tended to identify with management.

The key to the behavior-versus-treatment aspect of professionalism in management lies largely in the supervisor's initiative. To passively wait to receive professional treatment before extending one's best in the way of professional behavior is to hold one's own potential for ransom. Not only is such behavior unprofessional, it essentially establishes one as unpromotable for all practical purposes. The organization's hierarchy may never consciously consider professionalism a factor at all, but whether upper management is enlightened or not so enlightened they are still likely to be turned off by an attitude of passivity on the part of a supervisor. In most organizational settings, he or she who sits back waiting for something to happen is simply bypassed.

Thus the professional manager will constantly deliver his or her best professional behavior regardless of whether consistent treatment as a professional is extended in return.

## A NEVER-ENDING TASK

One of the surest marks of a professional manager is the demonstrated willingness to take the initiative in matters of organizational communication. A supervisor communicates with employees, superiors, organizational peers, and others, all in ways that differ from each other, some considerably.

It would be impossible to insert here volumes about communications with one's employees. However, for purposes of this discussion there is but one point of particular importance that must be made: The supervisor is the key communicating link between the individual employee and the rest of the organization. It is through the supervisor that instructions, procedures, policies, directions, corrections, and rewards all flow to the employee. The supervisor is the employee's primary source of information about the organization, and more than that, the supervisor is the personality or embodiment of the organization for the employee. Thus, as the individual employee sees the supervisor, so is that employee likely to see the entire organization. When this consideration is multiplied by the number of employees an individual supervisor has, it makes one realize that the supervisor wields a great deal of power in shaping the attitudes of employees toward the organization.

Supervisors of course have the clout of organizational authority behind them in their dealings with employees. However, the best of supervisors do not swing their clout, do not intimidate employees with the authority of their positions. The best supervisors do not order; they ask. The best supervisors have discovered that the mere possession of power and authority is quite enough and that these need not be applied directly.

Although considerable organizational communication flows from employees to supervisor because it must—because procedures and reporting relationships have made it so—there is also a need for information to flow readily in the other direction. The better supervisors will continually remember their employees and anticipate the employees' information needs, doing everything possible to keep employees advised as to where they stand and what is going on in the department and the organization as a whole.

In working with peers, the professional manager strives continually for an attitude of mutual cooperation, but realistically may settle for something less. As in dealings with people outside the organization and all others with whom one may not have a direct chain-of-command relationship, communications consideration must ordinarily be earned. The way such consideration is earned is by first and continually remembering others and extending to them every consideration in communication. In short, the manager who remembers others and their information needs is more likely to be remembered by those others.

It is in organizational communication within the chain of command—specifically, communication with one's immediate superior—that a supervisor's professionalism will have much of its impact. By and large, middle and upper managers are relatively busy people. Most of them have more than one subordinate supervisor reporting to them, and many have large numbers of other people also reporting directly to them. It is of course part of the role of a manager at any level to serve as a source of guidance and problem-solving assistance to subordinates. However, it is far too easy for many supervisors to interpret this as meaning that the boss is there to run to when there is a problem.

The professional supervisor will appreciate that he or she is but one of a number of people who report to the same boss. Realizing this, the professional supervisor will take appropriate steps to anticipate the boss's information needs and to make it as quick and easy as possible for the boss to act or to reply. In other words, the supervisor will not go to the boss simply with a problem and a plea for help. Rather, the supervisor will go to the boss with a problem that has been thought out, fully defined, analyzed, and provided with possible solutions, and for which a recommendation is offered. Thus the professional supervisor will make the boss's work as easy as possible, recognizing that the boss probably has far more work than meets the eye.

The true professional manager is one who recognizes that he or she is never completely finished when it comes to making organizational communication work better. The truly effective communicator is one who always, mindless of so-called fairness and without weighing "my part" versus "your part," goes more than halfway more than half of the time in communicating with others, fully realizing that not always will all of one's efforts be repaid in full. This may be a difficult posture to assume, recognizing that one is deliberately extending thoughtfulness to a number of others who will never reciprocate, so it pays to remember that the primary beneficiaries of improved communications are oneself and one's department. When the supervisor and his or her employees know and understand more, the department can work more effectively and can better help the organization serve its patients.

• • •

Management is much the same as many other lines of work in that the occupation can itself be referred to as a profession; but not all of its practitioners are professionals. In summary, the supervisor may be considered a professional manager if he or she:

- accepts "supervisor" as legitimately synonymous with "manager," and views self as a full-fledged member of management;
- is able to achieve an appropriate balance between one's own vertically integrated technical specialist role and the horizontally integrated role of the supervisor;
- strives to acquire and retain an amount of organizational authority consistent with the assigned responsibilities of the position;
- accepts as a primary role the business of seeing that the work gets done through the efforts of the total work group (which includes the supervisor);
- is willing to earn (or try to earn) treatment as a professional by willingly extending conscientious professional behavior to the organization; and

- constantly takes the initiative to improve one's own communications posture within the organization.

Being a professional manager does not require that one qualify under someone's particular definition of professional. Even the so-called "legal" definition of both professional and manager under the Fair Labor Standards Act leaves much to be desired. Rather, at the heart of becoming a professional manager should lie the individual's liking for the work, dedication to the role of supervisor, and willingness to continually learn and grow in the practice of management.

## REFERENCES

1. McConnell, C. Unpublished survey, 1971–1977.
2. Hill, A. "The Supervisor as a Manager: Contributions and Conflicts." *Personnel Administrator* 27, no. 6 (1982): 110.
3. Ibid.

# Building productive relationships with movers and shakers

*Howard L. Smith*
*Associate Dean*

*Richard A. Reid*
*Professor*
*Anderson Schools of Management*
*University of New Mexico*
*Albuquerque, New Mexico*

*Neill F. Piland*
*Director*
*Health Services Research and Education*
*Lovelace Medical Foundation*
*Albuquerque, New Mexico*

MANAGERS have numerous opportunities to interact with powerful movers and shakers who influence the direction of health care organizations. The prognosis is that these opportunities will increase as health care providers seek better integration of strategy and operations. Many managers may be inadequately prepared to take full advantage of these propitious trends. This article identifies pertinent characteristics of movers and shakers in order to help managers better understand the roles they play. It then examines several strategies for building productive relationships with movers and shakers. Managers are encouraged to formulate effective relationships as a means to enhance personal and professional goal attainment.

## COORDINATING STRATEGY AND OPERATIONS

A dynamic environment is shaping health care providers' service delivery efforts. Such

*Health Care Superv,* 1991, 9(3), 11–21

problems as financing, competition, and quality of care also have a profound impact on the services health care organizations' plans to provide in the future. As many organizations are discovering, traditional strategies for service delivery must be replaced with more innovative ideas to cope with these pressures. Although innovation is a major asset, it is seldom the sole ingredient in developing successful service delivery efforts. Health care organizations must be equally concerned with improving existing services to achieve high quality patient care, provider productivity, and fiscal viability.

Many health care managers have primarily been responsible for operations—that is, implementing strategies formulated by top-level managers and governing board members. Movers and shakers typically define an organization's vision and direction. Today, health care institutions are also seeking better coordination between strategy and operations. Managers can play a pivotal role in integrating vision with implementation. As health providers negotiate the transitions within a complex environment, they must better capitalize on the contributions of health care managers and operating-level staff. Productive relationships between staff and movers and shakers depend to a great extent on health care managers who function as intermediaries.

For example, the nursing director in a long-term care facility participates with top management in setting objectives regarding cost and quality of nursing care. The director informs nurse managers and staff members about the expectations set for the nursing department. Concurrently, the nursing director serves as a conduit to top management about strategic changes observed by the nursing staff. Perhaps the nursing staff recognizes that the facility is attracting older, more frail patients or that a competitor has adjusted nurse staffing to enhance marketing efforts. The nursing director must effectively manage current operations (for example, nursing services delivery) while contributing to the facility's competitive response (for example, communicating strategically relevant information to top management).

Opportunities for health care managers to participate in strategy-level issues are increasing. Such involvement implies that fresh perspectives may be incorporated in developing organizational strategies and that more avenues may exist for coordinating strategy with implementation. However, integration depends on how well operating-level managers work with strategic-level movers and shakers. Many health care managers may not be adequately prepared for such interactions.

## A PROFILE OF MOVERS AND SHAKERS

Movers and shakers can alter the strategic direction of an organization or program. They can also significantly affect service delivery. Such movers and shakers include leaders on the board of trustees, articulate and motivated providers (for example, physicians) who are formally or informally associated with an organization, capable or powerful top management staff members, and community leaders (such as politicians, volunteers, patients/consumers).

Movers and shakers are effective agents of change within organizations because they possess at least five powerful characteristics: (1) charisma, (2) experience in policy-level decision making, (3) expertise, (4) entrepreneurial orientation, and (5) willingness to confront facts. Figure 1 schematically illus-

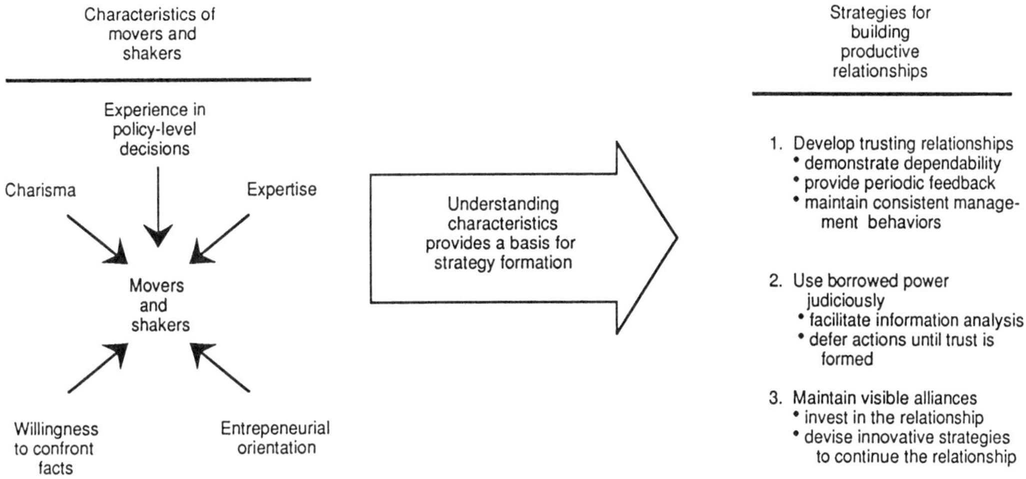


**Figure 1.** Understanding characteristics of movers and shakers as a precondition to building productive relationships.

trates these five characteristics and several strategies for building productive relationships with movers and shakers.

Movers and shakers may exhibit other prominent characteristics—such as political power, control of wealth or vast resources, and social or professional connections. Although this model is not comprehensive, it examines the characteristics most pertinent to health care managers and health care organizations.

From a health care manager's perspective, movers and shakers deserve respect because they affect strategy and operations. By influencing the governance of health care organizations, movers and shakers ultimately affect operating-level activities. As health care managers become increasingly involved in strategic issues, they will interact more often with movers and shakers. Health care managers should capitalize on these opportunities for themselves, their departments and their organization. Understanding the characteristics and qualities of movers and shakers is a prerequisite for forging such productive relationships.

***By influencing the governance of health care organizations, movers and shakers ultimately affect operating-level activities.***

## Charismatic qualities

Movers and shakers command respect merely because of their charisma and presence. This contrasts sharply with the respect accorded leaders by virtue of their organizational titles or positions. Charisma associated with movers and shakers is usually evident in their ability to communicate. Through effective communication (with individuals and groups), movers and shakers are able to influence people either directly or indirectly. People tend to listen intensely when movers and shakers speak.

Movers and shakers are especially capable of using charisma to win converts to their perspective. Informally before meetings or openly during conference discussions, they let their views be known. Although they often possess excellent verbal skills, they rarely dominate conversations or discussions, preferring instead to listen closely to the attitudes and opinions surrounding an issue. At opportune moments, they identify fundamental issues underlying the problem, summarize points of contention into two or three viewpoints or alternatives, provide evidence substantiating their own position, and then deftly acknowledge the least preferred options with a few salutary comments.

For example, a hospital administrator and governing board chairperson instruct a nursing director to assemble her assistants to discuss the problem of nurse turnover. The administrator restates the purpose of the meeting and initiates an open examination of factors leading to high turnover. After several team leaders have presented their ideas about salary and benefit problems, discussion centers around performance shortcomings by the dietary, pharmacy, and housekeeping departments that hinder patient care. Just as the conversation begins to focus on complaints regarding two recalcitrant physicians, the governing board chairperson speaks up. This mover and shaker underscores the preeminent problem of salary compensation, which is below market levels. She acknowledges that internal management control problems (by ancillary services department heads) and medical staff relations problems contribute to the situation. However, she also helps the group reach consensus regarding the impact of salary as the key contributor to turnover.

Movers and shakers provide listeners the opportunity to draw their own inferences. Avoiding extensive details, movers and shakers allude to general rationales that satisfy diverse constituencies within the decision-making body. Movers and shakers' charisma frequently inhibits listeners from challenging vague assertions or logically incomplete ideas. Consensus forms around the views of movers and shakers.

### Experience in policy-level decisions

Health care managers often propose ideas that produce change in hospitals. However, movers and shakers possess the requisite authority, either explicit or implicit, to make policy-level decisions. Their extensive experience in addressing significant strategic problems enhances their decision-making power. And many governing board and managerial staff members are often relieved that movers and shakers are actively involved. The process of building consensus around viable alternatives commences more rapidly when movers and shakers take charge. Although heated discussion surrounding certain issues may continue even after movers and shakers have spoken, most people realize that these verbal interchanges are either posturing or a way of resolving minor details.

The scenario of a medical staff meeting of clinical department heads in a multispecialty group practice illustrates the value of movers and shakers' experience. Assume that the contested issue is excessive assignment of managed care plan (that is, health maintenance organization) patients to new medical staff members. New staff members are expressing concern that the most economically rewarding patients are routed to more tenured staff members. The head of obstetrics discusses the problem of high malpractice insurance costs relative to the new physicians' income. The chief of urology notes that managed care patients have always been assigned to new staff members to facilitate building a patient base. The head of orthopedics expresses concern for senior staff members who have earned certain rights.

As the discussion begins to percolate, emotion dominates the verbal exchanges. The clinical department heads reach an impasse over the patient assignment problem. At this point an elder statesperson among the department heads expresses his view. He relates that this same problem has been encountered in other medical groups of which he was a member. He cites the same experience that the current group had with this problem 10 years before. He acknowledges the good intentions of both sides. Then he succinctly states that senior staff members in his clinical department will assume an equal responsibility for managed care patients. By example, this respected mover and shaker has used experience to delineate a feasible resolution and has challenged the other clinical departments to move toward an equitable reconciliation of the problem.

Implicit authority granted to movers and shakers reflects admiration for years of experience. Nonetheless, implicit respect must be maintained. Movers and shakers can renew their authoritative reputations by identifying basic issues in a situation. This frequently entails disregarding irrelevant arguments and concerns, delineating the problem, and identifying several alternative solutions in a form that can be readily supported by opponents. The ability to focus discussions on main issues engenders respect.

By relating current problems to past situations, movers and shakers can provide valuable insights. Additionally, since movers and shakers frequently have significant experience outside of the health care field, they are able to present meaningful analogies from a variety of settings. Analyzing relevant parallels can assist in formulating problems, generating alternative solutions, evaluating options, and selecting the best course of action.

### Managerial expertise

Many movers and shakers possess the ability to articulate a challenging strategic vision. Frequently, health care organizations become so focused on operating issues that they lose sight of their overall mission. Movers and shakers examine current problems relative to strategic mission. They analyze relationships between alternative solutions and the organization's strategic vision. Assessing alternatives from a variety of perspectives can produce better resolution of problems because they relate to the organization's strategic vision. The following example of a home health program serves as a case in point.

A hospital home health program has gradually reached fiscal solvency by attracting a clientele primarily composed of privately insured patients. Enough revenue is being generated to build an operating reserve. The home health agency director proposes to the governing board that the program diversify into durable medical equipment and intravenous therapy due to an apparent fit with home care. A mover and shaker on the board challenges this idea by observing that the strategic mission of the home health agency is to provide the highest quality home services attainable. Excursion into areas where the agency lacks distinctive competence is rejected because it would spread the agency's resources too thin. To solidify this argument the mover and shaker focuses the director's attention to falling productivity measures among home health aides.

Managerial expertise can contribute to improving the productivity of organizational resources. Movers and shakers support productivity by working with and guiding others. They are usually excellent motivators. Concurrently, movers and shakers recognize that a vision, not operating details, ultimately determines the fate of an organization. However, they will adopt a hard-nosed approach to managing to work toward realizing the organization's vision.

### Entrepreneurial orientation

Effective movers and shakers are accustomed to successful risk-taking. They know when a decision involves a gamble and are prepared to accept calculated risks to promote progress. They are well prepared for opportunities or contingencies, thereby allowing their organizations to respond positively to undesirable or unlikely events. Movers and shakers also recognize that chance favors the prepared manager and are active in systematic analysis and contingency planning.

***One of the ways movers and shakers think creatively about problems and their solutions is by challenging assumptions that underlie typical resolutions.***

Entrepreneurs are innovators; they tend to seek creative approaches in addressing new challenges. While drawing on experience is fruitful for resolving problems in many situations, movers and shakers also nurture entrepreneurial creativity. Only then can challenges within the competitive health care field be successfully addressed. Traditional approaches are often insufficient. Entrepreneurial thinking can improve the quality of organization strategy and its implementation.

One of the ways movers and shakers think creatively about problems and their solutions is by challenging assumptions that underlie typical resolutions. This approach develops new alternatives. Another strategy in creative problem solving is developing an ideal design. This technique relaxes constraints in the situation. Technically feasible alternatives are created that appear to be impractical from social, political, or economic perspectives. Finally, movers and shakers often enlarge the domain of their original problem. This may produce novel solutions, as binding constraints at one organizational level become controllable factors at a higher level of responsibility.

For example, a rural hospital's governing board is meeting to decide the future of a proposal to join a multi-institutional, for-profit chain. Discussion centers around the deteriorating state of the hospital's facilities, which have been almost fully depreciated. Given the declining revenue base and the prognosis that the hospital will be unable to cover substantial long-term debt, the board has entertained the option of joining the chain to acquire low-cost capital for new construction. Someone draws attention to the possible rate of financing and the prognosis for new management staffing should the proposal be accepted. Just when consensus is about to be reached, a board member who is publisher of the local newspaper shares her view. She underscores that joining a chain to acquire capital is a short-term solution (that is, good for the life of the new facility—25 to 30 years). She points out that the community will relinquish control. Furthermore, she directs thinking toward entrepreneurial ideas on service delivery—for example, involvement with urban medical centers, mental health services, managed care plans, etc.—that might broaden the hospital's revenue base and hence its ability to survive independently.

### Willingness to confront facts

Finally, movers and shakers are predisposed to making tough decisions. This characteristic is generally viewed as a willingness to bit the bullet, make hard-nosed decisions, or play hardball. This means that movers and shakers are not afraid to confront the facts. They recognize that the best approach for making decisions or resolving problems is one that meets facts, opinions, prejudices, forecasts and myths head-on. Avoiding the inevitable confrontation with reality only delays reaching solutions. Movers and shakers generally do not fear the consequences of making tough decisions. They fear the consequences of not making tough decisions. Their fortitude and desire to address problems as they arise has been rewarded in numerous ways, such as acquiring positions of authority in organizations and societies, membership on governing boards, community recognition. Such positive reinforcement only encourages movers and shakers to continue making what they believe to be the "right" decisions for a situation. They are not hesitant to take responsibility for the results of those decisions.

Consider the mover and shaker who is the chief executive officer (CEO) of a medium-sized, diversified, multi-institutional health care system. The system centers services delivery around its 35 affiliate hospitals. Prospective pricing has cut drastically into the system's profitability. The stock price has fallen precipitously and investment analysts predict a dire future. As the CEO assembles her top corporate staff during a weekend survival planning retreat, the climate of pessimism is undeniable. For most of two days staff members examine and reexamine options for the future. Finally, the CEO summarizes the situation and alternatives she has heard during the retreat. Her conclusion is crystal clear. Eighteen of the affiliates—all rural hospitals with consistent financial losses over four years and most in need of capital investments—will be divested immediately. The family of hospitals that enjoyed far-reaching repute will be severely diminished, but the productive core will remain. A base will continue from which a new system will emerge.

## STRATEGIES FOR DEVELOPING PRODUCTIVE RELATIONSHIPS

Since health care managers are increasingly involved in strategic issues, it is worthwhile to consider various strategies for enlisting cooperation from movers and shakers. By constructively utilizing the ideas, insights, and power of movers and shakers, health care managers should be able to more effectively discharge their responsibilities. A foundation for developing productive relationships resides in the concept of cooptation. Over 40 years ago, Philip Selznick[1] examined several methods by which individuals and organizations are able to subtly acquire power. He labeled this process *cooptation*. The term has since been expanded to include gaining power or influence by a wide variety of overt and covert methods. At least three methods exist for coopting the power and influence of movers and shakers: (1) developing a trusting relationship, (2) using borrowed power judiciously, and (3) maintaining viable alliances. Depending on their situation, health care managers may be able to adopt one or more of these approaches to increase their personal and professional effectiveness.

### Developing a trusting relationship

Trust between two individuals requires a strong commitment from both parties. Health care managers may have to invest considerable energy when developing trusting relationships with movers and shakers. Managers must first determine whether the gain is worth the investment in the relationship and then estimate whether such relationships can be established. If affirmative answers to these questions are attained, managers can then pursue a relationship-building strategy.

***Although they may not agree with health care managers on every issue, movers and shakers are more likely to feel comfortable around managers who are consistent and predictable.***

Trust between individuals is a time-dependent phenomenon. It requires periodic interactions and the positive reinforcement of behavioral patterns to mature. Numerous tactics can be used to develop a trusting bond with movers and shakers. For example, health care managers can demonstrate dependability by effectively performing job responsibilities valued by movers and shakers. Dependability is enhanced by providing regular follow-up and periodic feedback. Consistency is another attribute essential to a strong and trusting relationship. Although they may not agree with health care managers on every issue, movers and shakers are more likely to feel comfortable around managers who are consistent and predictable. Extreme fluctuations in thought processes, values, behaviors, or philosophies do not inspire their confidence. Well-established and stable behavior is more likely to elicit trust.

The example of the director of an agency offering intravenous therapy (that is, home IV services) shows how consistent behavior generates trust. The director meets with her corporate board on a quarterly basis to review revenues, expenses, and utilization trends. The corporate board has diversified holdings in hospice, durable medical equipment, home care, intermediate care, and residential care services. The director has adopted a policy of providing nothing but straightforward analyses of the agency's performance. She carefully explains the reasons for budgetary deviations and explains tactics planned or implemented to correct the deviations. She methodically reviews performance during the prior quarter before forecasting trends for the next period.

One of the movers and shakers on the corporate board silently listens to the director's diligent presentation. He is impressed with her forthright manner and concise explanation of tactics to resolve problems. Moreover, he admires the director's willingness to present facts clearly at every quarterly meeting. The mover and shaker gets the impression that the home IV services director has nothing to hide. In contrast, the mover and shaker recognizes that the hospice director steadfastly refuses to present a plan for controlling costs, the durable medical equipment manager is using voodoo inventory practices to create an illusion of low overhead, the home care manager cannot explain excessive staff turnover, the intermediate care facility administrator is manipulating patient funds, and the residential care services manager has no idea about how to respond to growing competition. Within a short period of time, the home IV services director is presenting shorter reports to the corporate board, is asked to function as an internal consultant to the hospice, and receives a salary increase. The mover and shaker who silently watched the IV agency director has developed trust in her capabilities and responded accordingly.

Trust is seldom expressed spontaneously. Health care managers must cultivate a sense of when they have acquired the trust of movers and shakers. Managers will receive periodic clues. For example, trust is often confirmed during critical meetings. At these moments, a mover and shaker may take a less active role and merely express approval of a manager's proposals or decisions. Moreover, movers and shakers may openly refer a query to a manager for further elaboration. Another indication of trust occurs when movers and shakers rise to support a beleaguered manager either informally or during meetings.

### Using borrowed power judiciously

Health care managers can coopt the influence of movers and shakers by capitalizing constructively on advice and counsel. Initially, movers and shakers are suspicious of individuals who seek to establish close relationships. They withhold trust at first. This trial period permits a cautious assessment of a manager's discretion in using borrowed power. For example, consider a hospital that is deciding whether to initiate a joint venture with a physician group practice for a magnetic resonance imager. A mover and shaker (for example, a physician) on the hospital's board of trustees approaches the hospital administrator over lunch to discuss the project. The mover and shaker presents a point of view and enumerates a series of arguments for rejecting the proposal. The conversation then gravitates toward discussions of the weather and plans for a coming holiday.

The administrator can respond in three ways to the physician's suggestion: accept the advice, ignore it, or react to it judiciously. In particular, the administrator could terminate further discussions with the group practice in view of this conversation, using the rationale that any further effort is probably futile because the board of trustees will likely disapprove the venture. Alternatively, the administrator could continue to meet with the physician group and thereby risk the fruitless consumption of additional resources. A third option is to postpone further meetings with the group practice, focus efforts on confirming or refuting the mover and shaker's assessment, and establish it as an agenda item for the next board meeting. Then, before the next board meeting, the administrator can preview the analysis and recommendations for the mover and shaker.

The last alternative reflects the prudent use of borrowed power. The administrator has minimized additional expenditures of resources needed for further discussion and negotiation. Attention can then be fully given to analyzing the issues raised by the mover and shaker. Furthermore, the administrator has maintained flexibility, allowing the mover and shaker to reconsider new information. In short, the mover and shaker retains decision-making power, while the administrator earns the respect and trust of the mover and shaker. Several experiences of this nature could solidify this coopted power base.

**Maintaining viable alliances**

A third method for coopting power and influence is for health care managers to maintain viable alliances they develop with movers and shakers. A significant amount of continuing contact can help transfer the power of movers and shakers. Once managers have developed alliances they should cultivate the relationships rather than let them fade. Admittedly, the ability to maintain a viable relationship may be beyond the control of health care managers. However, it is important for them to think creatively when formulating strategies and, above all, take the initiative. Waiting for movers and shakers to reciprocate is wishful thinking. Managers can use unobtrusive methods to win respect that ultimately are conducive to forming a long-term relationship.

Consider the example of a rural health clinic partially funded by a state health department. The clinic's director has received acclaim throughout the state and region for its prenatal care program. The program succeeds under conditions that cause most other clinics to fail. Additionally, the prenatal care program achieves this success without any additional resources than similar clinics of its type. The clinic director frequently travels to the capital to meet with the head of the state health department and other health providers. In time, the clinic director is lured away from his position by a lucrative offer from an urban-based multispecialty group practice. Nonetheless, the former clinic director continues to cultivate his alliance with the state health officer. By volunteering to serve on various public health committees and advisory boards, by periodically taking the state health officer to lunch, and by inviting the official to present state health views at the multispecialty group practice's grand rounds, the former clinic director maintains a valuable alliance with a prominent mover and shaker. At the proper moment (for example, if the former clinic director needs a personal reference or if the state is contemplating contracting with private medical groups for services), the relationship can be invoked for the benefit of the former clinic director.

• • •

Movers and shakers often demonstrate capabilities that health care managers should recognize before attempting to build productive relationships with them. First, the charisma associated with outstanding leaders is reflected in superior communication skills and presence. Next, a broad experiential base coupled with penetrating analytical skills allows movers and shakers to earn exceptional authority and power. Third, movers and shakers are able to focus on strategic visions. Movers and shakers work through other team members to select and implement solutions that are consistent with organizational mission statements. Fourth, their entrepreneurial mindset enables them to take calculated risks and design creative solutions in response to formidable challenges. Finally, movers and shakers are not reticent to face facts and make tough decisions.

Not all movers and shakers possess all of these characteristics equally. Nor are they all concerned about the same issues. As individuals, they bring differing interests and capabilities to health care organizations. Health care managers may strive to cultivate one or more of these characteristics themselves. Self-improvement begins with identifying personal deficiencies and systematically planning to overcome them.

Until health care managers mature into movers and shakers, they can coopt the influence and power associated with movers and shakers. By establishing a trusting relationship and using borrowed power constructively, they can earn the respect and confidence of movers and shakers. A third approach promotes power transfer through a continuing viable relationship. Health care managers may need to use some combination of these methods. Additionally, they can consider tailoring various methods into a coordinated strategy. Health care managers have a variety of promising strategies available for building productive relationships with movers and shakers. Pursuit of these strategies may improve personal prospects and promote the achievement of organizational missions and objectives.

## REFERENCE

1. Selznick, P. *TVA and the Grass Roots*. Berkeley, Calif.: University of California Press, 1949.

# Networking: A vital activity for health care professionals

***William Umiker***
*Adjunct Clinical Professor of Pathology*
*Pennsylvania State University*
*Hershey, Pennsylvania*

According to *Webster's New World Dictionary*, a network is "a system of interconnected or cooperating individuals." Luebbert expands this to "an informal group of contacts who share advice, facts, techniques, job leads, plans and dreams, and lend each other moral support."[1] Networking used to be referred to as "old boys'" networking or as having "connections" or "politicking." It takes place on golf courses, in corridors, offices, cafeterias, and parking lots. The cliche "It's not what you know but who you know that counts" is still heard from people who regard networking as anathema.

A basic tenet of networking is that people for whom you do favors will do them for you. Networking is building relationships. *Focused* networking is being able to know

*Health Care Superv*, 1989, 7(3), 65–69

and to influence key people who can accelerate your career.[2]

Networking grows in importance as the United States moves from a smoke-stack to a service society, with more "knowledge people" and fewer blue-collar workers.

## BARRIERS TO NETWORKING

Many health care workers feel uneasy about reaching out to others.[3] They were taught early in life that asking for help is a sign of weakness. Yet, in today's workplaces *interdependence* can represent a higher order of competence and value than independence.

Introverts, nonassertive persons, and indolent individuals have difficulty using personal support systems. Women are latecomers. Alina Novak describes a famous storybook character as a skilled female networker: "Cinderella used her stepsisters to give her information about a key event. Then, she plugged in to her mentor, the fairy godmother, who had resources that were utilized on her behalf. When she got to the ball, she was imaged appropriately and knew how to dance. And then she knew when to leave."[4]

Women are catching up fast. Just look around. Note the zeal with which women network in activist groups like the National Organization of Women (NOW), Planned Parenthood, Right to Life groups, and Mothers Against Drunk Driving (MADD). Witness the intensity of their efforts to penetrate all-male organizations. Many women feel that men have the right to have exclusive clubs, but not when these clubs are used for business networking.

## THE BENEFITS OF NETWORKING

### To obtain technical, professional, and fiscal information

Here are some examples: Louise, a radiological technician, calls a nurse friend on the night shift to find out how to handle Dr. Furious who explodes when his patients are in the radiology department while he makes rounds. Jim is upset with a new personnel policy. He gets together with other members of the physiotherapy department to decide what they could do about it. Steve, a chemistry supervisor, calls Dr. Jones, a laboratory consultant, for advice on the selection of a new analyzer.

Helpful information is not all job related. Newcomers appreciate learning about good restaurants, the best places to shop, and alternative routes for driving home when the traffic is heavy. Networker Alice has several associates whom she can call when her car is out of commission.

### To obtain advance information about trends, organizational changes, or new projects[5]

When it comes to speed, the grapevine beats all the formal channels hands down. These person-to-person systems also provide information that is not otherwise available. Sister Rita Mary, the chief executive officer, decides to make late night rounds. By the time she reaches the first nursing floor, every nurse in the hospital has been alerted.

### To get feedback

Network participants can provide positive and negative feedback. Sue has just written her first article for publication. She asks one of the old-timers to critique it. Grace, the new supervisor, has several colleagues look over a new policy she would like to introduce.

Getting feedback requires trust, frankness, and acceptance.[6] Participants must also be willing to be vulnerable.

### To get psychological support

There is an emerging awareness of interdependence as a mental-health imperative as well as a necessity for professional growth. Our emotional well-being depends on developing friendly and helpful associates.[7] We get emotional "highs" from a sense of belonging or power. Knowing that others share the same problems can be reassuring. The sharing of frustrations and victories is psychologically beneficial.[8]

### To learn about job opportunities

In many organizations, most job vacancies are filled on the basis of recommendations from their own employees. Applicants who are recommended via this channel tend to outperform those recruited through other modalities.

Much recruiting goes on informally at professional meetings and workshops. Good networkers are the first to learn about new jobs or opportunities to serve on key committees and task forces. They recommend colleagues for choice assignments or appointments. Joyce, the microbiology technologist, went out of her way to chat with Dr. Pitkin, a visiting consultant. Dr. Pitkin was so impressed that she recommended Joyce for an appointment as instructor at the medical school.

*Job applicants who are recommended by employees tend to outperform those recruited through other modalities.*

### To enhance careers

The sage advice about not hiding your talents under a basket is heeded by networkers. They use networking to get their feet in the doors of opportunity.[9] They find the means to continue their education, learn new skills, and put these new skills to use.

## WITH WHOM SHOULD YOU NETWORK?

### In-house colleagues and peers and local experts such as medical specialists, consultants, executives, and training specialists

These individuals precede or follow you in work flows. For a laboratory supervisor that would include physicians, nursing personnel, phlebotomists, and office or data processing personnel.

Members of support departments such as materials management, human resources, data processing, document duplication, visual aids, and so forth. Never underestimate the power of secretaries, security guards, or housekeeping personnel.[10]

### Professionals at meetings, seminars, workshops, committees, and task forces

The omnipresent lapel name tags on attendees are signs of networking in action.[11] The availability of teleconferencing, telemarketing, and computer networks have greatly expanded these connections.

### Customers and suppliers

Amateur networkers confine connections to fellow employees and professional colleagues. Expert networkers know that customers and suppliers represent a gold mine of information just waiting to be tapped. They encourage sales representatives to deliver their pitches, and they ask probing questions. They often write to manufacturers for technical information.

The most successful enterprises are those that maintain close contacts with their customers. Most hospitals have not yet developed sophisticated methods for getting patient feedback. This is changing rapidly as hospitals acquire marketing experts. However, department heads should not expect their marketing department to assume all of this responsibility. Laboratory supervisors accompany phlebotomists to observe their patient-handling skills. The office staffs of physicians are invited to wine and cheese meetings where problems are addressed.

In hospitals there are customers other than patients and physicians. Departments such as personnel, education, and materials management serve other departments. Too often these cost-center relationships are competitive, even adversarial. Effective networkers get to know these other people better, empathize with them, and develop a cooperative interdependency.

## WHAT THE BEST NETWORKERS DO

- They know how to communicate with people. They ask open-ended questions and listen attentively. They avoid asking stupid questions by finding out things beforehand. They respond promptly and enthusiastically to questions and requests from others. They try to give as much as they get.[12]
- They are selective. They focus on those who can enhance their chances of reaching their goals, but they do not neglect old friends.
- They keep their relationships businesslike.[13]
- They keep in touch with their contacts.
- They express appreciation for favors.
- They regularly attend major professional meetings.[14]
- They circulate at parties and at meetings. They introduce themselves rather than wait for someone else to do the honors.
- They are great joiners and try to attend the meetings of their organizations.
- They are cordial and courteous to everyone, but are somewhat selective about the people with whom they develop special rapport.
- They often volunteer for committees and task forces. They agree to give lectures and workshops.
- They share clippings, reports, articles, and information derived from seminars.
- They use coffee breaks and lunch times to chat with many different people.[15]
- They establish relationships with newcomers. They volunteer to help with indoctrination and job training.[16]
- They keep a file of the names, addresses, and telephone numbers of their contacts.

## WHAT THE BEST NETWORKERS DO NOT DO

- They do not take unfair advantage of fellow networkers. They do not abuse other people's time.
- They do not pass up opportunities. They are not afraid to ask for what they need.[17]
- They do not rely on only one or two people.
- They do not let networking interfere with their work responsibilities.

## MENTORS

Mentors are the linchpins of personal support groups. They are usually, but not always, individuals who have influence in an organization. Merlin was King Arthur's mentor in the movie Camelot.[18]

As counselors, mentors provide empathic support, encourage the development of problem-solving skills, and advise on contemplated career moves.[19] They share knowledge and experience, including the kind that would otherwise take years to accumulate like unwritten practices, idiosyncrasies of managers, policies that can be ignored, and those that must be followed to the letter.[20]

As sponsors, they increase the visibility of their proteges by seeing to it that they are appointed to certain committees, invited to give presentations, and introduced to influential people. Proteges consciously or subconsciously emulate the behavior and attitudes of their mentors.[21]

Why not take a second look at your network. Maybe it needs some mending, or just needs to be bigger.

REFERENCES

1. Luebbert, P.P. "Networking for Survival and Success." *Medical Laboratory Observer* 19, no. 6 (1987): 39–42.
2. Davidson, J.P. *Blow Your Own Horn*. New York: AMACOM, 1987.
3. Luebbert, "Networking for Survival."
4. Novak, A. *Keynote Address*. Annual Conference on Continuing Education in Nursing, American Nurses' Association Council on Continuing Education, Washington, D.C., 1981.
5. Luebbert, "Networking for Survival."
6. Puetz, B.E. *Networking for Nurses*. Rockville, Md.: Aspen Publishers, 1983.
7. Ollson, M., and Lipitt, R. "Networking for Support, Growth and Gain." *Training* 22, no. 2 (1985): 65–67.
8. Luebbert, "Networking for Survival."
9. Ollson and Lipitt, "Networking for Support, Growth and Gain."
10. Luebbert, "Networking for Survival."
11. Novak, *Keynote Address*.
12. Ibid.
13. Ibid.
14. Davidson, *Blow Your Own Horn*.
15. Ollson and Lipitt, "Networking for Support, Growth and Gain."
16. Ibid.
17. Novak, *Keynote Address*.
18. Ibid.
19. Umiker, W.O. "Mentoring: A Tool for Career Development." *Medical Laboratory Observer* 18, no. 8 (1986): 71–72.
20. Ibid.
21. Ibid.

# Part III
# Self-Help Is Where You Find It

# Supervisor, manage yourself

*Charles R. McConnell*
*Vice President for Employee Affairs*
*The Genesee Hospital*
*Rochester, New York*

THE CAPACITY for conscientious and effective self-management is one of the most valuable assets that a first-line supervisor can possess. However, the ability to effectively manage one's self is more often than not simply assumed to exist and is not given a fraction of the attention it deserves.

Supervisors who wish to improve their ability to manage the efforts of others—certainly a desire that most supervisors should have—need not look to management theories, modern management techniques and gimmicks for help. Rather, they must begin with some personal and common-sense fundamentals. These basics, truly fundamental to the extent that all generally accepted management theories assume their presence to a workable extent, relate only indirectly to the business of "getting things done through people" (as management is frequently described). Also, the basics are sufficiently per-

*Health Care Superv*, 1983,1(3),57–68

sonal that they can be acquired only through individual effort following the supervisor's recognition of the need to do so. In short, to become an effective manager of others a supervisor must first become, through personal effort, an effective manager of self. This must be accomplished solely by the supervisor; none of the basics can be implanted magically in the supervisor by higher management.

Neither can the supervisor constantly look to higher management to provide specific direction in all matters, to load, aim and propel the supervisor in productive directions. A certain amount of higher management direction is, of course, essential, but it is not always there when the supervisor feels the need for it; nor does it always take the specific form the supervisor would like it to take. Just as it falls to the supervisor to be self-managed as far as many important basics are concerned, so it falls to the supervisor to be self-directed a large part of the time.

For a base upon which to build one's self as a manager, the supervisor must start with self. The supervisors who have proven themselves best at managing the efforts of others are those who first captured and mastered the fundamentals of managing themselves.

Every employee in the health care organization is a manager of sorts. Even unskilled workers are to some extent managers of their own time, tools, talents, methods and supplies. Since all of these factors—time, tools, etc.—are brought together with human effort to determine output, every employee at every organizational level is a manager of output. It follows that the quantity and quality of an individual's output are largely functions of the person's success at self-management.

***The supervisors who have proven themselves best at managing the efforts of others are those who first captured and mastered the fundamentals of managing themselves.***

Self-management is considerably more important to the supervisor than it is to the nonmanagerial employee; the supervisor has considerably more flexibility in manipulating resources and applying individual effort. This appears to be so because a supervisor's work is considerably more results oriented, and thus less process oriented, than the work of the nonmanager is. That is, the worker is more likely to be guided by a finite number of specific procedures that limit self-management flexibility, but the supervisor, often simply responsible for "getting the work done," may take a variety of approaches as long as the work is indeed accomplished. The more results oriented the work is, the more flexibility the individual has; the more flexibility the individual has, the more important self-management becomes. (It follows as well that the higher in the management structure an individual rises, the more important self-management becomes, but this is beyond the scope of this article.)

The supervisor who seeks improved management effectiveness should do so by seeking to improve the use of his or her personal resources. In the last analysis, it will prove to be the capable management of self that enables one to most effectively manage others.

## A SUPERVISOR'S PERSONAL RESOURCES

A supervisor's personal resources fall under three broad headings: initiative, organization and time.

### Initiative

In his entertaining film *You, Yourself, Inc.*,[1] the late J. Lewis Powell told a story about a young manager who was preparing to take a self-study course entitled "How to Develop Initiative." Upon his boss's instructions, the young man had obtained the books and materials for the course. However, when contacted some time later, he was found to have done nothing yet—he was waiting for his boss to tell him to begin. In connection with this illustration, Powell made reference to the "wheelbarrow personality," the personality that may have plenty of capacity but is useless without someone else pushing it.

It is true, of course, that a supervisor cannot always take initiative in all directions because of the understandable limits placed on one's authority. In matters of self-improvement, however, the only limitations on one's initiative are those imposed by oneself.

Beyond matters of self-improvement, the degree of initiative available in task performance may admittedly depend on the attitude and approach of higher management. Indeed, some misguided higher managers discourage and even occasionally punish initiative and seem to prefer to function as "wheelbarrow pushers." Managers who function as pushers are committing some classic errors. Their subordinate supervisors may compound these errors by following the path of least resistance and becoming wheelbarrow pushers themselves. Only one small change in the management hierarchy is needed for a wheelbarrow-pushing manager to be replaced by a manager who expects all subordinate supervisors to be self-propelled.

In matters regarding the application of initiative in self-improvement, the supervisor may become involved in considering a number of personal attitude factors that come to focus in a single question: "How well do I like my job?"

Liking one's work is especially important to the supervisor. Of course, few people truly like everything they do all the time, and common sense suggests that they will not like everything they have to do every day on the job. It can only be hoped that they like their work more often than they dislike it. Chronic dislike of one's work usually leads to a poor attitude (certainly a self-defeating state for a supervisor), and poor attitude is more often than not reflected in the absence of initiative.

Liking the work and a healthy attitude on the job are essential for long-run success. These will lead the supervisor to *wanting* to be effective, and the supervisor will then be in a position to discover that the best way to improve as a supervisor is to take the initiative and seek self-improvement. Implicit in this is the belief that, as far as first-line supervisors are concerned, the only lasting form of motivation is self-motivation. Certainly, periodic pay increases do not appreciably motivate supervisory performance. Threats and punishment are even less effective as motivators and may even be demotivators much of the time. The effect of a swift kick by higher management will be temporary at best; the sting goes away quickly, but resentment and resistance are likely to remain.

The only lasting source of motivation lies within one's self and in one's relationship with the work. It follows that the best sources of learning and growth lie within the individual, and that these sources can be tapped effectively only by the individual.

Many supervisors are doubtless haunted by the feeling that they need to do a better job at what they are doing, and that they are probably capable of doing better than they are now doing. However, they tend to wait for a more appropriate time: "After the rush is over"; "As soon as the census goes back down"; "As soon as I get more staff"; or "Right after we get the budget done." However, there is always something to be done, and the proper time seems never to arrive. True initiative recognizes that conditions are rarely ideal and that self-improvement should not be delayed.

Once present, initiative requires a specific focus. The preferred focus for a supervisor's self-improvement initiative is found in personal organization and in the use of time.

## Organization

### *The time is now*

For years, a popular cartoon has hung on many office walls. It pictures two disheveled people seated on opposite sides of a table. They are slouched down in their chairs, both have their feet on the table, and the table itself is cluttered to overflowing. The area around the table, faintly resembling an office, is in general disarray. The caption of the cartoon is: "Next week we've got to get organized."

True initiative would suggest that it is *now* that the manager must get organized. In this sense of organization, the manager remains yet a great distance from "organizing" as the basic management function through which the framework for accomplish-

***True initiative suggests that it is* now *that the manager must get organized.***

ing the department's work is established. The manager must organize his or her physical surroundings and work approach in order to perform more efficiently.

These comments relate largely to organizing one's self; the organization of one's work is more appropriately considered under the management of time.

People differ greatly from each other in the extent to which they require order in their surroundings or are able to tolerate clutter and confusion. Some supervisors seem to function satisfactorily in the midst of clutter. However, all persons are subject to limits beyond which a lack of order in the work setting will prove counterproductive.

Consider a certain plant engineering manager who used his desk only as a repository for several tall, ragged towers of documents. These stacks included accumulations of everything from half-page memoranda and letters to lengthy reports, and from advertising brochures and catalogs to professional journals. These piles of material were the manager's only "file." The manager and his file were known throughout the institution; in spite of the imposing height of the stacks, the manager seemed able to thrust his hand into any particular stack and retrieve the item he was looking for. However, the institution expanded, the manager's scope of responsibility increased and material began to accumulate at a faster rate. Eventually, the number of stacks doubled, and unsorted documents were stored on every flat surface in the office. What was apparently a good memory became taxed beyond reason ("Let's see now, which stack did I put that in?"), and the manager began to lose the ability to retrieve items on a single try. More importantly, items began to get lost—and more than a few of them stayed lost. The manager was forced into a position where a complete reorganization of his surroundings was his only alternative, and this reorganization loomed as an overwhelming task simply because it was so long overdue.

### *General cleanup*

The first step to take in getting organized is to thoroughly clean and straighten the office or other immediate work area with one specific guideline in mind: Nothing will be retained unless it is truly useful, and everything retained will have a specific storage location. This means that all material that has been allowed to collect on desks, tables, file cabinets, window sills and other flat surfaces must be sorted and reckoned with. This means also that the contents of all file drawers and desk drawers must similarly be sorted and reduced to an essential minimum.

It has been said that the purpose of a refrigerator is to contain leftovers until they are old enough to qualify as garbage. Desks and file cabinets are frequently treated in the same manner; many things that are put away because of supposed potential usefulness are destined to become no more than needless clutter.

A thorough purge of the supervisor's accumulation of documentation should result in retention of just three clearly identifiable kinds of material:

1. A section of open or presently active projects. For most supervisors this may consist of a single folder filled with one- and two-page items that can be considered currently active, backed up with a single folder for each of several open projects of greater scope. These will constitute the supervisor's open file. This open file should be reviewed every day and items added or deleted as necessary.
2. A file for projects or problems that are pending, on hold or likely to become active in the near future. For most supervisors this file will not amount to more than a few folders.
3. A general storage and reference file. This file should include active reference material and project records (appropriately sorted and condensed) and correspondence that would appear to be in the supervisor's best interest to retain.

By far the largest single category of material emerging in a thorough cleanup of the office will be files and printed matter that *may* be useful *some day*. The supervisor should resist the temptation to retain this kind of material. The mere possibility of potential future use can be said to exist for everything in the office, and it is probably this consideration that caused most of the clutter to accrue in the first place. Many supervisors suffer from the pack-rat syndrome, retaining every item that may be of some value in the remotest of circumstances. A simple rule to follow in sorting such material is: If there is no *known* use for an item either now or in the future, it should be discarded. And in doing so, it pays not at all to agonize at great length over what to keep and what to get rid of. Since any future use of such material is unknown, it is highly likely that something of potential value will indeed be discarded. However, this will happen only by pure chance, a chance that the supervisor can readily afford to take. It should be recognized that one cannot possibly retain everything he or she may need in the future. Rather than having possession of all information, it is much more important for the supervisor to know where to go for current information when it is needed.

Every so often, perhaps twice each year, the supervisor should undertake to personally update his or her files. Two benefits are to be derived from this process: (1) the amount of material retained is automatically condensed, and (2) the supervisor purging the file is updating his or her memory relative to what is being retained and where it is stored.

It is all too easy to allow office clutter to accumulate. The supervisor should endeavor to prevent the accumulation from getting out of control. It pays to develop the habit of going through the material that has accumulated every few days and disposing of it according to the guidelines already suggested.

Surely, every supervisor has experienced the following thought while going through the in-basket: "Here is an item I should read (or would like to read), but I do not have the time right now. I'll set it aside and read it at my leisure." It is safe to say that most material set aside in this manner is never read. It would behoove the supervisor to adopt a more efficiency-minded attitude toward potential reading material. Something either is of sufficient importance that one can make the time to read it, or it can be discarded or perhaps passed along to someone who may find it useful.

The most inexcusable form of office clutter, inexcusable because much of it is automatically rendered useless upon retrieval, consists of unsorted and undated handwritten notes. If the notes resulting from a project or problem are of sufficient importance to retain, they should be thoroughly sorted and condensed before filing and should be fully identified and dated. This leads to the mention of one small but extremely important tip that can make much of a supervisor's informal documentation far more valuable than it would otherwise be: Never set pen or pencil to paper without dating the page and providing a brief identifying heading.

## Time

A management consultant once paid a visit to an acquaintance who was the dean of one of the divisions of a small college. When the consultant entered the office the dean was talking on the telephone and waved the consultant to a chair. With a few minutes to spare, the consultant idly surveyed the sizable conference table loaded to nearly overflowing with all manner of scholarly clutter. In the midst of all of this material there lay a copy of *The Management of Time* by James T. McCay (Prentice-Hall 1959).

The consultant was flipping through the book when the dean finished his telephone call and turned to his visitor. The consultant held up the book and said, "I was thinking of buying this book myself. Do you recommend it?"

The dean shrugged and answered, "I don't know. I got it two or three months ago, but I haven't had time to read it yet."

In so many words, the dean had given voice to some common feelings about improving the use of time: People would like to use time more efficiently, but they do not have sufficient time to learn how to do so. They might just as well admit that they are too busy being inefficient to take the time to learn how to be efficient.

### *Priorities*

It is essential to determine priorities and establish deadlines for one's own activities. Any task worth doing deserves a deadline, even if it is a somewhat loose deadline that must be changed a time or two. The supervisor will profit by developing the habit of assigning deadlines to all incoming tasks and working to stick to these deadlines as much as possible. One should get accustomed to this process and should get accustomed to accomplishing most tasks under a modest amount of self-imposed deadline pressure.

***It is essential to determine priorities and establish deadlines for one's own activities. Any task worth doing deserves a deadline.***

The process is simple. The supervisor asks: What is the most important task I must complete today? This most important task becomes priority number one, and it is assigned the nearest deadline. The remaining tasks facing the supervisor are questioned in the same way, and less immediate deadlines are established accordingly.

### *Paperwork*

The supervisor should deal with the paper accumulating in the seemingly bottomless in-basket on a daily basis. It is helpful to develop a routine sufficient to allow one to go through the in-basket at approximately the same time each day and separate all material into the following three categories:

1. Those items that can be acted upon at that moment, because they are urgent or are sufficiently short so as to be dispensed within a minute or two. A helpful rule to remember is: Whenever possible, handle a particular piece of paper only once.
2. Open items, those that require thought, analysis, assimilation, research or perhaps delegation. Many such items become part of the supervisor's current work load and soon find themselves on a list of active priorities.
3. Material that is of no use and can be immediately passed along or discarded.

One thought contained in the foregoing list is worth repeating: Whenever possible, a piece of incoming paper should be handled only once. Note that if the supervisor is following these three suggestions, all material in two of the three categories is indeed handled only once.

### *Telephones*

The telephone is sometimes extremely disruptive of the supervisor's workday. Although it is to the supervisor's advantage to take many of his or her incoming direct calls personally, there will be times when control of such calls is necessary. A call cannot be answered when the supervisor is not there; a call should not be answered directly by the supervisor who is engaged in a meeting or dealing with matters of personnel relations with an employee (unless, of course, the call is urgent).

As most supervisors have discovered, incoming calls not received at once are rapidly manifested in a stack of telephone message slips usually instructing one to call back. At times, it may pay to resist the temptation to immediately return the one or two calls that came in while one was away from the desk. Of course, calls identified as urgent should be returned as soon as the messages are received. However, the vast majority of call-backs can be taken care of at one time during the workday. The supervisor should select one time of the day to go through the accumulated messages and return all calls one after the other. Before doing so, all material that may have to be referred to during any of the calls (at least those calls for which the subject is known) should be laid out close at hand. Telephoning can be much like any other task in that it is more efficient to tackle a number of messages in a batch than it is to deal with them singly throughout the day.

### *Meetings*

Here meetings refer primarily to those the supervisor has convened and is running as opposed to meetings to which the supervisor is invited to attend.

The supervisor who is conducting a meeting should forever be conscious of the fact that the amount of clock time involved is automatically multiplied by the number of attendees at the meeting. If even five minutes are wasted in a meeting of six persons, the result is a half-hour lost forever. To ensure that the most value is obtained from the time spent in meetings the supervisor should:

- be certain of the need for a meeting and call a meeting only when one is clearly justified;
- clearly identify the objectives of the meeting before gathering participants and convening;
- make certain the appropriate participants are invited—those persons with both the knowledge and authority to act on the problem at hand;
- if the meeting involves more than a single topic, make certain an agenda is supplied and that all necessary reference material is ready to hand to the participants;
- make certain of the availability of proper facilities in advance of the meeting;
- start the meeting on time;
- provide active meeting leadership, drawing all participants into the discussion but controlling the agenda so as to prevent wandering from the subject; and
- summarize the results of the meeting for those present and see that all necessary follow-up activity is specifically assigned.

### *Planning*

At the end of each workday, the supervisor should reexamine and as necessary realign the priorities to be dealt with the following day. The process takes only a few minutes a day and consists of no more than rearranging a half dozen or so items on the next day's page of the calendar. It is rare that a full day's planned activities will proceed exactly as planned. This is to be expected; plans are not static requirements, cast in concrete. Rather, a plan is a moving, growing, shifting, changing approach to the job. Because much of what occurs in the working life of a supervisor is unexpected, it is usually necessary to replan much of what was to be done today into tomorrow's intended work load. It is important that the plan be kept live and up to date each day; and the supervisor can rest assured that even though the day's list of activities was far from complete at the end of the day, he or she was at work on the most important tasks at hand.

### *Delegation*

As a supervisory skill, delegation probably receives more verbal tribute and less sincere practice than any other process. There are a number of reasons why many supervisors fail to delegate properly or completely. Some of these reasons—such as basic insecurity, fear of competition from one's subordinates and lack of self-confidence—lie beyond the scope of this discussion. However, one of the most frequently encountered reasons for failure to delegate is a reason already touched upon: the lack of time to do so properly.

More than any other supervisory skill, delegation requires sincere and determined effort aimed at habit formation. The process to be followed, again and again until it is incorporated into the supervisor's habit pattern, is summarized as follows:

1. Determine what tasks can be delegated.
2. Determine which people in the work group are capable of dealing with specific delegated tasks.
3. Organize the tasks so they can be handed over to subordinates.
4. Assign, instruct and motivate the employees who will perform the delegated tasks.
5. Monitor subordinates' progress relative to results expected.

It is generally true that the supervisor most strongly feels the need to delegate at times when the backlog of work is the greatest and the pressure is on. It is at precisely these times that the supervisor cannot usually delegate effectively because of reservations about taking the time needed to do so. Invariably, the time crunch will be most apparent when the need to delegate is felt most strongly. However, since effective delegation indeed takes time—very often a great deal of time—the major hurdle the supervisor must clear is the acceptance of the need to spend more time without immediate results. That is, delegation takes time here and now, time that is not returned in the form of time saved until much later.

### *Finding time*

A simple exercise is suggested for supervisors sincerely interested in improving their use of time, an exercise primarily concerned with revealing how one's time is spent.

For a period of at least two weeks the supervisor should endeavor to record every activity undertaken in such a way that all work time is accounted for. The figures need not be precise or attempt to isolate every miniscule task, but should focus on tasks of significant size or groups of smaller activities that can be identified with blocks of time rounded off to perhaps the nearest five minutes. A simple log sheet should be sufficient, indicating activities undertaken and amounts of time consumed. Sample entries might be: "Write incident report—15 minutes"; "Return Monday's telephone messages—20 minutes"; "Attend unit managers' staff meeting—1 hour"; "Interview job applicant—45 minutes."

When at least two weeks' worth of log entries are accumulated, all items should be sorted and rearranged according to three task definitions:

1. *Routine tasks* are tasks for which the *what* and *when* are both known; they are known jobs that can be expected to occur at fairly regular intervals. For example, the time a supervisor may spend approving time cards each Monday falls under the routine tasks definition.
2. *Unscheduled tasks* are tasks for which the *what* is known but the *when* remains unknown. They are known activities that do not occur with predictable frequency. For instance, for the supervisor expected to write incident reports, writing the reports is a known task, and rarely will the supervisor know in advance when it will be necessary to write one.
3. *Emergency tasks* are tasks for which neither the *what* nor the *when* are known in advance. The supervisor simply knows that emergencies will arise and must be dealt with.

A two-week time record created in the foregoing manner and subdivided into the three task categories just described can allow the supervisor to gain significant information that will help in the planning process. For instance, if the supervisor discovers that an average of 30 percent of the time is spent dealing with emergencies, then he or she should appropriately leave 30 percent of all available time open for emergencies. Likewise, knowing how much of the total available time is generally taken by routine tasks and unscheduled tasks, the supervisor can come much closer to realistic planning than would otherwise be possible.

## THE SELF-MANAGEMENT FOUNDATION

A great many endeavors in supervisory self-improvement lead quickly to failure because of one or more of three common errors:

1. The supervisor strives to accomplish too much too soon, vowing to become more efficient and accomplish more, delegate fairly and improve communications, plunging in in an effort to

achieve massive improvement at once.

2. The supervisor fails to recognize the power of habits in the work pattern, and fails to recognize that supervisory improvement involves breaking old habits and forming new habits—a task not readily accomplished.
3. The supervisor fails to follow through with the self-reinforcement essential to the process of incorporating changed behavior into one's work pattern.

Supervision can be a life-long career involving a never-ending process of learning. Management is sufficiently open ended that one is never completely "there" in terms of having arrived. Since the process is indeed never ending and the basics involve a great deal of habit formation, it pays for the supervisor to begin by pursuing modest but lasting improvements in small increments.

The supervisor who is serious about self-improvement need acquire only some simple guideline information about the basic processes of supervision—delegation, decision making, handling personnel problems and so on—and practice the processes at their simplest levels until these are indeed part of one's behavior pattern. Take, for instance, the matter of planning out one's day every day. The process is described in a paragraph or two, yet it requires conscientious application and self-enforced repetition many times before this takes its place as something that is done as a matter of habit.

Good advice is available in published form from almost everywhere. Working supervisors—and for that matter, most managers at all levels—need only the simplest of guidelines and the most basic of straightforward advice. There is little need for weighty references or esoteric management theories; most of the time these serve only to accentuate the gap existing between theory and practice.

Time invested in learning how to manage one's self will pay back many times over in problems solved, problems avoided and time saved. Learning how to effectively manage one's self is the best possible preparation for learning how to manage others.

Effective management—much like charity—begins at home. One is most likely to succeed in managing others if one first succeeds in managing one's self.

***Time invested in learning how to manage one's self will pay back many times over in problems solved, problems avoided and time saved.***

REFERENCE

1. Powell, J.L. *You, Yourself, Inc.* Washington, D.C.: Bureau of National Affairs.

# Time management: from victim to victor

*Victor J. Morano*
*Director*
*Victor J. Morano Consulting Services*
*Shrewsbury, Massachusetts*

WHAT IS IT that most people stretch, use, kill and abuse, that also has the power to fly, slip away, drag and heal all wounds? Sometimes there is too much of it, and at other times there is not enough. It is the topic of this discussion: *time*.

Every health care supervisor stands to benefit by gaining improved control of his or her time. There are specific methods one can apply to learn how to manage time. Simply described, time management is self-management. As such, it requires a major change in one's attitude and perspective regarding time and demands a new focus in the way one deals with time. One must move from being a victim to becoming a victor.

## FROM VICTIM TO VICTOR

Victim and victor are most appropriate expressions to use in describ-

*Health Care Superv*, 1984,3(1),1–12

ing the human impact of time. Countless supervisors sacrifice their lives, as well as their health and happiness, to the god of time. Each day is spent in jumping from one crisis to the next in the service of this unreasonable deity.

At the other end of the time management spectrum there is the victor. The victor is the health care supervisor who takes charge and gives direction to the use of time. However, the difference between victim and victor goes far deeper than the applied techniques of time management, involving the self-awareness one must develop to eventually arrive at self-management. A conscious effort is required to recognize the vital importance of being self-directed as opposed to being other-directed.

### The problem with time

There is no problem with having enough time. Every person has at least eight hours to accomplish his or her work. The major question is: How to best use those eight hours. This is a reasonable question that deserves to be addressed, but there are other questions that should be asked first, such as: Why bother? Why take on another task with time as short as it already is? What benefits can be expected?

### Payoffs from time management

As a health care supervisor, one realizes that it is nearly impossible to motivate anyone unless he or she stands to have some personal need filled. If one seriously strives to become time-conscious, there are several positive benefits that may result.

1. **Greater personal job satisfaction.** It is not by chance that greater personal job satisfaction is listed as the number one payoff. From this, all of the others follow naturally. If one can eliminate the debilitating effects of time anxiety and focus on positive accomplishments, there will be an increase in enthusiasm for one's work. More needs will be met. Greater personal satisfaction will result from being self-directed.

2. **Increased productivity.** Yes, it is possible to do more in less time. This can come about through self-awareness, a positive attitude and proper motivation. Highly motivated employees accomplish a great deal more in less time than those who just put in their eight hours. Planning carefully, selecting those tasks that are appropriate and eliminating those that are not also have an impact on increased productivity.

3. **Improved interpersonal relations.** This is a key area for supervisors. A supervisor under the stress of time anxiety often has little time or patience for communication and for working effectively with others. However, a supervisor who is personally satisfied in his or her work and has a relaxed and reasonable time schedule will certainly have a greater opportunity to relate more successfully with others.

4. **Better future direction.** An unhappy consequence of being a victim of time management is the frequent

absence of direction in one's work. When objectives or long-range goals are requested from a harried victim, the response may be: "Objectives? You've got to be kidding. I'm just trying to keep my head above water for today." Victims are often myopic, having limited vision regarding work goals. Victors, on the other hand, make the time to know the directions in which they are moving, both now and in the distant future.

5. **Reduced stress.** Our era has been labeled the Age of Stress and Anxiety by many. A major contributing factor to this dubious honor is time anxiety. According to a survey report on executive stress published by the American Management Association, the major source of stress for both middle and top management is a combination of heavy work load, time pressures and unrealistic deadlines.[1] To reduce one's stress and time anxiety is certainly a worthwhile goal and an important step to becoming a master of one's time.

6. **Improved personal health.** As a result of the foregoing payoffs, one may feel better mentally, emotionally and physically. Obviously, time management as self-management is not a panacea for the ills of humankind. However, chances are that with the seemingly relentless burden of time anxiety lifted, one's personal health may improve.

## A PLACE TO START

To start the process of becoming a victor in time management, there are several areas that must be explored. First, one must examine how his or her time as a health care supervisor is spent. This does not mean to study the official job description, if one exists, but rather to look realistically at what is actually done. Are the activities and projects the same things that one's superior expects or wants done? Is much time being spent on those projects that are of a top priority, or is time being wasted on low priority activities? Does one's list of priorities agree or disagree with those of one's superior? Are there tasks that are an important part of one's job on which no time is being spent? All of these are vital questions that must be answered in order to effectively manage one's time.

## THE TIME INVENTORY

First, some basic yet essential data should be acquired through an inventory of one's time. Frankly, doing a time inventory is far from an enjoyable experience; however, it can be most productive. Use a very simple format—a long sheet of paper with columns labeled for date, activity, time started, time ended, total time and notes. Reproduce several sheets of the form and put them on a clipboard. For a minimum of two weeks, record the necessary information and any notes regarding the activity that are important. *Every* activity should be recorded, including interruptions. At the end of the two weeks, the time analysis may begin. Patterns will develop and common time robbers may be identified. For example, the same kind of interruptions from the same person or source may occur again and again.

At the end of each day, total up all the time in the total time column. Often, people find that the total does not equal eight hours. A careful analysis should reveal some valuable clues as to how time is actually spent; what time of the day is most productive; whether too much time is spent on low-priority tasks, or too little time on high-priority items. The time inventory also serves as a superb document for giving the health care supervisor specific direction for immediate and long-term improvements in his or her time management program.

***The time inventory also serves as a superb document for giving the health care supervisor specific direction for immediate and long-term improvements in his or her time management program.***

Finally, a note of caution: One may find countless reasons why it is impossible to do the time inventory. Despite these, do initiate and complete the inventory. Do not join those who lament: "But I haven't got the time to inventory my time." This may be a sure sign of the person who needs it most.

## THE TIME CONNECTION

In dealing with time, there is an important reality that must be faced. Every supervisor has a boss. This is the person who is most interested in how the supervisor spends his or her time and what it is that is actually accomplished. In fact, he or she may be the one the supervisor feels is responsible for much time anxiety. One cannot talk about time management as self-management if this major influence on one's time is overlooked. There must be a time connection between the supervisor and the superior. Mutual expectations and understanding regarding the use of time must be clarified. Some technique is required whereby one's own job tasks and priorities may be clarified and connected with those of one's superior. There is such a technique, developed by a 19th-century economist named Vilfredo Pareto. He discovered that 20 percent of the people in Italy controlled 80 percent of the wealth. Today this is known as the 80/20 rule. With some minor adjustments, the Pareto Principle may be adapted for time management purposes. To use the Pareto Principle, one must do the following.

### The job and all its duties

1. Find a quiet place, preferably away from work. Be sure to do this at a time when interruptions are unlikely.
2. Randomly list everything that one does as a health care supervisor. This may be a long or short list, as long as it is complete. The list should not be limited to activities accomplished in two weeks or even a

month, but should be as all-inclusive of your duties as possible.

3. Next to each activity, estimate as closely as possible the approximate percentage of work time spent on each. Of course, the total must equal 100 percent.
4. Now carefully draw up a second list. This time the activities should be written in the order of importance as one sees them, starting with number one as the most important and so on. Remember, these are according to one's own priorities. Write down the percentage of time spent next to each as on the first list.
5. The top 20 percent of the list of activities are the critical few that should occupy most of one's time.
6. The remaining 80 percent of the list are the trivial many, which should be delegated, altered or eliminated. One may discover that much time is spent on activities that are low in priority and too little time on those of high priority.

**The superior's view**

To make the time connection, the supervisor should now involve his or her superior:

1. Suggest that the superior take the original list and put the activities in the order of importance as he or she sees them.
2. Ask the superior to include additional duties that may not be on the list.

**The comparison**

At this point, the supervisor and superior should meet to compare their lists of job priorities. After some discussion, mutually agreed-upon priorities are established. Total agreement is not guaranteed. It will, however, become quite clear what it is that the supervisor is expected to do and how his or her time will best be used. This will also result in an educational experience for both. The supervisor will fully understand what the superior considers important and the superior will get a better appreciation of the supervisor's expectations and view of the job.

The Pareto Principle provides an excellent illustration of the difference between the victim or victor approach. Too many health care supervisors set impossible expectations for themselves. Adding to this situation, their superiors add more responsibilities, since they may be unaware of the extent of the supervisor's work load. But it does not have to be that way. The supervisor who is the victor of time will take the necessary steps to maintain control over his or her work life. Mutual and reasonable goals will be established with one's superiors through the time connection.

There are many other tools that are available to the victor. Some of these are discussed below.

## THE MAGIC OF NAMING

There is a certain amount of magic in naming something. It seems that somehow in the process of naming something, one not only becomes aware of it but also has power or jurisdiction over it. It is said, for example, that the ancient Jewish religion did not have a written or verbal name for God. The people feared that somehow in the naming of God there would be a reduction of God's omnipotence. This concept is not alien to our present-day culture. There are times when one may be feeling poorly and cannot identify the source of the physical ill. When the physician finally declares that one has a particular ill, there is a sigh of relief. Once it is named, one can deal with it. One can begin to have power over it. In the field of counseling, there is a term to describe an elusive yet very real anxiety or depression. It is called a "free-floating" anxiety. Much of the anxiety is the result of not being able to identify one's illness. If one can name the problem, one can deal with it and work toward resolving the problem.

To become a victor, one must begin to carefully examine his or her use of time and seek to name those people, tasks or circumstances that are time robbers. Once the robbers have been named, one must then determine and implement some specific strategies to prevent further thefts of time.

## TO CATCH A THIEF

It will be helpful at this point to look at a list of time robbers that are common to health care supervisors. They are ranked so that the first time robber is the one that steals the most time, and so on. Suggestions for possible solutions are also given.

### The terrible telephone

The constant interruptions of the telephone create havoc with scheduled work tasks in two ways. Not only do telephone conversations steal time in themselves, but the interruptions also cause a disruption in the flow of work. The latter may be even more destructive to effective time management than the actual time spent on the telephone. To deal with this, one may wish to review the results of the time inventory, including the number, origin, nature and time of calls received. Once a major source of telephone interruptions is identified, one may then deal with it. One supervisor reported that his telephone log showed he was constantly being interrupted by a fellow supervisor from another department. Both he and the other supervisor were surprised to learn that they interacted so frequently throughout the day. They resolved the problem by establishing a regular time to meet for ten minutes each day to discuss their mutual concerns. This drastically reduced the telephone interruptions and resulted in a better use of their time.

Another means of dealing with continual telephone interruptions is to set up a protective system to screen calls. If there is a secretary or some other person who usually answers the phone, he or she may be carefully instructed as to those calls that will be accepted and those that will not, where the rejected calls might be directed and what times of the day one is not available to accept any calls. In other words, the supervisor becomes the self-directed victor, not the victim, of the telephone.

**Have you got a minute?**

All supervisors have experienced the unhappy aftermath of this seemingly innocent remark. Unfortunately, the minute frequently extends well beyond its defined limit of time and becomes a major time robber. This is the curse of the deadly drop-in visitor. These are usually the sort of people one would welcome, but not in the middle of a busy day, unannounced and strictly at the visitor's convenience. This situation can create a dilemma for those who want people to feel welcome to approach them—particularly employees. Once again, a well done time inventory will expose the antics of the visitors and help to identify who they are, when they drop in and how often they intrude.

How does one deal with this time robber? The key word is schedule. Do not permit valuable time to be at the mercy of people who drop by—be they subordinates, peers or even superiors. People who casually drop by must be made to appreciate that one would be delighted to see them but that it should be at a time of mutual convenience. This is where a diplomatic secretary may function best. As the drop-in visitor is being scheduled, the secretary may add, "And when you return in one hour, you will be able to get her undivided attention at that time." If one has no secretary, time must be taken to personally educate the drop-in visitor. It will be time well spent.

Our final word on this topic concerns the wish of many supervisors to maintain an open-door policy. Although certainly a worthwhile goal, this policy is to be regarded with caution if it means that anyone who has a question or a comment or time to kill may arbitrarily interrupt the supervisor's work. An open-door *attitude* is a preferable alternative. The supervisor establishes the policy that he or she is always willing to listen and help whenever possible. The difference is that people will be scheduled to meet with the supervisor. The obvious exception will be those rare times when there is a genuine emergency. One would be wise to discuss and define with others exactly what constitutes a genuine emergency.

**Meaningless meetings**

Myriad and meaningless meetings rank high on the time robbers' list. To avoid the theft of valuable time, each meeting to be attended must be carefully evaluated. Again, there is a choice. A supervisor may be victimized by the demands of countless meetings or may evaluate their usefulness and take control of his or her time. There are several things one may do to evaluate meetings:

- Never attend a meeting that does not have an agenda. In order to achieve a specific goal in the least amount of time, some direction is required. Many meetings have no specific objective. Meeting agendas should be distributed to all participants prior to the meeting so that thinking and preparation can be done before, not during, the meeting. This same principle applies to any background information or data required to be read by those attending the meeting.

- Do not attend a meeting that does not have a definite starting time and ending time. Work is indeed elastic and will fill the time allotted to it, but if it is determined that a meeting is to last only one hour, somehow those present will manage to complete the business within that time.
- Attend only those meetings that are relevant to the work that one does. This is where the supervisor must personally evaluate the worth of the meeting. It may be helpful to review the notes of past meetings, if available. One should question whether the results of the meetings are usually productive; whether things are accomplished, decisions made and problems solved; and whether attending these meetings is a good use of one's time. If the supervisor finds that the answers to these questions are clearly negative, then a course of action should be chosen and taken. The supervisor may, for example, choose to improve the content of the meeting so that it does become productive. If one chooses not to, or it is impossible to do so, the decision may be to not attend. But what if it is a required meeting? Again, as the victor of one's time, there are options available. The supervisor may put his or her evaluation into writing and present this evidence to the person requiring attendance. Discuss with this person how the meeting might be more productive or how one's time may be better spent elsewhere. If this approach does not work, then the supervisor should continue to attend and work to improve the quality of the time spent there.

Another possible option is to send a representative to attend the meeting and report back to the supervisor.

### Go forth and multiply

This is not intended to be a biblical dictate to propagate the earth, but simply a recognition of the need for effective delegation in order to manage time well. A common time robber for many supervisors is ineffective or nonexistent delegation. One may recall that in the Pareto exercise, there were the trivial many or 80 percent of the tasks from which one may delegate. Yet there are supervisors who jealously guard the things they do and refuse to delegate them.

There are several reasons why supervisors may choose not to delegate. Some may feel insecure in permitting others to do the work they once did. Others may be untrained in how to properly delegate. They may feel there is no one to whom they may delegate. The most frequently given reason is that many supervisors feel that it is easier or quicker to do the job themselves. Initially, it *is* easier and quicker to do the task oneself. Yet, if a task is properly delegated, this advantage is short-lived. The amount of time a supervisor may save through delegation will convince even the worst skeptic.

Delegation not only gives the supervisor more time to attend to higher-priority tasks, but also permits employee growth and increases the employees' level of responsibility. Although space does not permit a detailed description of how to delegate properly, there is one word of caution regarding the process: Delegation does not mean dumping. Too often, subordinates object to being delegated work because it is viewed as the supervisor dumping unwanted jobs on them. How the delegation is perceived and conducted by the supervisor makes all the difference between acceptance or rejection by the employee.

### The firefighting supervisor

For a firefighter, it is quite admirable to be a firefighting supervisor. For the vast majority of supervisors, fighting fires is not appropriate. A major time robber is at work when a supervisor pursues his or her job by frantically running from one crisis to another, attempting to put out "fires," or crises. With a lack of objectives or priorities, time and work become fragmented. Things are left in varying stages of incompletion and disrepair. The result is often frustration and anxiety for the supervisor as well as the staff. There are several steps one can take to avoid the firefighting syndrome.

#### *Plan each day*

The ancient bit of wisdom to plan each day is agreed upon by all and followed by few. At the end of each day, the supervisor should make a list of things to be accomplished the following day, with tasks listed according to priority. Supervisors should identify their times of peak efficiency during the day. Schedule those projects that require one's best efforts at the time of day that coincides with one's energy peak. Another important aspect of the daily plan is to schedule a healthy mix of those things one must do or ought to do, along with those that one wishes and likes to do.

***An important aspect of the daily plan is to schedule a healthy mix of those things one must do or ought to do, along with those that one wishes and likes to do.***

Too often the imaginative and creative aspects of one's job are overlooked. Supervisors should realize that it is equally important to spend some time each day doing those tasks that exercise their creative minds. These things usually represent the projects that one would really like to get to "some day." Make some day today.

*Management by objectives*

Supervisors may better organize their jobs and manage their time through the use of management by objectives (MBO). MBO is often concerned with long-term objectives, i.e., goals for the next few months or years. There are several formats one may select for implementing MBO. The following is a brief representation of the basic elements of the program:

- identifying one's key job duties;
- stating specific objectives to be accomplished regarding each key job duty (what are the results expected?);
- listing the methods by which each objective is to be attained (how is one to accomplish a specific objective?); and
- selecting the means by which one will measure the success of attaining each objective (how will one know when an objective has been reached?)

A most important aspect of MBO is that all of these steps are undertaken with specific due dates in mind. To manage one's time, specific dates for meeting objectives must be established and adhered to. Without due dates, no MBO program and in fact no successful time management approach will work.

Making use of a daily plan for short-term tasks and employing some form of MBO for longer-term objectives can be an effective remedy for the firefighting supervisor. The supervisor who actively seeks to control his or her time through planning and establishing objectives is responding as a self-directing victor.

## SOME VICTORIOUS STRATEGIES

There are numerous suggestions for saving time. The following are brief recommendations on using time to one's own advantage. Although it is not possible to put all of these into effect immediately, *now* is the time to start.

- Eliminate paper. Do not allow it to accumulate. The best advice regarding paper control is to pick it up once and dispatch it. Assign it to someone else, make a decision, give it to one's secretary or use the "round file."
- Conduct regular staff meetings. Establish a set time, day and place for regular meetings. Say it once to 20 people rather than saying it 20 times to each individual. Also, remember the earlier discussion about meetings.
- Block your time. Some projects demand uninterrupted time. Plan and prepare for these by setting aside a block of time to complete the task. In some institutions a quiet hour is observed. During this time telephone calls,

visits and interruptions of any kind are not permitted for those people involved. The results have proven to be most rewarding.

- Take time to train. The time spent in effectively training one's staff pays great dividends in both time saved and increased productivity. This ties in with proper delegation.
- Relinquish ownership. A common time trap indigenous to supervisors is accepting problems that are not theirs. Determine who owns the problem and graciously return it to its rightful owner. Also, involving employees in the art of problem solving will help them to grow.
- Simply say no. The victor of time management does not try to be all things to all people. Persons who attempt to do this end up being nothing to themselves. Learn the fine art of saying no. Refuse to accept those things that are not one's responsibility or that one cannot handle at that time.
- Plan your emergencies. Despite the apparent contradiction in terms, it is possible to carefully plan one's time so that marginal emergencies are controlled. For the supervisor who schedules and plans ahead, it is possible to expect the unexpected. Most health care supervisors are able to predict the time of day, week, month or year when their workload increases. One can anticipate when budgets are due, when reports need to be submitted, and so on. Many emergencies are somewhat predictable and supervisors can plan the time to deal with them.
- Be complete. A real and insidious time robber occurs without one being aware of it. It is work that is left unfinished: the stopping and getting back into the project again, working at an uneven pace that shifts from slow to frantic and the missing of deadlines. To combat this time robber, one must be complete and finish fully what is initiated. Work should be accomplished at a reasonable and controlled pace. Deadlines should be set and met.
- Get away. Minivacations are a strong deterrent to time anxiety. These are selected brief interludes during the course of the day to "get away from it all." Selected means that these minivacations should be scheduled at specific times. What one does during the five- or ten-minute respite is up to the individual. The only restrictions are that it not be work-related, and that it be something one enjoys. It may be a brisk walk around the block, listening to one's favorite music, reading poetry or whatever. A minivacation is to be taken daily, perhaps once in the morning and again in the afternoon. It will help to reduce stress and revitalize a person so that he or she may continue to take charge of time.

## NOW IS THE TIME

There is no mystery about how to manage one's time. Time management is self-management. If a supervisor is being directed by other people and surrounding events, he or she is a victim of time. If a supervisor is autonomous, setting the pace and direction, he or she is a victor of time. The greatest reward derived from time management is a sense of personal satisfaction in one's work and life. Thoreau said: "We have lived not in proportion to the number of years that we have spent on the earth, but in proportion as we have enjoyed."[2] A major influence on this enjoyment is how one uses, or is used, by time. As a health care supervisor, there are several specific things one can do to help manage time. Take the time to initiate a time inventory. Carefully work though the Pareto exercise alone and then with your immediate superior. Identify and analyze those time robbers that may be stealing the treasure of time. Most important, determine and undertake some definite means by which one may become the victor of time. *Now* is the time to begin.

## REFERENCES

1. Kiev, A., and Kohn, V. *Executive Stress.* New York: Amacom, 1979.
2. Thoreau, H. D. *Thoreau on Man and Nature.* New York: Peter Pauper Press, 1960, p. 43.

# A new look at delegation: The supervisor's personal approach

*Charles R. McConnell*
*Vice President for Employee Affairs*
*The Genesee Hospital*
*Rochester, New York*

EFFECTIVE delegation has long been a subject of considerable preaching. It is the basis of numerous seminars and workshops, and one need review only a small sample of current management literature (this article is but one more example) to obtain a reasonable impression of how often delegation is discussed in print. Despite its frequent presentation, however, delegation is often treated once over lightly, if at all, even by supervisors who are genuinely interested in becoming better managers.

## A MISUNDERSTOOD ACTIVITY

Although subject to a great deal of preaching, delegation is frequently overlooked when it comes to conscientious practice. All too often one's ability to delegate is unconsciously taken for granted.

*Health Care Superv*, 1987, 5(3), 77–89

Many people responsible for the work of others take delegation for granted because

- they do not fully understand the true nature of delegation;
- they do not recognize, or at least do not fully appreciate, the extent of the power of one's habits in preventing improvement in delegation; and
- they have not yet come to view delegation from the perspective of the employee to whom the work is delegated.

### The nature of delegation

Delegation is far more than simply assigning work to a subordinate. That particular description—assigning work to someone—is of course a simplistic description of delegation as a process. However, delegation is both a process and a condition. The process is applied when a particular task is assigned to an employee, and the employee performs as expected and completes the task on time. The condition of delegation, beyond the simple process, exists only when the employee automatically accepts the delegated task—whether it be a single one-time task, a series of tasks, or a periodically repeating task—as a legitimate part of his or her job.

There are two kinds of delegation: one so simplistic and automatic that it goes without saying and another that we consciously identify as delegation. The first is the delegation implicit in the employee's job description. A supervisor is responsible for the accomplishment of a certain amount of work. Since the supervisor cannot do all of the work alone, employees are assigned, consistent with the amount of work to be done. However, the supervisor remains responsible for the performance of this work; in that sense the work is the supervisor's.

The employee's job description consitutes organizational delegation; all the tasks in the job description are delegated more or less permanently to that employee, and a change in this status requires alteration in the structure of the employee's job; thus, the job description changes.

The second kind of delegation is that which is ordinarily given the label of delegation. This consists of the assignment of tasks that fall generally outside of the job description, or are lumped together in the job description under a statement such as "performs all other duties as directed." It is these tasks that lie beyond the employee's expected or regularly recurring duties that are delegated.

True delegation also involves the surrender of authority. When a particular tasks lands on the desk of the supervisor, the supervisor is expected to assume authority in accomplishing that task. The implied message that arrives along with the task is, "Your position gives you the authority to get this done." When such a task arrives you have two choices: perform the task alone or assign it to an employee. When you perform the task you are exercising some of the authority of your position. When you assign the task to an employee, however, that employee is given a sufficient amount of your positional authority to allow that person to perform on your behalf. However, having surrendered this portion of authority you nevertheless remain responsible for the completion of the task. (Authority and responsibility are explored further in a later section.)

### The power of habit

Nowhere in this discussion are there steps to follow for effective delegation. There are steps to follow for effective delegation in dozens, if not hundreds, of conventional treatments of the topic, and most of the advice in these process-oriented listings is sound. That is, it is sound advice if it is followed. However, most of the time it is not followed, or if it is followed at all it is not conscientiously pursued for a sufficient amount of time to become ingrained in the supervisor's habit pattern.

Time and habit are two major obstacles that must be overcome to improve our effectiveness as managers. Time has a considerable impact on delegation. All of the steps required in proper delegation—matching the person with the task, instructing and removing obstacles and providing assistance, providing essential motivation, and allowing for follow-up and correction—require more time than may seem to be available. However, supervisors tend to be most strongly aware of the need to delegate at those times when the workload is heaviest and the time available to properly instruct others and bring them up to speed is limited or nonexistent. Regarding delegation and time, one can say only that there is rarely a "best" time to concentrate on delegation, because proper delegation itself takes considerable time. One can only accept the belief that the true time savings of delegation do not occur now but rather lie in the future, in the weeks and months to come. Simply put, it is invariably necessary to spend more time now for the sake of saving time later.

Aside from the ever-present pressures of time, however, the biggest single barrier to effective delegation is habit. If one is to attempt to adopt a new approach to delegation—any of the good-advice delegation steps available—one must change one's ways of doing things. Such change means altering habit patterns, shedding old habits, and replacing them with new ones. Anyone who has put forth conscious effort to change a deeply ingrained habit should have a full appreciation of how difficult this can be. It can certainly be done, depending on how much effort is applied, how long this effort is sustained, and how deeply ingrained the old habit is. Attempts to improve the way in which one delegates frequently go the same way as attempts to apply what one learns at a time-management seminar about improving effectiveness; a flurry of initial activity is followed by stops and starts that diminish and eventually vanish as old ways take over again. This ordinarily occurs because one is only dimly aware, or has perhaps not thought at all, of the immense barrier presented by habits that may have become so deeply ingrained through years of practice that they are now second nature.

***The key to improving one's skill at delegation lies in the constant awareness of the need to overcome old habits.***

The key to improving one's skill at delegation lies in the constant awareness of the need to overcome old habits. It is necessary to start on a small, or at least modest, scale, consciously applying the new process to one well-defined task or project at a time and doing this over and over again until the new way becomes a habit that is strong enough to keep the old habit from returning.

### The employee's perspective

The supervisor who wants to become better at delegation should be looking both downward and upward: downward toward the employees to whom he or she will delegate and upward toward the manager from whom delegated tasks are received. The supervisor who must delegate to employees—and surely this includes every supervisor—should develop a delegation pattern based on an idealization of how the next highest level of management should be delegating downward. The term "idealization" is important, because middle managers have the same delegation problems that supervisors have, and one's boss may not always be an effective delegator. In short, the way the supervisor delegates to his or her employees should be based on the way the boss ought to be delegating to the supervisor.

## THE PERSONAL APPROACH

Put yourself in the position of your employees and consider, by looking upward at the same time, how your superior should, or perhaps does, delegate to you. It helps to look toward your boss regarding delegation because your employees similarly look toward you. Although the motivational forces that cause people to work exist in a complex mix that may vary dramatically from person to person, the net effect of these motivating forces is often not all that different between you and most of your employees. For the most part the majority of your employees will want many of the same things that you want; many of them will perhaps aspire to supervision, wishing to rise from the ranks of the work group, as perhaps you did.

Surely not all of your employees will aspire to management, and not all of them will seek challenge in work, as perhaps you do. Generally, however, their motives will parallel yours so that you can deal with them in a manner similar to the way you would like your boss to deal with you.

You are therefore on a reasonable course if you try to pattern some elements of your relationship with each individual employee after an idealized working relationship with your boss. Attempting to do so will put you in a position of being able to work on improving delegation both upward and downward—that is, while you strive to become better at delegating, you can work to achieve a more appropriate delegation relationship with your superior. This is a highly personal approach, because it finds you looking out for your own best interests—as well as the best interests of your employees and the organization—by improving the effectiveness with which you delegate and simultaneously improving your communicating relationship with your superior.

## IDEAL VERSUS REAL

In an ideal relationship with your boss, you and that higher manager would know fully where you stand with each other at all times and on all matters. In the real world, of course, this relationship may be somewhat less—perhaps even significantly less—than the ideal. However, it is possible to use your knowledge of your needs as a supervisor and your concept of an ideal relationship with your boss to

- reshape and generally improve your relationship with your boss, actually guiding your boss along the path toward a more effective delegation relationship with you; and
- establish a new and more effective pattern for how you delegate to your employees.

Accomplishing such bidirectional improvement means actively working on authority relationships both downward and upward at the same time.

## CLEARING THE WAY FOR EFFECTIVE DELEGATION

It is necessary to determine initially how you want to be treated by your immediate superior concerning delegation. This usually means deciding how, as realistically as possible, you need to be treated so that you can fully meet the requirements of your job. What follows after your needs have been defined is the application of the same line of thought to your relationship with each employee in your work group. The following paragraphs describe major considerations that can be applied to delegation both upward and downward.

### Differing perspectives: Up versus down

The upward view between two adjacent points in the chain of command is not the same as the downward view between those same two points. Looking upward you are likely to see your superior as a single point of information, advice, and assistance; looking upward, your employees probably see you in the same way. The upward view between adjacent points in the chain of command focuses on a single person, and more often than not that person, an organizational superior, is seen as a source of support. However, the downward view is quite different. The superior, whether it is you looking downward at your employees or your manager looking downward at you and your peers, sees not one point of contact but several. Furthermore, the superior frequently sees these several points of contact as sources of problems and grief. Every person in the chain of command has one primary upward channel of communication; however, every managerial person in the chain of command has as many primary downward channels of communication as he or she has direct-reporting employees.

As the person in the middle of three consecutive points in the chain of command, the supervisor needs to appreciate the differences between the upward perspective and the downward perspective. Therefore, the most constructive view to take when looking up the chain of command is: I am but one of a number of people reporting to this superior, and my needs may be only the tip of the iceberg, so I need to make it as easy as possible for my superior to communicate with me. Conversely, the downward view suggests: Each of these people who report to me are looking to me for guidance, so I must show them how to relate to me so that I can meet their needs as well as possible.

Whether rank-and-file employee, supervisor, or middle or upper manager, the person looking up the chain of command sees a single point of contact and thus a single and presumably dedicated source of assistance. However, the person looking down the chain of command invariably sees multiple points of contact that, taken together, are capable of making overwhelming demands.

**Homework: Not just problems, but solutions too**

A large part of becoming an effective delegator consists of teaching employees to do their homework before bringing problems and other matters up the chain of command. However, the business of homework, or thorough staff work, can be dealt with both upward and downward by the individual supervisor. The reaction of many employees to the presence of a problem is to take that problem to the boss and ask for advice and assistance. The boss, however, whether it is you, the supervisor, or your immediate superior, does not need problems. Rather, the boss needs solutions.

***The way not to communicate with a superior is to say in effect, "I have a problem; I need your help."***

The way *not* to communicate with your superior is to say in effect, "I have a problem; I need your help." Rather, it is necessary to first do some homework: Analyze and isolate the problem, identify causes if possible, develop alternative solutions, and identify specifically what is needed from the boss. Then go to the boss and say, "Here is a problem. This is why I think it is a problem and what might have caused it. Here are two or three possible solutions, and the solution I like the best and why. This is what I believe I need from you in order to proceed. What is your advice?" Often the boss may need only answer "yes" or "no" or "do this" or "do that." Just as often the problem will be very nearly self-solving once you have subjected it to analysis. In any case, you will have made it as easy as possible for the boss to communicate with you, without intruding on the boss's time to analyze the problem and without transferring ownership of the problem to your superior.

In parallel fashion the supervisor should encourage individual employees to do the same kind of homework to the extent of their abilities. Whether dealing with a specifically delegated task or a problem encountered directly by the employee, the supervisor should instruct the employee in techniques of analyzing and refining everyday problems, offering alternative solutions, and making recommendations. The employee who does the necessary homework does not always relieve the supervisor of sometimes extensive involvement; the supervisor may have input to offer beyond the reach of the employee. However, the employee who does the necessary homework has accepted partial ownership of the problem and has focused the problem so that it can be dealt with more efficiently. At the heart of effective delegation is the need to teach the employees to do as much as possible on their own before calling for help. One highly successful supervisor expressed management's needs well by saying, "Don't bring me more problems, bring me solutions."

### Reasonable deadline and follow-up

Although your superior may be lax with you regarding deadlines and follow-up—no level of management is exempt from such weaknesses—there is no need to be similarly lax with your subordinates. This is another area of supervisory behavior in which you can do much for yourself in improving how you work both upward and downward.

The superior who is lax concerning deadlines and follow-up shapes subordinates' expectations accordingly. If the boss says simply, "Take care of this when you can," the subordinate may respond immediately, within days or weeks, or never. And if the superior says, "Let me have this by this Friday," but the subordinate knows through past practice that the boss is not likely to mention it again for two weeks, it will probably be two weeks before the work gets done. Such managers have, through their actions over time, conditioned their employees to expect this kind of behavior. Add to this conditioning the fact that some time-related instructions—"When you get a minute," "Whenever you can," "Sometime soon"—can mean anything from right this minute to never, depending on the employee's interpretation.

No matter how nonurgent or unimportant it may be, any task that is worth assigning is worth assigning a reasonable deadline. Once a deadline is assigned, regardless of the task's significance, that deadline should never be allowed to pass without some kind of closure taking place. If closure does not occur in the form of delivered results, then the manager who assigned the task and set the deadline should immediately follow up with the employee.

If your manager does not set deadlines for you, set them for yourself. Commit yourself to such deadlines, if possible by promising results to the boss by some given day and time. Do not be too tough on yourself by promising immediate results, but rather allow yourself all reasonable slack. (If your boss is at all effective he or she will quickly say that you are allowing yourself too much time.) If you are unable to deliver when you promised because of circumstances beyond your control, do not wait for the boss to follow up; rather, inform the boss of the delay and its causes.

This notion of applying reasonable deadlines and faithful follow-up is even more important in the supervisor's relationship with the employees in the work group. These are also the steps that ensure the thoroughness and effectiveness of proper delegation. One can assign a thoroughly defined task to a well-instructed employee and still get nothing if there is no specific requirement for completion or no follow-up. As previously suggested, the supervisor who assigns no deadlines projects a casual attitude toward timely accomplishment of work that can permeate the group. Worse still, if the supervisor usually assigns deadlines but lets them slide by without saying anything, the employees will come to see the supervisor as lax, disorganized, and possibly uncaring. It is this latter condition that is most likely to occur. Apparently, it is easy to assign a deadline when a task is assigned, but it is not quite as easy to remember to follow up on that deadline. Many managers fail to follow up on the deadlines they set, and in doing so they create credibility problems and other difficulties for themselves.

Assigning reasonable deadlines and following up on them probably represents the area of performance in which a supervisor can considerably improve his or her managerial effectiveness with little effort. The supervisor can simply set a reasonable deadline for every task that is assigned and faithfully follow up every time a deadline is missed.

### The right tasks

Employees may find themselves in the fairly common position of being unable to appreciably influence the kinds of tasks their managers delegate to them. Furthermore, the managers may not delegate any tasks outside of what the employees are normally expected to do. They can of course make suggestions and let their manager know they are willing to take on greater responsibilities. If the requests and suggestions fall on deaf ears, employees may not be successful in getting their managers to delegate some of the right kinds of tasks to them. Managers, however, can look within their own work groups to ensure that they do indeed delegate the right kinds of tasks to their employees.

The right tasks are those jobs that the employees can be made to see as reasonably interesting, challenging, or otherwise enlightening or instructional, as opposed to tasks that are likely to be seen as menial, monotonous, or otherwise undesirable. Successful delegation depends to a considerable extent on positive motivation. All too often, attempts at delegation engender only resistance and resentment, because employees view delegated tasks as work they have to do because the boss considered it too lowly or too dull to do personally. Certainly almost every job has its less desirable elements, but often these can be rotated among several employees or otherwise divided up so that those in the group can feel that this is something they need to get done together, and no one or two persons need to feel that they are being dumped on. Often the best approach to the dull assignments that inevitably occur is to bring several employees together in a joint effort to look for more efficient and more tolerable ways of getting these things done.

If at all possible supervisors should avoid inadvertently fostering the notion that delegation really means, "I'm giving this to you because I don't want to do it." Rather, delegation should be used whenever possible to provide the employees with more interesting and more challenging work, more variety in their daily routine, and more opportunity to learn new things that will help prepare them for possible advancement in the future. Delegation of the right kinds of tasks also holds an added advantage for supervisors: The process teaches you more about your employees and their capabilities, thus giving you information that may help in making promotional decisions and also allowing you to develop capable backup personnel who can act in your absence in certain matters.

***If at all possible supervisors should avoid inadvertently fostering the notion that delegation really means, "I'm giving this to you because I don't want to do it."***

### Boundaries

Without good, clearly defined boundaries—limits on authority that define the territory within which one can act—an employee at any level of the organization can either work inside a safe but narrow area within which work life may be dull and unsatisfying, or wander into the gray areas and take some risks. Some employees, workers and supervisors alike, will opt for risk taking; some employees, again workers and supervisors alike, will choose to remain narrowly contained.

For many employees, and certainly for supervisors and managers, a reasonable amount of boundary testing should be encouraged. Although a thorough treatment of boundary testing and its many implications lies largely beyond the scope of this discussion, for present purposes, boundary testing can be described as deliberately entering the gray areas surrounding one's job and attempting, through positive action, to learn where one's boundaries actually lie. Such testing should always be gentle and should never involve intrusion into some other person's territory. Most of the time, however, an employee finds a boundary only when others perceive that employee to be overstepping authority.

Looking upward in the chain of command, the supervisor can define and often slightly broaden his or her authority by simply testing boundaries and picking up problems that have fallen through the cracks and otherwise clarifying gray areas. Looking downward, the supervisor should ensure that the employees' boundaries are sufficiently well defined so that boundary testing would rarely be necessary. Ensuring that, the supervisor should next ensure—at least for those reasonably professional workers who are capable of governing many of their own actions—that the boundaries are as broad as possible.

In considering the matter of boundaries and the differences one might see between looking upward and looking downward, the preferred posture of a supervisor can be described as follows: Although your superior may have provided you with the barest of job descriptions or no job description at all, this does not prevent you from providing your employees with complete job descriptions that clearly spell out the limits of their authority. Within the health care organization, and especially in the many departments employing large numbers of technical and professional people, probably the best approach to authority limits is to clearly define the employees' boundaries (again, making these boundaries as broad as possible) and to turn the employees loose to function within those limits.

**Speaking up or talking back**

There is little practical advice to offer to the supervisor whose manager appears closed to criticism and disagreement or who will hear nothing contrary without actually holding it against the dissenter. Many supervisors have managers with whom they may speak freely and bluntly; many supervisors have managers who have demonstrated that they react to criticism or disagreement of any kind with resentment, disfavor, and prejudice. If you cannot speak critically with your boss you will ordinarily have to live with that condition and make the best of it. However, since you are in a position to frequently make the boss look better and occasionally keep the boss out of trouble, your inability to speak up is more your boss's loss than yours.

Even if your superior is closed to criticism and disagreement, you can remain open to the same from your employees. A crucial part of the communicating relationship with each employee is employee feedback, and for feedback to be complete it must include the bad along with the good. The only way to consistently receive any of the bad—those comments that might be construed by employees as being critical of your decisions or actions or as disagreeing with you—is to demonstrate that such comments are received in the helpful spirit in which they are offered. Employees who learn through experience that their supervisor can gracefully receive and tactfully deal with negative information will eventually feel completely free to share such information without fear of repercussion. An atmosphere in which the employees feel free to speak up or talk back is clearly to a supervisor's benefit for at least two important reasons: Employees who do the day-to-day work of the department have far more intimate knowledge of the inner workings of the department's tasks than the supervisor does, so they can see problems that the supervisor cannot see; and since the supervisor cannot possibly know everything at all times, the employees, as extensions of the supervisor, can help the supervisor avoid certain difficulties and, to put it bluntly, stay out of trouble.

## The freedom to fail

When an employee fails in the performance of a delegated task it is often a shared failure. Often the failure is largely the employee's for doing something incorrectly or for not following instructions; at other times the fault lies with the supervisor in bringing task and person together and providing direction and support. Since delegation failure must be shared, and since we all learn from our failures often far more than we learn from our successes, it makes little sense to over-punish an employee who makes a mistake. Criticism should of course be delivered when deserved, but it should always be of a constructive kind, including the means for correcting one's behavior and avoiding a repetition of the error. In many patient-care situations there is no room for error and, thus, little if any room for the tolerance of mistakes. However, in nonpatient-care functions and in many support and administrative activities there is indeed room for error, and errors occur frequently.

***The employee who is soundly punished for making a mistake will likely shy away from further exercising initiative for fear of punishment.***

The employee who is soundly punished for making a mistake, especially a mistake made while exercising reasonable individual initiative, will likely shy away from further exercising initiative for fear of punishment. Errors are a natural part of one's career growth, and one might eventually say the employee who never makes a mistake is not doing much growing. The employee who never makes a mistake—and especially the *supervisor* who never makes a mistake—is the one who never exercises initiative or never tries anything new or different.

## AUTHORITY AND RESPONSIBILITY

No discussion of delegation, traditional or otherwise, is complete without a few words about whether it is actually authority or responsibility that is being delegated. In spite of the many authors and speakers who deal repeatedly with the supposed delegation of responsibility, it is actually authority, and only authority, that is delegated. Delegation is the actual handing over of something, a task of one's own or piece of one's own job description, something that the delegator then no longer has. If one's job and one's authority to perform that job can be envisioned as a physical object, such as a pie, delegation may rightly be described as cutting a slice from that pie and handing it to another person. The missing piece is simply no longer there; it is handed over—it is delegated. The responsibility for task performance, however, is not handed over. Rather, the task performance responsibility is replicated at a lower level. That is, the employee is made responsible to the supervisor, but the supervisor remains responsible to his or her superior for the performance of that task.

This relationship between authority and responsibility lies near the heart of the reasons why many supervisors have trouble delegating thoroughly to their employees; they know they remain responsible and fully answerable for the performance of tasks that now lie completely in the hands of another.

The final point to be made concerning authority and responsibility is that these two characteristics must exist in equivalent amounts. An employee who is given the responsibility to accomplish a particular task should possess all the authority necessary to permit the accomplishment of that task. To give the employee responsibility with less than full authority is to tie that person's hands and make it necessary to get the job done by depending on uncontrolled outside forces. Conversely, to give an employee task performance authority without concurrent responsibility is to allow the individual to operate without accountability and without risk.

## THE UNDENIABLE NEED TO DELEGATE

The justification for frequently reminding supervisors and other managers of the importance of effective delegation is simple: Delegating effectively is essential if one is to manage effectively.

At times, especially when the frustrations of dealing with certain employees get in the way, it is easy to fall back on the old saying: If you want something done right, do it yourself. However, one person can do only so much and still continue to do things well. The supervisor who continues to take on more and more without carefully and selectively delegating to others is courting diminished effectiveness, departmental morale problems, and personal problems of various kinds, including eventual failure. When you examine the full scope of that for which you are responsible, not just the tasks that are yours alone but the work of the entire group, you can appreciate that there is no way to do it all alone. Delegation, therefore, lies at the center of management itself—getting things done through people.

Regarding the view of delegation both up and down the chain of command with which this discussion began, one might formulate a simple golden rule of delegation. That is: Delegate to your employees in the manner you would have your superior delegate to you.

# Improving performance appraisal from the bottom up

*Charles R. McConnell*
*Vice President for Employee Affairs*
*The Genesee Hospital*
*Rochester, New York*

As ANYONE WHO has risen from the ranks into supervision can attest, there are many significant differences between working as a supervisor and working as a nonsupervisory employee. Supervisors and nonsupervisors must do a great many things differently from each other; however, the requirements placed on them are identical in four important respects:

1. Supervisors and nonsupervisors alike are subject to the same organizational goals and policies.
2. Supervisors and nonsupervisors alike must be intimately familiar with the tasks of the department. Supervisors, while perhaps performing these tasks at times, must understand, teach, and judge task performance, whereas nonsupervisors will of course perform them regularly.
3. As are all employees at all organizational levels except the very top, supervisors and nonsupervisors are

*Health Care Superv*, 1990, 8(2), 73–83

subject to the delegation of tasks by their immediate superiors.

4. Supervisors as well as nonsupervisors are subject to performance appraisal by their immediate superiors.

Just as it is possible for supervisors to improve the effectiveness with which they delegate duties to employees by examining their own delegating relationships with higher management, it is also possible for supervisors to become better evaluators of employee performance by examining and improving on their own performance appraisal relationships with higher management.

Most instruction or advice given to supervisors about performance appraisal is presented with a downward perspective; that is, such comments focus only on the relationship between supervisor and subordinate. It is the goal of this article to suggest how the supervisor can become a better evaluator of employees by working to improve his or her own appraisal relationship with higher management. Whether the individual supervisor's appraisal by higher management can be substantially improved by this process depends entirely on the attitude and receptivity of higher management. However, regardless of the supervisor's success in improving his or her own appraisal, the insight gained in the process will make the supervisor a better evaluator of employees.

## SIMILAR NEEDS

The first-line supervisor or manager is simply another employee of the organization who happens to be one level removed from the rank and file. As rank-and-file employees are subject to the requirements of the supervisor, so too is the supervisor subject to the requirements of the next highest level of management.

As employees of the organization, the supervisor and the nonsupervisor bring similar, perhaps even largely identical, needs to work with them. It has been generally accepted for many years that humans are motivated largely by their desire to fulfill the needs that drive them. For example, by seeking and maintaining an income, people acquire the means to fulfill certain physiological needs; by obtaining approval and acceptance as a member of a group, people fulfill certain sociological needs; by seeking job satisfaction and approval, people fulfill certain psychological needs.

***Since performance appraisal is far from being the most comforting activity for most managers, there is a tendency for many managers to run late with appraisals.***

Although the mix of needs varies from one person to another, the needs of supervisors and nonsupervisors are not all that different from each other. That is, although the mix varies from person to person, the kinds of needs that motivate rank-and-file employees are generally the same kinds of needs that motivate supervisors. Therefore, if you carefully consider what you wish to obtain from your own performance appraisal, you can gain considerable insight into what most of your employees wish to learn from their appraisals.

Although there are secondary objectives concerned with employee development, the primary objective of performance appraisal is for the employee to maintain or improve performance in the job he or she presently holds. That is the organization's primary objective of performance appraisal, and it is the objective the supervisor should have in mind when evaluating a subordinate. However, the manner in which you pursue the objective makes a difference. The objective should be pursued in a manner that as completely as possible gives the employee what he or she needs to obtain from the process. Consider some of the information and results that you, and therefore most of your employees, wish to carry away from the appraisal interview:

- a sense of having been dealt with fairly,
- appreciation of your contribution to the organization,
- recognition of special effort or exceptional accomplishments,
- an indication of how your performance can be improved, and specific direction that will help you to improve,
- an honest assessment of your future prospects,
- a sense of having been fairly rewarded materially (primarily in terms of pay increases) relative to others who are similarly situated, and
- the feeling that you have been allowed to contribute constructively to your appraisal discussion, and that you have been listened to and taken seriously.

The foregoing list may seem to represent a tall order, but it is not overly idealistic in terms of the desires, perhaps largely unarticulated, that each of us carries into our performance appraisal discussions. These several points can be examined in two ways. First, are they being satisfied for you in *your* performance appraisal? If not, there are steps you can take that may help to improve your own appraisal. Second, are you doing the best you can do to fill these needs for each employee you evaluate? If not, you can begin now by adopting these factors as guidelines for evaluating your employees.

Having thus increased your awareness of what both you and your employees wish to obtain from the appraisal process, you can then proceed to examine the manner in which your manager evaluates you and determine whether you can inspire any constructive change.

## APPRAISAL TIMING

Most employees, supervisors included, are keenly aware of their scheduled evaluation dates. Does your own appraisal always occur on time? If yes, you fare better than many others in this respect; it remains only for you to apply this strict schedule adherence to your employees' evaluations. But if your own appraisal rarely occurs on time, see if you can do something to correct this practice.

Since performance appraisal is far from being the most comforting activity for most managers, there is a tendency for many managers to run late with appraisals. This condition is aggravated if the organization's performance appraisal system is not conscientiously administered. Some central function, ordinarily the human resource department, is usually responsible for keeping the system moving, distributing forms, sending out reminders of due dates, and following up on delinquent appraisals. If system administration is lax, many managers tend to run even later with appraisals.

If your performance appraisal is chronically late, try reminding your manager shortly before the next one is scheduled.

Most managers will take no offense at a reminder such as, "I see my evaluation date is just two weeks away. Is there anything you would like me to do in the way of preparation?" Or, noting that your evaluation date is coming up, you might innocently ask your manager if your appraisal interview has been scheduled yet so you can get it on your calendar. Such diplomatic reminders will not offend most managers, and a manager who might not yet have thought of your appraisal or who had simply assumed that you were giving it no particular thought might respond by giving you your appraisal on time (or at least not as late as might otherwise have been the case).

Regardless of your degree of success in improving the timing of your own appraisal, however, do not forget that timing means as much to most of your employees as it does to you. If you have tended to run late with employee appraisals in the past, do not be offended if employees give you subtle reminders of upcoming review dates; they are probably using the same techniques with you that you are using with your manager.

## CONSIDER SELF-APPRAISAL

If you enjoy a reasonable working relationship with your manager, and if you are not uncomfortable in doing so, offer to do a complete appraisal of your own performance using the same forms and criteria the manager will use. If you get to perform a self-appraisal, make sure that it is unbiased from either direction; that is, you should not see your manager's appraisal of you until after you have done your own, and your manager should not see your self-appraisal until after he or she has written your evaluation.

Should your manager be one who sometimes forgets appraisal interviews altogether, your self-appraisal will help ensure that a performance discussion does indeed occur. However, a self-appraisal's major benefits arise from an examination of the differences between your appraisal of yourself and your manager's evaluation of you. Consider, for example, that you are evaluated on 12 different job criteria. If the manager's evaluation and your self-appraisal are reasonably close in the assessment of 9 or 10 of the 12 criteria, then you immediately know that your discussion of performance will be focused most constructively on the remaining 2 or 3 criteria on which you are not so much in agreement.

You may want to consider the use of self-appraisal by your employees, especially if you supervise primarily technical or professional workers. However, it is suggested that self-appraisal be presented as strictly optional, with absolutely no pressure perceived by employees who do not wish to participate. Many employees, uncomfortable with performance appraisal to begin with, are easily threatened by mandated self-appraisal. An employee who feels threatened will be trying so hard to second guess you that a useful self-appraisal will not be possible.

## MAKE SURE THE INTERVIEW OCCURS

It is not unusual for the occasional manager to hand a completed appraisal to an employee while saying, "Here's your evaluation; we'll talk about this sometime soon," or even, "Here's your evaluation; see me if you have any questions." The appraisal handed to the employee under such circumstances is ordinarily a "no-fault" review; that is, overall it will be favorable, if somewhat nonspecific, and anything it contains that might be described as criticism will be buried in vague terminology.

***If you do nothing to make it into something else, your appraisal interview by the manager who is looking to get off the hook for another year will consist of little more than general compliments and complimentary generalities.***

Should you receive a completed performance appraisal form under the circumstances just described, your manager has, simply by handing it to you, given you an open invitation to request an appraisal interview should one not be scheduled for you soon. The no-fault review, the kind that generally says you are doing a fine job without providing any particular detail, serves but a single purpose—it gets your manager off the hook for another year as far as your appraisal is concerned.

Take steps to ensure that your appraisal interview happens. Make a direct request of your superior to talk about your appraisal. It is rare that a manager will deny or find a creative way to avoid such a direct request from an employee.

In dealing with your employees, you should of course schedule timely appraisal conferences. Do not wait for them to have to prompt you in the manner suggested for you to prompt your delinquent manager. Always remember that the behavior that stymies and frustrates you when you encounter it in your manager will also stymie and frustrate your employees when they encounter it in you and do your conscientious best to avoid passing along inappropriate behavior. Once you have been granted an appraisal interview, whether it is automatically scheduled for you or scheduled at your urging, take whatever steps you need to take to get the most out of it.

## WORK FOR A CONSTRUCTIVE INTERVIEW

If you do nothing to make it into something else, your appraisal interview by the manager who is looking to get off the hook for another year will consist of little more than general compliments and complimentary generalities. However, although a few minutes worth of nonspecific praise may be much easier for you to take than a few minutes worth of criticism, a goody-goody, nonspecific appraisal will do nothing for you in your growth as a supervisor. Neither will goody-goody nonspecific reviews do anything constructive for your employees.

### Go armed with questions

Prepare several questions—at least three or four—to take with you to your appraisal interview. Do not ask questions like, "How do you think I'm doing?" Rather, prepare some pointed questions that deal with specific aspects of your performance, especially questions that stem from tasks and task elements covered in your job description. For example, in an effort to determine what your boss thinks about the way you are fulfilling your staff education responsibilities, you might want to ask something like, "What did you think of the departmental safety program I conducted during the last quarter? And do you think I could make it more compact without reducing its effectiveness?"

If your manager is conscientiously attempting to give you an honest and realistic appraisal, you may not have to use your prepared questions at all unless they deal with topics that you genuinely want to discuss over and above the points your manager raises. Your advance questions exist mainly in case your manager is inclined to fill the interview time with harmless generalities and friendly chitchat. If your manager is clearly trying to avoid the hard part—which is also the constructive part—of the interview, you will need your questions to get the discussion focused along construction lines.

### Challenge general statements

British author G.K. Chesterton is reputed to have said that "All generalizations are dangerous, including this one." Do not automatically accept generalizations about your performance, even highly complimentary ones. Challenge them.

Be especially wary of statements that hinge on the words always and never, as in "You always do this" or "You never do that." Rarely, if ever, are such statements completely true.

If, for example, your manager says to you, "Your group's productivity looks fine," you can then question whether productivity was better in some respects than others, and where the differences lie; whether you appear to have maintained adequate productivity over the peak vacation period; whether it was evident in productivity during the last quarter that you had one employee on medical leave; and so on. Virtually every general statement your manager might make can be particularized by a series of specific, constructive questions from you.

Keep in mind that your objective during the appraisal interview should be to get your manager to talk about specific aspects of your performance. You do exactly that when you pose specific questions. Many managers, especially those who tend to think out loud better than they think on paper, will deliver a far more constructive appraisal when they can simply converse with you about the specifics of your performance.

You should expect, however, that as you challenge positive general statements, you run the risk of drawing out some negative commentary. Perhaps your manager is indeed largely pleased with the way you are performing overall, but as you focus the discussion point by point and deal in turn with narrow aspects of your performance, the chances that negatives will emerge increase dramatically. Be prepared to accept the negatives, because after all, if you are serious about having a real performance appraisal, you will want to hear the honest negatives. Also, be prepared to ask how the negatives can be turned into positives in the future.

### Request corrective guidance

Any specific criticism of your performance should be accompanied by constructive guidance on how you can go about improving that aspect of your performance. No criticism is constructive unless it includes the means for effecting correction, and criticism that is not constructive is not valid.

When your performance is criticized during your appraisal interview, consider taking the following action:

- If the criticism is general, ask for specifics. For example, if your manager says, "You've been a little sloppy in controlling overtime," ask for your boss's perception of how much you are off, what time period it applies to, and what he or she believes the cause might be.
- Ask for specific guidance, as in, "Okay, exactly what can I do—in addition to what I've already been doing—to help hold overtime down?"
- Secure a specific target. Whether suggested by you or your manager, your target for improvement should be discussed between you and should ideally be one on which you both agree.
- Agree on a specific time frame for improvement.

In any discussion with your manager about some aspect of your performance that needs improvement, whenever possible, you should know what is to be done, how much must be done, and by when it should be done. Pursuing the overtime example, rather than agreeing that you will "work to bring overtime usage down," you might, for instance, agree that you will "reduce overtime usage (what) to no more than budgeted levels (how much) by the end of the second quarter of the year (when)."

**Negotiate your evaluation score**

Your performance appraisal goes into your personnel file and thus becomes part of your official record of employment. It will remain there as long as you remain with the organization, it will probably stay there long after you have left, and it will perhaps be accessed for reference purposes. Therefore, you have an interest in the indicated level of performance that becomes part of the official record. Also, if your organization operates a merit-pay program and if some portion of your merit increase depends on your evaluation score, you have an additional, as well as a more practical and immediate, interest in what goes into the record.

***If there is money at stake, you might wish to challenge the scoring—diplomatically, of course—to determine whether you can improve the outcome of your appraisal.***

Regarding the commentary that might appear on your evaluation, do not be overly concerned with one or two weak spots if the overall rendering of your performance is favorable. These days there is less and less likelihood of specific appraisal comments being used in references unless they are wholly positive. The most one is likely to see about performance on the majority of present-day references is a check mark indicating that performance was, for example, above standard, at standard, or below standard.

Regarding evaluation scores, your score should do you no long-run damage as long as it indicates your performance to be at or above your organization's defined level of standard performance. If there is money at stake, however, as in a merit-pay system that provides higher raises for higher evaluation scores, you might wish to challenge the scoring—diplomatically, of course—to determine whether you can improve the outcome of your appraisal.

Challenging your appraisal score falls solidly under the heading of nothing ventured, nothing gained. It cannot hurt to try to negotiate a slightly higher score, especially if you sincerely believe (without ego-tripping) that you have done a better job than the score reflects and if you feel that you have convinced your manager that there are some important considerations he or she may have overlooked.

It is difficult to predict how your manager might react to your attempt to negotiate a higher evaluation score. Some managers feel totally committed to the comments and scores they have set to paper before the appraisals are discussed and behave as though changing an evaluation score indicates weakness or indecisiveness on their part. Some managers deliberately allow room for negotiation in their scoring simply to see whether certain employees will take the initiative to challenge them and ask for more. Still other managers, ordinarily those who are totally unthreatened by participative process, will recognize that employees have valid input to supply to their reviews and will thus remain open to new information. Regardless of the style of management you work under (unless you report to the most autocratic of managers, whose style you will recognize in an instant), you have nothing to lose by opening the subject of a negotiated increase in your evaluation score.

When the shoe is on the other foot, be extremely careful how you react to an employee who tries to negotiate a better evaluation with you. It is easy to experience immediate resentment for the employee, especially with one you feel you have already rated justly or even generously. Some employees, especially those who do not fully understand performance appraisal, feel they are being downrated if their scores are anything less than perfect. Or perhaps they feel they are not making progress if their scores are not higher with each subsequent evaluation. You need to use great care in sorting out these employees from those others who have valid, specific input to bring to the appraisal process. Be sufficiently open and broad-minded to recognize that an employee you are evaluating will sometimes be able to legitimately point out things that you missed. In letting the negotiation work for an employee who has a valid point, you can demonstrate your belief in participative processes and can show that you are sufficiently flexible to change your mind when given additional facts.

## KNOW THE SYSTEM

Everyone in the organization should know exactly how the appraisal system works. Everyone from the level of first-line supervisor on up should also know exactly how to apply the system to others. However, rarely does either of these circumstances exist completely throughout the organization.

All managers at all levels who appraise others should have received basic instruction in the use of the performance appraisal system, and this instruction should be periodically reinforced. In most organizations, however, it is common to find managers who have never received more direction in applying the system than they get from a single, rapid reading of the instructions. If you know your organization's appraisal system from the inside out and are thoroughly familiar with how it is applied, you will make your own appraisal easier for yourself and your manager.

Outside of the mechanics of timing and the scheduling of interviews, the features that all employees should know and understand may be encapsulated within the following three considerations.

First, every employee should know the criteria against which he or she will be evaluated. This means that all specific responsibilities, all specific tasks, and all specific kinds of behavior that will be evaluated should be known to the employee in advance, as well as the standards of performance or the measurements that will be applied. In other words, the employees should be well aware of the expectations of the system.

Second, every employee should know how scores are applied to each individual element of an appraisal, exactly how the final score is tabulated, and what that overall score translates into in terms of an overall relative description of performance (i.e., "standard," "satisfactory," "unsatisfactory," "outstanding," or whatever descriptive terms your particular system uses).

Third, it is of critical importance that every employee understand the difference between standard performance (or satisfactory performance, or whatever your system calls it) and average performance. Although many of us tend to think of performance in terms of averages and tend to place ourselves somewhere relative to average, we remain better off if our appraisal system never involves the use of the term average at all. The average performance of a work group is just that; it is the average of the overall scores of a number of people. However, standard performance—that performance level implicit in doing what one is expected to do in a reasonable manner with expected results under reasonable supervision—tends over the long run to be the lowest level of performance prevalent in the organization. After all, someone who is performing below the standard of the job is not doing what he or she was hired to do, and substandard performance should have been dealt with along the way (this is what the employment probation period and certain other corrective measures are for). Therefore, true average performance in a work group will invariably lie somewhere above standard performance.

However, people who do not have a problem with the use of the term standard performance may nevertheless, strange to say, have difficulty with the term average as applied to their performance. Most of us have the tendency to think of ourselves as no less than average and perhaps a bit better than average, and we may tend to react negatively to average ("Me? Only average?"). The focus of the system should be on at least maintaining standard performance and achieving above-standard performance as possible, without reference to averages. However, a great many employees see the terms standard or satisfactory and think of them as meaning average; this notion must be corrected if appraisal is to work as intended.

## KEEP THE APPRAISAL ALIVE

Do not allow your performance evaluation to simply vanish into your manager's files, never to be seen again until the following year when it is time for your next appraisal. Rather, at one or two points during the year, secure some time with your manager to talk about an item or two from your most recent appraisal. The ideal item for you to address at such an interim discussion would be one for which your manager had some legitimate criticism and had offered you some guidance for corrective action. If you feel that you have made progress on this item, or if it is an item for which you had agreed on a shorter time span than one year before reexamination, then this item is appropriate for an interim performance discussion. A topic also suited for an interim performance discussion would be one for which, although your work was judged satisfactory at your last appraisal, you believe that you have shown some significant improvement.

In point of fact, any aspect of your performance that you honestly believe you can improve can be used as an opener for an interim performance discussion. If you set some modest improvement objectives for yourself—two or three miniobjectives for which you have developed a reasonable statement of what, how much, and when—you can use these to initiate a performance discussion with your manager that can be far more than just an exercise in keeping communication lines open.

***At one or two points during the year, secure some time with your manager to talk about an item or two from your most recent appraisal.***

Do likewise for your employees without them having to suggest it. That is, schedule one or two sessions for each employee between performance appraisals to discuss a few points relating to each one's last appraisal. Until your employees become well accustomed to this practice, give them plenty of advance notice as to which past appraisal points you would like to discuss. In this manner you will encourage your employees to think about serious efforts to improve at times other than appraisal times, and you might even discover that you have inspired them to set self-improvement objectives on their own.

## A TRUE TWO-WAY STREET

Effective performance appraisal is a two-way street that carries a considerable amount of traffic in both directions. However, if left totally up to the evaluator at all times, appraisal can and often does become a purely mechanical process that can be almost totally one-way. In far too many traditional approaches, the process is active for the appraiser, but is passive for the employees being evaluated. To fulfill its maximum potential, appraisal should be very nearly as active from the bottom up as it is from the top down.

The guidelines presented in the preceding pages deal largely with ways in which you can take a more active role in your own performance appraisal. Having done everything you can reasonably do to take an active role in your own appraisal, it remains up to you to then apply a common-sense, golden-rule approach to appraisal overall: Evaluate your employees in the manner in which you would like to be evaluated by your manager. Recall what was said earlier about the applicability of basic human needs to most people. Then appreciate that, as far as performance appraisal is concerned, the appraisal approaches (or lack thereof) that leave you frustrated and discouraged are very nearly identical to those that will leave your employees frustrated and discouraged. There may be times when you have to tell yourself that your employees deserve better than what you are receiving yourself.

As supervisors, we acquire a great deal of what we know about managers from our management role models and especially from our immediate superiors. However, rarely should we allow our role models to dictate all that we do. As we learn by example what we should be doing, we should learn also by example what we should avoid doing. As far as *your* performance appraisal is concerned, develop the best possible appraisal relationship you can develop with your manager. Then address the elements of that relationship that are weak or absent, and do your best to ensure that each of your employees is given the opportunity to develop the kind of performance appraisal relationship that you yourself would like to enjoy.

# Does your resume do you justice?

***William Umiker***
*Professor*
*Pennsylvania State University*
*Hershey, Pennsylvania*

NEW GRADUATES must now compete with displaced employees for jobs. Recognizing this, educational institutions teach new graduates how to write resumes, or they urge students to get professional help.

Humanistic organizations soften the blows of reductions in force by providing outplacement services. In these, resume preparation is emphasized. Therefore, the job seeker who dashes off a perfunctory resume leaves the starting block with a major handicap.

The primary purpose of a resume is to get interviews with potential employers. It can also give you a competitive edge. The ideal resume makes the hiring official think "This is exactly the kind of person we're looking for." To achieve these two purposes, you must come up with something that stands out from the rest.

*Health Care Superv*, 1988, 7(1), 50–53

## THE COVER LETTER

The cover letter introduces your resume, so strive to make it do just that. It should state the position you seek, your work objective, and why you should be considered (see box, "Example of the Body of a Cover Letter").

## THE RESUME

After you list your educational accomplishments, list your previous positions. Arrange these chronologically, the most recent position first.

Your knowledge, skills, attributes, and experience are the heart of the resume. Prepare a generic group of skills and experiences. This group will be in every resume you send out.

Add to this basic group special items that are congruent with specific jobs.

Select action words in your descriptions here are some that pack power:

| | | |
|---|---|---|
| Advise | Indoctrinate | Save |
| Conduct | Introduce | Solve |
| Coordinate | Lead | Teach |
| Develop | Plan | Train |
| Formulate | Publish | Troubleshoot |

Karen Good plans to send out a dozen resumes. She knows of two openings right now. One is a technical job in a large institution; the other is that of night supervisor. The latter position calls for both performing technical procedures and directing three other employees.

Karen decides to try to get these jobs. She prepares a dozen generic documents, holds ten copies, and modifies the remaining two for the two positions she is pursuing.

Here is Karen's basic list:

- Trained in all aspects of—
- Has reputation as a "can do" person

**Example of the Body of a Cover Letter**

Through a former associate, I have learned you have a supervisory opening. I am interested in that position.

For the past six years I have been an assistant supervisor in a large inner-city facility. While I enjoy my present job, I seek more responsibility and challenge. Also, my two sons will soon be of school age. A suburban location such as yours is very attractive.

While I am not familiar with the details of the position, I believe that my training and experience qualify me for the position. Please see the attached resume.

For the past several years I have made a special effort toward developing my supervisory skills, while not neglecting technical and professional development.

I could be available within a month of the date of selection.

May I have an interview to establish my credentials?

- Likes challenge of working with minimal supervision
- Eager to take on additional training and to develop new skills
- Respected for competency and integrity
- Innovative and flexible; welcomes change
- Cost and quality conscious
- Highly productive
  - Extensively experienced in instrumentation
  - Regularly attended seminars and workshops, often at own expense
  - Cross-trained to substitute for personnel in other work sections
  - Consistently earned outstanding performance ratings
  - Developed and implemented several new procedures
  - Accepted assignments as quality assurance and safety coordinator.

Additional items Karen added to the resume for the technical position in a large organization were as follows:

- Comprehensively trained in—
- Specialist in—
- Expert trainer
- Flair for applied research
  - Usually assigned the most difficult technical tasks
  - Selected by students as outstanding instructor
  - Developed extensive file of new techniques
  - Assisted in exhibits at national meetings
  - Published several articles on—
  - Regularly conducted workshops and seminars

Karen inserted the following elements into the resume targeted for the night supervisory job:

- Good balance between performing and managing
- Effective leader
- Competent generalist; can pinch-hit in all sections
- Excellent practical application of knowledge
- Familiar with, and enjoys, after-hour assignments
- Skilled in instrument trouble shooting

**What to Avoid in a Resume**

All-purpose resume
  Tailor each resume for the job sought.

Brief resume
  The resume should be more than an outline.

Lengthy resume
  Do not bury your strong points in trivia.

The pronoun "I"
  "I" is acceptable in the cover letter.

Education prior to college entry

Negative aspects of your present or past job

Salary desired
  The organization may have a larger amount in mind.

Excessive praise
  Avoid flowery adjectives and superlatives; stick to facts.

References
  They will be requested if desired.

- Performed broad spectrum of tasks, often under pressure
- Indoctrinated new employees and taught new procedures
- Gave advice often sought by fellow workers
- Frequently represented supervisor at meetings

Amplify two or three items that deserve special mention. Select accomplishments you think the employer would be most impressed by. For example, Karen could add under the item "Cost conscious": In 1987, the implementation of procedural changes suggested by applicant resulted in savings of $25,000.

Check your rough draft for errors listed in the box "What to Avoid in a Resume." Edit for content, form, spelling, and punctuation.

If you want professional help, do not look for it until you have gathered all of the information described above. Then get assistance in converting all the information into an attractive package.

If you choose to forgo the professional route, type your resume on white, off-white, or ivory bond 8 1/2-by-11-inch paper. The author highly recommends a word processor. It simplifies modifications. Leave plenty of white space at the margins, top, bottom, and between lines.

If you do not get a response, select new targets and customize a few more resumes. If faster action is needed, send out batches of the generic resumes.

## SUGGESTED READINGS

Bostwick, B.E. *Resume Writing*. New York: Wiley, 1980.

Brill, L. *Business Writing Quick and Easy*. New York: AMACOM, 1981.

Day, C.M. "Market Yourself to a Better Job." *Medical Laboratory Observer* (April 1982): 77–86.

Stimac, M. "Writing a Skills Resume." *Journal of Society for Advancement of Management* (Summer 1977).

# The supervisor's guide to oral presentations

*Charles R. McConnell*
*Vice President for Employee Affairs*
*The Genesee Hospital*
*Rochester, New York*

"ELEANOR, WE'VE been asked to supply a speaker for a regional conference on nursing management issues and problems. Since your flextime scheduling project represents some innovative thinking, I'd like you to consider accepting this assignment. What do you say?"

How does Eleanor respond to her manager's question? How should any of us answer a similar question from the boss, especially if our speaking experience has been limited to brief reports at meetings? How would any of us react to an unexpected request to speak before a group?

Consider one particular supervisor. Today, her reaction to such a request would probably be based on a quick assessment of her personal workload. However, a few years ago she might have reacted with something near panic, suffering stress and anxiety for

*Health Care Superv*, 1983,2(1),53–62

every waking moment until the presentation became history.

It is easy enough to say that a speech should be treated as any other assignment, to be approached with confidence and given the best effort. However, this may not help Eleanor; she may be highly confident of her technical ability and yet lack confidence as a public speaker. Eleanor's circumstances are not unusual. Most health care supervisors have been well-trained technically but have had little or no training in oral presentations.

As a nurse, Eleanor considers herself a professional. However, Eleanor considers herself an amateur as a speaker, so she needs to apply conscientious effort to building the confidence essential to her functioning as an effective speaker. Confidence is one of the keys to effective public speaking, and the key to confidence is thorough preparation.

## PREPARATION

> *No person not inspired can make a good speech without preparation.*
>
> —Daniel Webster

It is possible to improve on Webster's statement and suggest that few if any people, inspired or not, can speak well without preparation. It is the rare individual who can deliver a compelling presentation extemporaneously. A certain amount of preparation is usually required; the fewer speeches one has made, the more preparation will be required.

Instead of worrying about facing an audience, one should spend the time getting ready. Most practiced speakers have found that nothing but accumulated speaking experience will eventually minimize prespeech nervousness, but sound preparation will go a long way toward calming the butterflies in the inexperienced speaker's stomach. Preparation begins where the speaker should be most comfortable: with knowledge of the subject.

### Knowing the subject

> *The first rule for speaking well is to think well.*
>
> —Mme. de Lambert

One must know the subject well, but even this is not enough. What is known must be delivered in an organized fashion, intended to accomplish certain results. The knowledge of the speaker has been obtained in bits and pieces, sometimes in random order. To transfer some of this knowledge to the listeners, a speaker needs to be selective about what is conveyed and the order in which it is offered.

A new speaker, especially a first-time presenter, should always prepare more material than the situation seems to call for. One should figure on the worst case likely to be encountered. Perhaps it will be necessary to stretch and fill some extra time, and audience questions will not be forthcoming as hoped. Even the normal case, in which the time available is what had been expected, should be bolstered with plenty of material. The supervisor who has never given a presentation is likely to be surprised at how rapidly his or her material is covered.

A speaker should never underestimate the value of thorough preparation. Eventually, one may decide there is little point in devoting major preparation time to a minor presentation, but first presentations, regardless of their importance, are worth extra time and effort for the sake of gaining confidence.

## The audience

*If the speaker won't boil it down, the audience must sweat it out.*
—Raymond Duncan

Technical professionals speaking on technical topics must give special consideration to the composition of the audience. Two critical factors are the technical level of the presentation and the intended purpose of the speech.

### *Level and purpose*

A technically mixed audience is the most difficult for a speaker. If the listeners range from the newest nursing assistant to the vice-president in charge of patient services, a problem exists. If all remarks are pitched at the level of the vice-president, many listeners will be bewildered; if the speaker addresses the nursing assistant, much of the audience is likely to become bored—and lost to the speaker.

The safest course lies in settling on an average, based on an assessment of those who will hear the presentation. Consider the level of education and technical familiarity most prevalent in the audience, for example registered nurses, nursing administrators or educators, and plan to speak to that level. Not everyone's interest may be captured, but the speaker will be doing the best job possible under the circumstances.

Also influencing language and technical depth will be the intended purpose of the presentation. Essentially, speeches are intended to instruct, stimulate, explore or persuade.

Before beginning to assemble material, it is best to decide on the purpose of the speech. For instance, instruction consists largely of reporting and explaining. One communicates specific information but does not necessarily direct the manner in which the listeners interpret that information. In instruction, there is a strong emphasis on facts.

A presentation intended to stimulate may emphasize facts to a considerable extent or not at all. Facts as such may be unimportant or may be already known and accepted by the listeners; the speech is meant to provide inspiration or insight, strengthen loyalties, create interest or appreciation or simply entertain.

The exploratory presentation finds its use in situations that are not best resolved through solitary thought and action. The supervisor using a speech to explore a problem may present several solutions or possibilities for audience consideration. Exploratory speech is the principal tool of the discussion leader at group problem-solving sessions. The intent is to refine and expand on alternatives through the participation of others.

All speech is persuasive in that it modifies each listener's perception of reality to at least some extent. As a purpose of speech, however, persuasion means to use speech in such a way as to lead the listeners to change their beliefs or behavior in some predetermined way. A speaker "sells" a solution to a problem because he or she believes it is the best solution, or persuades the right group of people to take an interest in a particular problem. The purpose should be clear, and the facts presented and words employed should support that purpose.

Not all presentations have a single purpose; they cannot simply instruct or stimulate or explore or persuade. As medical equipment salespersons have discovered, it is often necessary to instruct the customer in the product's characteristics, to stimulate interest and to persuade the buyer. Although persuasion may be the primary purpose, the specific speech situation calls for attention to other considerations as well. Thus it is necessary to decide on the primary purpose of a presentation—instruction, stimulation, exploration or persuasion—and select and present the facts or arguments accordingly.

### *Size and status*

Two additional factors to consider in assessing the audience are the size of the group and their professional position relative to the speaker and the topic. The larger the group, the fewer the opportunities for keeping the speech on a personal, conversational level. In addition to assailing the new speaker's just-budding confidence—the thought of facing two or three hundred people instead of a dozen can be appalling—there may be restrictions on voice and movement (for instance, it may be necessary to use a microphone). Given a choice, it is best to make first speeches to groups of no more than 20 people.

As to the listeners' professional position relative to the speaker and topic, little more can be said than was said about audience mix—pitch all remarks to the prevailing level of education and technical familiarity. The listeners' professional positions will probably have the greatest influence on the speaker's degree of confidence.

A novice speaker will probably feel most comfortable talking to people who are less thoroughly versed in his or her specialized field, and perhaps not quite so comfortable speaking to educational and professional equals. One may be justifiably frightened into making elaborate, painstaking preparations should one have to face an audience more advanced in the topic than one happens to be.

The foregoing comments suggest that the best situation for the beginning speaker has the following characteristics:

- All listeners are of about the

same technical level, that being less than the speaker's level.
- The group is small.
- It is necessary to concentrate primarily on instruction.

In short, given any choice in the matter, one should start with a teaching assignment in one's chosen field. The best audience for a new speaker is usually a class of students exhibiting the foregoing three characteristics.

**Organizing the material**

One problem experienced by many new speakers is not that they know too little but rather that they know too much. Or they try to reveal too much in too little time and in no particular order. What the presenter has to say must follow a pattern.

***One problem experienced by many new speakers is not that they know too little but rather that they know too much.***

There are numerous ways to organize material. Most applicable to the health care field are the topical formats, including the time-honored scholarly paper format of background, problem, methodology, findings and conclusions. Using this outline, the speaker offers pertinent background information, defines the problem, discusses the approach to alternative solutions, reveals what was discovered and offers conclusions or recommendations. Other topical designs include arrangements of criteria, for instance quality, price, service and appearance, and the general questions of who, what, where, when, how and why.

Health care professionals' speech needs are often also served by simple logical arrangements such as: cause, effect and correction; problem, damage and solution; need, desirability and practicality; and past, present and future. Patterns may also be spatial or geographic, such as: federal, state and local; hospital, west wing and coronary care unit; and left, center and right.

Using the past-present-future pattern and adding to it as appropriate, a broad topical outline for Eleanor's flextime scheduling presentation can be developed (see box). There should be considerably more substance to an outline than Eleanor's contains, and many more points and subpoints as well. Regardless of the amount of detail employed—and it is better to err on the side of too much rather than too little detail—the speaker should take care to have all main points identified in their order of presentation.

Proper main-point structure offers another benefit besides providing the essential organization of a presentation. Time is frequently a critical consideration; the speaker suddenly discovers that it is necessary to either stretch to fill or trim to fit. With clear main-point headings available, it is possible to appropriately expand or condense with less risk of unbalancing the presentation by omitting some important points.

**Broad Topical Outline**

1. Introduction
   A. Opener (anecdote, appealing or revealing statistics, or challenging question) to introduce speaker and topic.
   B. Preview (revealing the theme in brief, enumerating the main headings to be developed).
2. Body
   A. *Past* (perhaps problems and weaknesses in traditional scheduling techniques for certain classes of personnel; the stimulus prompting recent efforts; the conditions needing improvement).
   B. *Present* (the flextime-scheduling project—where it stands and what it is accomplishing).
   C. *Future* (the directions in which current developments are likely to lead this hospital and the health care industry).
3. Conclusion
   A. Summary (a recapitulation, emphasizing the theme of the speech).
   B. Closer (a hard-hitting restatement of the theme; it may be an anecdote or quotation, or it may tie back to the Opener and offer new insight).

## PRESENTATION

### Text or notes?

*I always dislike using a manuscript in making a speech. It's like courting through a picket fence. Everything that is said can be heard, but there isn't much contact.*

—Eugene Smith

Reading a prepared text robs a presentation of spontaneity. It does not hurt to write a text; this forces thorough organization, and it fixes many remarks in the speaker's mind. It is possible to develop excellent speaking notes from a text, notes that are far more complete than those made from an outline. However, to put life into a fully prepared speech, one must be more actor than speaker. Also, much audience contact is lost because the speaker's eyes are frequently on the paper. A prepared text is recommended only when the topic is so sensitive or controversial that every word must be weighed and reweighed before delivery.

Three- by five-inch note cards containing the topic outline are best. One method is to write each point or subpoint on a separate card along with whatever reminders or other backup information may be needed. With a little practice, it is possible to capture all the information needed on a pack of file cards that will slide into a pocket and fit neatly into the palm of one hand when needed.

Note cards should be typed or legibly hand-lettered, because you will need to find each word at a glance. Use all capital letters and triple spacing between lines. Other gimmicks include using a two-color underlining scheme to note a shift to another point or the need to turn to visual aids for support.

One word of caution about note cards: number them in sequence so that none will be missed and there will be no confusion about their order. Many experienced speakers have grim recollections of dropped notes. (Picture a handful of unnumbered cards gently fluttering to the floor like so many autumn leaves while the audience awaits the next remark.)

## Visual aids

Depending on the formality or structure of the presentation, the speaker may want to use slides, overhead transparencies, a chalkboard or other visual aids. It is important to remember, however, that visual aids should supplement a speech, not attempt to carry it.

Color slides—35 mm transparencies—are helpful in formal presentations, especially those that must be given repeatedly. For a one-time speech, however, slides generally entail too much trouble and expense, unless the speech is a major event. The principal hazard of slides (other than the risk of projector malfunction) is darkness. There is no better way to encourage nappers than to turn the lights down low.

The most easily used visual aid is an overhead projector and 8½-by-11-inch transparencies reproduced on an office copier from masters made on a typewriter (all capital letters of the largest available type) or done by hand using lettering guides or rub-on type. Avoid the tendency to put too much information on a single sheet; seven or eight well-spaced lines of a few words each should be the limit. The audience should hear the speaker as they see a key word or a pertinent picture; they should not have to read full passages of fine print while listening.

## Verbal tics

The supervisor who wants to develop as a speaker should make a tape recording of himself or herself doing a presentation and analyze it with brutal frankness. Listen especially for nonword sounds that may be used, the "verbal tics" that fill the conversations of so many people (listen to a half-dozen taped interviews on any news broadcast to know exactly what is meant here).

The serious would-be speaker should work to eliminate all verbal tics. Becoming aware of what one is doing when speaking is more than half the battle; the rest is the conscious control of every sound that comes from one's mouth. Verbal tics are "thinking time" for many speakers, but that essential time does not have to be sacrificed. Pauses of two or three seconds are normal, and sometimes a brief silence is as compelling as a shout. In any case, two or three seconds of silence are much to be preferred over two or three seconds of "and-uhhhh!"

Also, listen for what happens to words uttered without care. Does *for* come out *fer*? Does *to* sound more like *ta*? This is not to suggest that elocution lessons are needed before giving one's first job-related presentation. However, listening to one's own voice and correcting glaring inconsistencies will vastly improve one's speaking style with very little effort.

### Timing

*It isn't the first-hand information that makes the best speech, but second-hand timing.*

—Hal Chadwick

As suggested earlier, with plenty of material and a good outline, a speech can be expanded or contracted according to the demands of the clock. A new speaker who is concerned about the extent of preparation and wants to know how long a speech will take should make a dry run against the clock. This should not be done silently; if you just "think your way through," the material will be covered too quickly.

An actual speech situation is needed. A small audience—perhaps two or three associates or family members—will hold the speaker to a speed closer to that of actual delivery. A speaker who is using a prepared text or falling back on a fully written speech to estimate time should use the rule of thumb employed by many professional speech writers: 150 words of text equals approximately one minute of speaking time.

### Humor

*True humor springs not more from the head than from the heart; it is not contempt, its essence is love; it issues not in laughter, but in smiles, which lie far deeper.*

—Thomas Carlyle

A presentation may lend itself to the use of humorous anecdotes and illustrations; the topic may have its lighter side. However, do not force the use of humor. Humor in a speech ought to occur naturally, related to the topic or theme. Then, when a supposedly funny comment fails to get a laugh, it may still have contributed toward making a point.

In speaking as in writing, humor is difficult to handle well. It defies consistent treatment. What is funny to one person may vary from time to time and also be influenced by the mood and surroundings of the moment. And what is funny to one person may not be funny to another.

Regardless of the so-called permissiveness of the times, it is still best to keep remarks as inoffensive as possible. A speaker has no guarantee that he or she will never upset a listener with something said in jest. But ethnic or even slightly off-color remarks will certainly meet with someone's disfavor in the average listening group.

If you are going to poke fun at anyone, be your own target. Take care, however, to portray yourself as a normal human being with normal shortcomings. It is easy to go overboard and look foolish.

In short, humor in a speech should flow from the topic and the situation and serve a purpose other than simple entertainment. A speaker should not try to be a stand-up comic—the "act" could open and close with a single appearance.

### Style

With time and experience, each speaker will develop a style that is in some ways unique and that tells the audience a great deal about the speaker as an individual. It would be presumptuous to dictate what a particular speaker's style should be; however, there are ways to make each speech more effective than the last.

***With time and experience, each speaker will develop a style that is in some ways unique and that tells the audience a great deal about the speaker as an individual.***

Always be aware of the verbal tics discussed earlier; work to eliminate them until they are no longer an automatic recourse during speech. Develop a preference for the concrete word over the abstract one. For instance, avoid saying "machine" when actually referring to a "volumetric infusion pump," and avoid saying "early morning" when "6:00 A.M." will send a clearer, more specific message.

Watch out for loaded words that create unintended impressions. Control your words, so that most of the impressions created are intentional, to make or reinforce points. For example, "eager beaver" says one thing to listeners; "interested and tireless worker" says something quite different.

Use anecdotes and case histories whenever possible to illustrate points and keep the topic firmly linked to the real working world. Speak in personal terms—you, we, us—to establish and maintain the necessary interrelationship of speaker, topic and audience.

Remain aware of other factors influencing the manner in which speaker and material are received: vocal range, varied rather than monotone; enunciation, especially of key words intended to register strong impressions; body movements, with at least some limited movement; and facial expressions, which often say more than the words about the speaker's enthusiasm for the topic.

Finally, practice establishing eye contact with members of the audience. Look directly at numerous listeners in turn throughout the presentation. Visually sweep the room, but frequently linger a few seconds on first one person and then another. Ultimately, the speaker should cause each listener to feel that he or she has been communicated with personally.

## FOLLOW-UP

After completing a first speech—or any presentation for that matter—the speaker's attention should turn to self-evaluation. The all-important word is feedback. The speaker should stimulate feedback, by encouraging questions and in discussions after the speech. The speaker should use such feedback to strengthen the material and refine speaking techniques. Also to be assessed is timing, through a comparison of estimated delivery time with the time actually required to give the presentation.

The feelings experienced by the speaker while speaking and immediately after speaking should indicate the adequacy of preparation. It is only during and after the speech that one will know whether the preparation was sufficient.

If the talk was recorded, after two or three days the speaker should play it back and critically analyze his or her technique. Once past the humbling experience of hearing himself or herself as others do, the speaker will be able to spot mistakes and go about correcting them.

## PRACTICE

As a group, health care personnel are neither better nor worse communicators than other professionals. Most health care professionals, however, are not trained speakers.

There are numerous supervisors and other health care personnel who are excellent public speakers, but most of them did not come by it naturally. They faced speaking assignments head-on, sought advice or assistance and refused to concede to stage fright. And they kept at it, presentation after presentation, until they attained a commendable degree of speaking skill.

Public speaking can be an extremely useful tool for health care supervisors to have. Those who happen to get an assignment, such as the one Eleanor received, should not regard it as a calamity. It is actually a golden opportunity for professional growth and development.

# From idea to print: writing and publishing a journal article

*Charles R. McConnell*
*Vice President for Employee Affairs*
*The Genesee Hospital*
*Rochester, New York*

EVERY JOURNAL reader who has experienced the desire to write an article for publication should find encouragement in one simple statement of fact: The overwhelming majority of people who write for professional and management journals are working professionals and working managers. Like most of the readers of this journal, these journal writers are pursuing full-time careers in the fields they have chosen to write about.

Most active journal writers cannot be called professional writers in any sense of the word. Although many of them produce writing of professional quality, they do not depend on writing for part of their income. Relatively few journal writers are actually part-time professional authors who earn a portion of their living by way of the written word, but even these active authors pursue full-time nonwriting careers that require most of their time and attention.

*Health Care Superv*, 1984,2(2),78–94

What is the primary difference between the writers of journal articles and the readers of journal articles? For the most part, the writers are simply readers who have discovered that a significant amount of personal satisfaction lies as close at hand as their typewriters.

## WHY WRITE A JOURNAL ARTICLE?

It is certainly not for financial reward that one ordinarily writes a journal article. Most technical and professional journals do not pay their authors. The author of a published journal article usually receives only a copy or two of the issue the work appears in and perhaps a number of "off-prints" (copies of the article itself). Seldom is there any money involved. Occasionally an author will be paid if an article is specifically requested, but this practice is generally reserved for persons who are recognized authorities in their fields and who have established themselves as authors.

Since the process usually results in no financial reward, why should a supervisor, manager or working professional put forth the effort required to write a journal article and secure its publication? For some people, this question may be answered through consideration of the advantages one may enjoy in writing an article and having it published. Following is a list of these advantages.

- Publication provides one with the opportunity to share one's knowledge or ideas with others.
- Publication may also provide the opportunity to make a positive contribution to one's chosen field.
- Depending on the individual, there is sometimes considerable ego gratification involved in publication; one acquires "publication credits" and is able to see his or her name in print.
- Publication may provide an immense feeling of satisfaction relating to the successful completion of a difficult task.
- The research that must often be done in the development of a journal article frequently expands the knowledge and insights of the author.
- Finally, the author who has seen a journal article through to publication has experienced valuable practice in working with the written word.

Whenever one encounters advantages, however, there are often offsetting disadvantages to be reckoned with. The greatest practical disadvantage, often outweighing all of the apparent advantages for some persons who would like to see themselves in print but who have not followed through, is the considerable amount of sometimes difficult and frustrating work involved in developing an article and seeing it through to a form in which it is publishable. There can be a considerable amount of work involved, especially for the first-time author. In addition to the major visible disadvantage of this work, there is another, more subtle disadvantage in

***In submitting an article, one is exposing one's self to criticism and possible rejection.***

attempting to write for publication: In submitting an article, one is exposing one's self to criticism and possible rejection.

Stemming from thoughts of rejection, some additional comments are in order about the previously cited advantage of acquiring writing practice. As is the case with many other human skills, writing skill is developed primarily by working at it. False starts, multiple drafts, roadblocks and frustrations may all be part of the writing process. Development of one's self as a writer requires discipline, determination, the ability to deal with criticism and rejection, and a great deal of self-criticism.

Most of all, the would-be author must like to write or must at least have the desire to *learn how* to like writing. Many people will openly admit that they do not like to write. These people, who will write no more than an appointment note or a grocery list if left to their own preferences, tend to labor with great difficulty when trapped by the necessity to write an occasional letter or memorandum. These people do not like to write, and writing is difficult for them. However, they are caught in the classic chicken-or-egg situation: Do they dislike writing because it is difficult for them, or is writing difficult for them because they dislike it? If an individual's case is the former—writing is disliked because it is difficult—a liking for writing can be developed by working at writing and allowing conscientious practice to make the process easier and thus more likable.

People vary markedly in how rapidly they are able to develop their writing skills. However, there are relatively few "natural writers" in the world, and what is often referred to as "talent" for writing is usually a level of skill that has emerged as a result of hard work. For many would-be writers the first successfully completed article may turn out to have been a chore of immense proportions. However, one can count on the process becoming both easier and more satisfying as one gets better at it.

## THE IDEA VERSUS THE WRITING

Which major element of an article is more important, the idea or the writing? Both are obviously of considerable importance, but if forced to make a choice between the two, the writing should be considered more important than the idea.

In view of the majority of editors and probably the majority of published writers as well, useful ideas are far easier to come by than good writing. A sound, appealing idea may be completely obscured and rendered virtually unpublishable by poor writing. On the other hand, an idea that is weak or thin can be given life by lively, intelligent writing.

In most cases, the conception of the idea and the making of the decisions regarding its specific treatment are but a small part of the work involved in generating a publishable article. Though the task of writing may come to naught or may never begin in the first place if a usable idea is not generated, once the task of thoroughly developing the idea on paper is begun it becomes evident (at least to the person manipulating the words) that the overwhelming proportion of the actual work lies in the writing.

As one of the most elemental acts of communication, writing is the process of transmitting ideas by way of visible symbols (words) to persons who are separated by time and distance from the person who has generated the ideas. The best idea in the world will amount to nothing if it is not put into a form in which it can be understood and used by others. There is a saying, old but destined to remain pertinent as long as thought must be transmitted by way of language: "The genius who cannot communicate an idea is fully as hampered as the fool who cannot conceive one."

The idea that one may use for writing a journal article need not be an idea that has never been used before. Truly original ideas, one will discover, are extremely few and far between. Rather, it is the idea taken together with the particular slant, approach or treatment that determines usability. More often than not, a "new" idea for a journal article results from a different twist on an old idea, a juxtaposition of old ideas, or an old idea that has simply been brought up to date with new information. A simple brainstorming exercise or a modest amount of research can be counted on to reveal numerous ideas that could be developed into articles. No matter how diverse, however, all of these ideas will have one thing in common: They will all require clear, literate writing to turn them into published articles.

## KNOWING THE AUDIENCE

It is essential that the would-be writer have some knowledge of the persons making up the readership of the journal for which he or she would like to write. One must acquire a reasonably accurate grasp of a number of characteristics of this audience, including their educational level, the depth and breadth of their knowledge of the author's subject, their needs as readers, their desires in terms of the things they would like to see in print, the problems they most commonly encounter on the job, the likely level of language they are most comfortable with, and the degree of variation in all of the preceding factors likely to be encountered within the audience. One must write for the journal's primary audience, those readers at whom the publication is targeted. Most journals also serve secondary audiences—and anyone outside of the journal's target audience who picks up a copy and reads an article can be included in a secondary audience—but it is the primary audience to whom the writers are addressing their comments.

The primary audience for a journal may be relatively narrow, limited to one specific technical field. For example, physicians make up the primary audience for the *Journal of the American Medical Association.* Or the primary audience may encompass persons with a variety of specialty backgrounds who nevertheless have a common interest. For example, *The Health Care Supervisor* (*HCS*) serves as its primary audience all persons employed in supervisory or managerial capacities in health care institutions (with health care institutions being the common tie).

A journal article must be directed toward the appropriate audience, and knowing as much as possible about the audience is a large part of knowing about the publication itself. Each publication takes a particular approach to serving its audience. This approach is evident in the kinds of topics the journal presents and the manner in which these topics are dealt with. Through reading and study the would-be writer must absorb the particular journal's specific approach and reflect that approach in his or her writing.

The major purposes of written communication can be said to be *information, instruction, persuasion* and *entertainment.* Although two or three or perhaps even all four of these purposes may be served by a specific piece of writing, only one of these will stand as the primary purpose. For example, the primary purpose of a work of fiction is to entertain, although in entertaining it may also inform, instruct and persuade to some lesser extent. The primary purpose of a piece of sales literature is to persuade, but the persuasion may be accomplished at least in part through information, instruction and entertainment.

The primary purposes of journal articles are information and instruction. An informational article provides the reader with the means to knowledge, awareness, explanation or some other form of information. For example, within this present volume of *HCS* the article, "Principles of Accounting and Finance for the Nonaccountant" is an informational article. Instructional articles are those that have a "how-to" flavor to them; the advice they provide is intended to be applied by readers. This article which the reader is now perusing is an example of an instructional article.

## WRITING STYLES

Because it deals with business and scientific information in a number of forms, journal writing is, in a broad sense, technical writing. There are three major styles of technical writing, two of which are highly applicable to journals.

### Pure technical style

The pure technical style of writing usually involves business or technical professionals writing for other business or technical professionals in the same specialty field or some closely related field. The *Journal of the American Medical Association* is an example of a journal written in the pure technical style; it primarily features physicians writing for other physicians. Likewise, a journal such as *Topics in Health Record Management* may be said to be assembled in the pure technical style because its focus is largely on health record practitioners writing for other health record practitioners.

Within the pure technical style authors are generally able to make free use, without the need for definitions, of all the terminology of the specialty field and even much of the jargon and "in-language" associated with the field. When writing in the pure technical style the author may assume equivalent technical knowledge of all members of the primary audience; essentially, the author is communicating peer to peer. Also, the pure technical style is marked by the use of relatively formal English; that is, it is written in the third person and is free of slang and contractions and other elements of conversational language.

### Middle technical style

The middle technical style is characterized by authors of a variety of technical and professional backgrounds writing for readers with a variety of technical and professional backgrounds, with all parties possessing some unifying factor that brings them into the journal's scope. The common ground will not be as narrow as a single technical specialty; rather, it will be of sufficient breadth to encompass the involvement of a variety of specialty backgrounds. The most common unifying characteristic found in journals of the middle technical style is concern with a given industry or subindustry. As an example, again consider *HCS*. Members of the primary audience have diverse technical backgrounds, but all have a common interest in supervision or management in the health care setting. As another example, *Hospitals*, published by the American Hospital Association, serves a primary audience of people of varied specialty backgrounds but all of whom are united in their interest in running hospitals or major functions in hospitals.

When working within the middle technical style it is extremely important for the author, who will probably be writing about a given technical specialty, to avoid overpowering the reader with the specific terminology, jargon and other in-language of that

***When working within the middle technical writing style it is extremely important to avoid overpowering the reader with the specific terminology, jargon and in-language of the specific field.***

specific field. This represents the key difference in the execution of the middle technical style versus the pure technical style—in the middle technical style, the writer cannot assume that the reader is fully conversant with all of the terms that he or she might ordinarily use. The writer may of course make some assumptions about the knowledge of people who work in the hospital setting—they will likely be familiar with *admission, X-ray, health maintenance organization, hospice* and other generic health care terms. However, the biomedical engineer laboring as an author had best not make mention of *telemetry* and move on without at least briefly describing the process and the equipment. Also, the computer specialist-turned-author had best not make fleeting reference to *RAM* and move on without explaining that RAM stands for random access memory and briefly describing how it works. In the middle technical style the author can assume no more than surface knowledge of the language of any particular technical specialty. In writing in the pure technical style, the computer specialist may refer to the *CPU* (and not even have to say that this means central processing unit). However, in writing in the middle technical style, this same computer specialist should probably avoid central processing unit altogether and refer to the *main computer*.

Although more terms must be explained in more detail in the middle technical style, writing done in this style is similar to writing done in the pure technical style in that the language employed is relatively formal.

### Popular technical style

Although the popular technical style is generally not pertinent to journal writing, brief mention of the style will round out the discussion of the technical writing styles. The popular technical style is used for consumption by the general public. In this style all but the most commonly known terms are explained, most technical elements are described in everyday words, and very little common bond among readers is assumed other than the ability to read English. Related to the health care field, some examples of material presented in the popular technical style are articles appearing in publications such as *Health and Fitness, Today's Health* and *Reader's Digest*. The language employed in the popular technical style is often informal and considerably closer to conversational language than the language of the other styles.

To reiterate, the key difference between the two styles of technical writing applicable to journals—the pure technical and the middle technical—lies in the level of the technical language employed. The pure technical style assumes thorough, inside knowledge of the terminology of a specific field; the middle technical style assumes superficial knowledge only of the terminology of any specific field. Beyond this surface knowledge, the middle technical style assumes only a broad common bond among the readers.

## THE PROCESS: FROM IDEA TO PRINT

Having established the background relative to audience and style, attention will now turn to a brief examination of the major steps involved in taking an idea from its conception to the finished product on the printed page.

### Idea, slant and market

It is necessary to jointly consider the idea, the slant and the market because the approach to be taken in writing an article will be dictated by the requirements of the publication for which the article is intended. The idea must be of relevance to the readership of the specific journal, and the writing style must be consistent with that which is characteristic of most of that journal's articles.

One can always proceed to write an article first and then attempt to find a journal that will publish it. However, once written, the article exists in a form that may be inappropriate to some, many or perhaps all of the possible markets. One will certainly not lose completely by writing the article first—the writing practice is always valuable—but if one is serious about publication, it is better to first locate an interested journal and then pattern the article according to that journal's requirements.

### Article proposal

One's idea for an article should be thought out and developed to the stage at which it may be succinctly expressed in a proposal letter. This letter, written in the form of ordinary business correspondence and preferably no longer than one typewritten, single-spaced page, should include the following:

- a theme statement in the form of a one- or two-sentence encapsulation of the basic idea;
- a compelling statement about the approach to be taken, clearly stating how and why the author's treatment of this idea will in some way be new, different or special;
- a clear statement as to why the topic is important to the journal's readers (in effect, the author's brief "sales pitch");
- a working title for the article (called a "working" title because it will be carried through the writing stages but will remain subject to change because a more appropriate title often suggests itself as the work progresses);
- a reasonable amount of time, usually stated in number of weeks or months after receipt of approval to proceed, for the writer to deliver a finished manuscript;
- approximate length of the finished article as presently envisioned, in number of words or number of manuscript pages (in lieu of this or perhaps in addition to this the author may offer to

produce the article at a length to be specified by the editor);

- a statement of the author's qualifications to write the article (this should not consist of "resumé attached"; all that is required is a brief paragraph of perhaps two or three sentences revealing a bit of the author's background pertinent to the article's topic);
- mention of the author's previous publication credits (that is, if there are any; an author who is yet to be published should simply remain silent on this point);
- a request for the journal to provide a copy of any writer's guidelines that they may desire their authors to follow.

This proposal letter should be addressed to the journal's editor. The editor's name can be found, in most journals, on one of the first two or three pages of any issue along with the address of the journal's editorial offices.

A proposal letter is generally more appropriate than a complete, unsolicited manuscript. In addition to saving the writer the mailing cost of the shot-in-the-dark submission of a complete article, the proposal letter saves time. Whether the idea is appropriate or not, the editor can usually react more quickly to a proposal letter than to a manuscript. A proposal letter also accomplishes the following.

- It helps the author avoid a great deal of work that may prove to be unnecessary if the idea is unacceptable to any journal serving the author's field.
- If the idea is favorably received by the editor, the proposal letter gives the editor the opportunity to make suggestions aimed at helping the author shape the article to the journal's needs.
- An accepted proposal, perhaps accompanied by suggestions for developing the article, can provide added motivation for the author to complete the project.

Even if one has an article completely written and ready to submit, it may often be better to describe the article in a one-page proposal letter and use that to attempt to stimulate an editor's interest.

Ideally, a proposal letter should be accompanied by a self-addressed stamped envelope (SASE). In the world of commercial book and magazine publishing the SASE is a firm requirement—proposals not accompanied by one are discarded and manuscripts not accompanied by the SASE are likewise discarded. This seeming hard-line stand is fully accepted throughout general publishing; if it were not, most publishers would go broke in short order simply returning the staggering number of unusable manuscripts and proposals they receive. Conditions are somewhat different in journal publishing, however, because the flow of proposals and manuscripts is considerably less than it is in general publishing. Nevertheless, journal editors do get swamped with mail from time to time, and one may find that the intelligent proposal accompanied by the SASE is the easiest to respond to.

Also, some journals are produced on a relatively tight budget, and a rash of proposals or manuscripts can generate considerable mailing expense.

Working with a journal, and whether submitting a proposal or sending a complete manuscript, it is best to include the SASE with the first submission to an editor. If this first contact is successful and results in a go-ahead on the proposal or an acceptance of the article, one may omit the SASE from future correspondence. Also, authors who have established themselves with a particular journal through repeated successful contributions can ordinarily omit the SASE altogether.

## The article

On receipt of the acceptance of the proposal the author should proceed with writing the article, incorporating any suggestions that the editor may have offered.

It is important to be mindful that the acceptance of the proposal is simply an invitation for the author to write the article "on speculation." That is, the author is not guaranteed in advance that the article will be published. Most editors will not capriciously approve proposals and ask that articles be written only to reject them on submission. An editor will usually be serious about asking an author to proceed with an article; but even though the idea may appear sound and appealing in proposal form, the author may not be able to translate the idea into a publishable finished product. Quite simply, an invitation to write an article "on speculation" means that acceptance and publication depend entirely on the quality of the finished product.

***Quite simply, an invitation to write an article "on speculation" means that acceptance and publication depend entirely on the quality of the finished product.***

In developing the article, the author should conscientiously follow the journal's editorial guidelines relative to language and style and even to much more mechanical requirements as manuscript length or the number or type of illustrations that are permitted. Most journals, and especially the book-type quarterly journals such as *HCS*, have a specific number of pages to work with in each issue. A journal will frequently specify a target length or at least a length range for submissions. By doing so, the journal's editorial staff is able to determine in advance the approximate number of articles it will be working with in a given issue.

It has often been said that writing cannot be taught but it can be *learned.* This reflects a bit of reality that authors have been discovering and rediscovering since someone first set words to parchment (or perhaps to stone): Most of what one learns about writing is self-taught, absorbed by reading the output of good writers and brought out and refined through the practice of putting countless words on paper.

Whenever an author approaches a piece of written work, he or she must be trying to do the best possible job. One cannot expect to simply throw ideas at the paper and "let the editors clean it up." Admittedly, journal editors, much more than editors in the general publications field, will work with an author to help develop a finished product. This is so because, as pointed out earlier, most journal authors are not professional writers. However, an author should still attempt to submit the best possible finished work even though he or she may face a high probability of the need for revision.

This brief presentation is not the place for a writing course or a course in basic English. Suffice to say that decent command of the language is required in writing a journal article. If one has reasonable command of the language, one has a good start at writing for journals. Even if one lacks such command of the language, this can be developed with conscious effort.

Without resorting to a lecture on the rights or wrongs of language usage, some pertinent style guides are offered for consideration by the would-be journal author.

**Strong opening**

State the essence of the theme at the beginning, and attempt to draw the reader immediately into the article with a device such as an anecdote that illustrates the theme; a dramatic pronouncement; a compelling statistic or some other evidence; or a strong problem statement. Let the opening of the article speak for itself. Avoid such openings as, "This article will discuss. . . ."

**Effective ending**

An article should not be allowed to end in midair simply because the author has run out of things to say or has covered the last planned point. An ending statement should be provided that either briefly summarizes the conclusions to be drawn from the article or ties the article's finish back to its opening.

**Abbreviations and acronyms**

Few people involved in health care need to be told that the field abounds with abbreviations and acronyms. When using such, write out each such term in full the first time it is used, follow its written form with the acronym, and then feel free to apply the acronym alone in subsequent mentions. For example, one might mention the Joint Commission on Accreditation of Hospitals (JCAH) near the beginning of an article and, for all subsequent mentions, use JCAH only.

**Subheadings**

Use frequent subheadings to highlight the development of the article's topic. This helps to break the material into distinct parts and makes it easier for the reader to stay in step with the progression of the material.

**Language**

Journal writing need not necessarily be "scholarly" writing—applying here the popular notion of scholarly writing as writing that uses a great many big words, lengthy meandering compound sentences, seemingly endless paragraphs and much general stuffing. There are many prevailing misconceptions regarding what is true scholarly writing and what is simply "purple prose." It is true that the journal writer, especially working within health care, will find it necessary to use some big words. However, regardless of the length of the words that must be used, the basis of all good journal writing is the simple declarative sentence.

The writer who is looking for assistance in learning how to handle the language better should consult some of the many books available on language and writing technique. One of the best such references, perhaps best because it is one of the most compact and easily used, is *The Elements of Style*, 2d ed., by William Strunk, Jr., and E.B. White (Macmillan Publishing Co., 1972).

Following are some additional pointers pertinent to *HCS* and thus to most journals written in the middle technical style.

- Avoid contractions. Instead of the conversational *don't* and *can't*, use *do not* and *cannot*.
- Completely avoid the use of the first person (*I*, *me*), and avoid more than token use of the second person (*you*). Rather, write in the third person referring to the likes of *the supervisor*, *managers*, *they*, etc.
- Avoid the use of the slash construction—two supposedly interchangeable words divided by a slash, as in *and/or*, *he/she* or *this/that*. Not only is this clumsy construction, in most instances it is unnecessary.
- Avoid sexism in writing, but do so through appropriate structure rather than by creating other problems. The use of *he/she* can usually be avoided by restructuring the sentence, or the slash construction can be replaced without difficulty by *he or she*.

Also, there is a related problem that has become prevalent since many people have begun to consciously avoid sexist language—the use of a plural pronoun in reference to a singular noun simply to avoid sexism. Years ago, for example, a writer might have said, "Each and every manager should respect his employees." However, this conveys the sexist assumption that all managers are male. To avoid being sexist, many writers and speakers are now saying the likes of, "Each and every manager should respect their employees." One does not have to be a language purist to know that this is wrong. More importantly, however, to many readers it is a glaring transgression that disrupts the flow of the material as surely as a pot hole disrupts one's trip down an otherwise smooth road. All sexism can be avoided in the writing process, usually with no more than simple restructuring of sentences. For one who is interested in ways to effectively eliminate sexism from writing, a helpful book is *The Handbook of Non-Sexist Writing,* by Casey Miller and Kate Swift (New York: Lippincott and Crowell, 1980).

**The article, revised**

The author's first and harshest critic should be the author. A draft, especially if set aside for a day or two after completion, will reveal many of its flaws and shortcomings on careful reading by the author. It is in the process of revision prior to initial submission that the author is called on to exercise the most discipline and determination. The revision process may require two drafts, three drafts, or four or more drafts. The key to this process is that the author should not commit the article to final manuscript form until convinced that it represents the best job that he or she can do.

**Manuscript preparation and submission**

If working on a go-ahead from a journal, the author should follow that journal's requirements for manuscript preparation. If the article is being written with no assignment in hand or no particular journal's requirements in mind, the following generally applicable guidelines should be considered.

- The finished article should be typed, double-spaced, with at least one-inch margins on all sides of the page.
- Pages should be numbered sequentially.
- The paper should be $8\frac{1}{2}'' \times 11''$ only, and always white. No pastels or other colored papers should be used (many of these do not copy cleanly). The writer should also avoid the crinkly, so-called "erasable" bond papers; these smear easily in handling, and a manuscript must be handled considerably during the editing processes. The best paper to use for manuscript typing is the plain white paper used in most of the dry photocopy processes.
- The finished manuscript should simply be paper-clipped. No fancy covers, binders or even staples are necessary; these must all be discarded when the manuscript goes into production.

The finished manuscript should be mailed flat in a $9'' \times 12''$ envelope with first-class postage affixed. Although it should usually be accompanied by a cover letter, this letter should be brief and in most cases need not say, in effect, more than, "Here it is." A cover letter should *never* be used to justify something that was said in the article or to explain why a particular approach was taken. Rather, the finished article must speak completely for itself.

**Requested revisions**

Although it may be disheartening to see one's article returned thoroughly marked up, very often the extent of the comments reflects the amount of time and effort given the manuscript by the editor.

It is to the advantage of the author to attempt to comply as thoroughly as possible with the revisions suggested by the editor. In the process of doing so one may have to see one's favorite phrase or that "perfectly beautiful sentence" vanish from the article. One should rest assured, however, that the editor's primary purpose in suggesting changes is to render the article publishable by making it as useful as possible to the journal's readers.

***It is to the advantage of the author to attempt to comply as thoroughly as possible with the revisions suggested by the editor.***

Also, it is appropriate at this point to again mention that editors of journals will often go out of their way to offer detailed constructive criticism. In this way they will work with new writers to an extent that editors of many other publications cannot afford to do.

In submitting requested revisions, the author should make every effort to meet the editor's timing. Often when a manuscript has reached this stage it is under serious consideration for a particular issue and the editor will have specific schedules in mind. Once having agreed to a date to deliver a revision, or for that matter to deliver any stage of a project, the author should make every effort to meet the promised date. If one sees that a promised date cannot be met, the editor should be notified as soon as this is known.

**Publication**

For a considerable time it may seem as though the accepted manuscript over which one labored so long and hard has been swallowed up in the system and forgotten. Much must take place after all of the articles for a given issue have been assembled and the editor has begun work on the next issue, and it could take anywhere from perhaps a minimum of three or four months to a year or longer before the issue including one's work is distributed. At the time the issue is released the author will receive whatever author's copies are provided according to the policy of the journal.

## WHAT ABOUT REJECTION?

Nearly all writers, including full-time professional authors, part-time professional writers and once-in-a-while writers of journal articles, have experienced rejection. Although all writers are likely to suffer a significant rate of rejection when they are first learning the processes of writing and marketing their work, even many established professional authors are regularly rejected.

One should never regard a rejection as a crushing defeat or a personal affront. Rather, one should analyze the rejected work to determine why it was adjudged unsuitable for publication and try to determine what one can do to either rewrite the rejected piece for submission elsewhere or make one's next article a better piece of work. What one does with a particular article will of course depend on the reasons why it was rejected. Rejection will ordinarily mean one or more of the following.

1. The article did not measure up to the standards of the publication. This may imply that it is simply not well enough written to make it worth working with.
2. The idea on which the article is based may be too weak or too thin for article-length presentation.
3. The idea or topic may be inappropriate to the specific publication.
4. The journal may have published an article on the same theme or topic in the recent past.
5. The specific journal may have a similar article planned, either somewhere in the preparation process or perhaps even finished and in or awaiting production.

The first two of the preceding reasons are understandably the most difficult for an author to accept because they say, in effect, that the idea was no good or that the writing was poor. But also, understandably, editors may be reluctant to address the real reasons head-on—so the author should examine his or her own rejected work with an extremely critical eye, perhaps even comparing it with successful published work, and be brutally honest about assessing the quality of the writing and the idea.

The remaining three reasons do not necessarily mean that the article was substandard as a piece of writing. The third reason, concerning the inappropriateness of the idea for the journal, may simply mean that insufficient care was taken in selecting a target publication for the idea. In this case rejection may have occurred because the author simply submitted to the wrong publication.

The fourth and fifth reasons suggest that the target publication may have been the right one but that the author's timing was wrong. One can minimize the chances of being trapped by the fourth reason, submitting to a journal that used a similar article in the recent past, by screening the past several issues of the target publication. Journals will of course repeat the use of similar themes and topics in their articles, but they will do so only at respectable intervals (perhaps one to two years between appearances of the same specific topic).

The fifth stated reason for rejection, that the publication has a similar article in work, can present problems because the author has no way of knowing what is indeed in work until an attempt is made to find out by submitting either an article or a proposal. This is one of the best reasons for making use of proposals. A proposal allows one to minimize the chances of wasting much of the work involved in writing an article to the style of a specific publication if that publication already has an article on the same topic in the hands of another writer. Periodical publications tend to work several issues ahead because of the time involved in some of the processes. Consider what may be happening at any particular time with a quarterly journal: One issue is in the process of being distributed to readers, the next issue is completely packaged and about to enter production, the following issue may be partly in the hands of the editor and partly in the hands of individual writers, and articles for the next issue and subsequent issues may be in the hands of numerous other writers. It is not unusual for a quarterly such as *HCS* which uses perhaps seven to ten articles per issue, to have 20 to 30 projects in the hands of writers, most of these assigned on speculation.

If an article shows promise but obviously needs work, the editor may suggest how it may be improved. Such comments are an encouraging sign, so the author should remain open to the editor's suggestions and follow them as closely as possible. When it comes to having to alter one's "deathless prose," the author should remember that one is not writing to please one's self but rather to please the *readers*. And it is the editor's job to be the judge of what will please the readers.

The aspiring writer should keep in mind that most editors are writers as well, and it is likely that they were themselves often rejected. However, they got to be published writers by working with other editors and following suggestions. Furthermore, they became published writers also by learning to match the style and the tone of the publications they were writing for.

To offer a final word about rejection, the would-be author should regard it not as the end of the road but simply as a single step on the way to publication. Rejection is but one of several obstacles that must be overcome.

## IS IT WORTH THE EFFORT?

It is only the author who can say, once the words are on the page forever and the author's name is in print, whether it was all worthwhile. However, for one to be able to decide whether it is truly worth it really requires at least one writing project that is seen through to publication. After doing so, one may quite legitimately decide that the results are not worth what they cost in terms of time and effort and that one is happy to be out from under the work and away from the pressure of deadlines. This is the case with a fair number of people; many journal issues carry the work of one-time authors.

On the other hand, one may discover that all of the work and all of the frustration has led to an immense feeling of satisfaction from a difficult task successfully completed. Chances are that the first-time author who experiences this immense satisfaction is going to appear in print again. And again.

# Index

## P



## Q



## R

# *Notes*

# *Notes*

# *Notes*

# *Notes*

# *Notes*

# *Notes*

# *Notes*

# *Notes*

# *Notes*

# *Notes*

# *Notes*

# *Notes*

# *Notes*

# *Notes*

# *Notes*

# *Notes*

# *Notes*

# *Notes*